ANDREW YOUNG AND THE MAKING OF MODERN ATLANTA

MERCER UNIVERSITY PRESS

Endowed by

TOM WATSON BROWN
and
THE WATSON-BROWN FOUNDATION, INC.

ANDREW YOUNG

AND THE MAKING OF

MODERN ATLANTA

ANDREW YOUNG, HARVEY NEWMAN

and **ANDREA YOUNG**

Mercer University Press | Macon, Georgia | 2016

MUP/ H921

© 2017 by Mercer University Press
Published by Mercer University Press
1501 Mercer University Drive
Macon, Georgia 31207
All rights reserved

9 8 7 6 5 4 3 2 1

Books published by Mercer University Press are printed on acid-free paper
that meets the requirements of the American National Standard for
Information Sciences—Permanence of Paper for Printed Library Materials.

ISBN   978-0-88146-587-7
Cataloging-in-Publication Data is available from the Library of Congress

CONTENTS

Preface

In 1996, Andrew Young, in collaboration with his daughter Andrea Young, published a book titled *An Easy Burden: The Civil Rights Movement and the Transformation of America*. This was the story of his life as a key figure in the civil rights movement where he served as executive director of the Southern Christian Leadership Conference under the leadership of Martin Luther King, Jr. Little was said about the next phase of his life as a public leader in Atlanta, Georgia.

In 2008, Andrew Young addressed Leadership Atlanta, an annual convening of leaders designed to transmit the "Atlanta Way" to new and emerging leaders in the city. Andrea Young was a member of the class and recognized that her classmates were not familiar with many of the stories and leaders who created the Atlanta they knew. It was clear a book was needed to tell the story of Andrew Young's contribution to the city of Atlanta. This book is an effort to fill that gap, but it does not focus exclusively on the work of Andrew Young since one of the important lessons of the city's political history is how he was able to build on the efforts begun by others.

Those lessons began with Mayor Bill Hartsfield's political coalition of white businessmen and members of the city's educated black middle-class. Hartsfield continued to win elections with the strong support of African-American voters from the 1940s until his retirement in 1962. His successors, Ivan Allen, Jr., and Sam Massell, continued the bi-racial coalition with support from business leaders. Both mayors made major contributions to the growth of the city with the dedication of a new airport, the construction of a major league stadium, and voter approval of the rapid rail transit system. Mayors Allen and Massell continued the process of desegregating a Southern city in a relatively peaceful manner, in contrast to other places in the region.

Politics was but one of the lessons that Andrew Young learned from earlier leaders in Atlanta. Long-time civic leader and unofficial "Mayor of Auburn Avenue" John Wesley Dobbs used the three B's—the *ballot*, the *book*, and the *buck*—as tools to uplift African Americans. Dobbs spearheaded the voter registration drive that led Mayor Hartsfield to hire the first black police officers in 1948, years ahead of most other Southern cities. These same voters would, during the decade of the 1970s, use the *ballot* to elect Andrew Young to the US Congress and Maynard Jackson as the city's first African-American mayor.

Another of the three B's, the *book*, emphasized the importance of education, and Atlanta was the home of a collection of black colleges and universities known as the Atlanta University Center. Within a segregated city, these institutions produced the ministers, teachers, and business leaders who formed the black middle-class that was key to making the city special.

The *buck* was also critical to making Atlanta. When Maynard Jackson took office as mayor in 1974, less than on half of one percent of the city's contracts went to minority firms, in a city with a majority African-American population. Jackson's policies for minority business development at the airport and elsewhere changed the opportunity structure for black and women-owned firms in the city. These controversial policies were continued under Mayor Young and afterward in the preparations for the Olympic Games. Using all of the three B's, Atlanta followed a path different from many of its neighboring cities in the South. Mayor Hartsfield had proclaimed that Atlanta was "the city too busy to hate." His successors helped make those words come closer to the truth. This book is an effort to pass on these lessons to others.

Acknowledgments

First, and foremost, we would like to thank our spouses, Carolyn McClain Young, Patricia Hewitt Newman, and Jerry Thomas, Jr., who deserve special mention for their patience and support, as well as their insights, over the course of the research and writing of this work. One of the joys of working on this book was the opportunity to record the views of many of the participants in the making of the city of Atlanta. We interviewed more than sixty people, and their observations provide new insights into how the leaders of the city made crucial decisions. Preparing the documentary film *Andrew Young's Making of Modern Atlanta* provided opportunities for video recording some of the same individuals, as well as, numerous others. Many of their insights found their way into the book, and we plan to make them available for future scholars to use as part of the Special Collections and Archives, University Library, Georgia State University. The authors express their thanks to all who gave their time to sit down and record their thoughts. Andrew Young was especially generous with his time, and the multiple interviews he recorded enrich this collection of materials. Thank you to the following for generously sharing their stories in the interviews: Billye Aaron, Hank Aaron, Stacey Abrams, Cecil Alexander, Elaine Alexander, Inman Allen, William Allison, Henrietta Antonin, Richard Arrington, Clara Haley Axam, Samuel Bacote, Carolyn Long Banks, George Berry, Lisa Borders, Marva Brooks, Raphael Cassimere, Anne Cox Chambers, Leah L. Chase, William Clement, Toni Coleman, Robert Corley, Ann Cramer, Emma Darnell, Anita DeFrantz, Eugene Duffy, Brooke Jackson Edmond, Duriya Farooqui, Austin Ford, Shirley Franklin, Douglas Gatlin, Pat Glisson, Frank Glover, Dan Halpern, Laura Jones Hardman, Azira Hill, Julius Hollis, Bob Hope, Tom Houck, Walter Huntley, Jr., William Ide III, Beni Ivey, Valerie Richardson Jackson, Leroy R. Johnson, Tom Johnson, Blaine Kelley, Sylvia Sanders Kelley, Lonnie King, Mitchell Landrieu, John Lewis, Michael Lomax, Charlie Loudermilk, Herman Skip Mason, Sam Massell, Charles (Pete) McTier, Michael Mescon, Ceasar Mitchell, Mark Morial, Carol Muldawer, Paul

Muldawer, Monica Pearson, Alicia Philipp, John Portman, Erica Qualls, Morris Redding, Kasim Reed, A. J. Robinson, Herman Russell, Sr., Rita Samuels, Maria Saporta, Mickey Steinberg, Richard Stogner, Rodney Strong, Kazua Sunaga, Jerry Thomas, George Turner, Ted Turner, Alex Wan, Carl Ware, Jimmy Williams, Raymond Williams, Sam Williams, Diane Wisner, Carolyn Young, Frank M. Young III, and Sam Zamarripa. Their stories bring life to policies and insights into the practice and ideas of leadership.

There were some who had passed away, but we appreciate the family members and friends who shared photos, invitations, letters, and other materials with us to illuminate this work and helped us to recapture precious stories. We thank Judith Augustine, Andrea Boone, Marian Jones, Rubye Lucas, Donata Russell Ross, and Sylvia Russell.

Many talented doctoral and graduate students from the Andrew Young School of Public Policy contributed their time and energy to our project, and we are grateful for their research: Kelechi Uzochukwu, Jung-In Soh, Teresa Taylor, Nicole Blount, Shaquille Bolden, Kimberly Chiltoskie, Robert Hovenkamp, Rebecca Linnear, Josh Merfield, Jonathan Smith, Catlin Smyke, and Tricia Whitlock.

Donald Bermudez, Andre Jones, Kay Jackson, Carmen Holman, Marian Jones, Beni Ivey, Carolyn Moore, Michael Ross, Susan Ross, Graylian Young, Sarah Steely, Kelly Callen, Patra Marsden, and Elsa Gebremedhin were among those who worked behind the scenes to help the authors in ways large and small.

A project of this size, scope, and duration is not possible without philanthropic support. For their gifts we thank Chevron, John Portman (who believed in this from the beginning), AFLAC, the Cox Foundation, Ronald and Vicki Canakaris, Georgia Pacific, Wells Fargo, Donata Russell Ross, Michael Ross, and B. Franklin Skinner.

We drew from many important public and private collections, but we would like to give special mention to institutions and their archivists that are invaluable to the preservation of Atlanta's history: the Auburn Avenue Research Library on African-American Culture and History, Atlanta-Fulton Public Library; the Atlanta History Center; the Robert W. Woodruff Library, Atlanta University Center; the Robert W. Woodruff Library, Emory University; the Portman Archives; and the

Special Collections and Archives, University Library, Georgia State University. Public policy and private philanthropy protect these treasure troves of inspiration for present and future generations.

Mary Beth Walker, dean of the Andrew Young School of Policy Studies, Georgia State University, and the members of the board of the Andrew J. Young Foundation also gave their assistance and support. We are also indebted to friends such as Jamil Zainaldin of the Georgia Humanities Council for his wise counsel and to Marc Jolley, the director of the Mercer University Press, for his willingness to publish our work. Finally, we wish to thank the many leaders in Atlanta. Many of these leaders are well known while others are less familiar, but who, nevertheless, made significant contributions to the making of the city. Uplifting the stories of people such as Clarence Bacote, Henrietta Antonin, George Berry, and Susie LaBord made this process such a rich experience for us since these were people who helped make the city a place with lessons for newcomers and for others elsewhere to learn from the "Atlanta Way."

ANDREW YOUNG

AND THE MAKING OF

MODERN ATLANTA

Foundations of the "Atlanta Way"

"We have raised a Brave and Beautiful City," said Henry Grady, the first of the great Atlanta boosters. Only a little more than a century later, his words seemed true as the bright skyscrapers overlooking Olympic Centennial Park saw the city host more than two million spectators, journalists, and athletes from around the world converging on Atlanta. This was beyond even the eloquent promises Grady made more than a century before to the New England Society in New York: "The New South presents a perfect democracy, the oligarchs leading in the popular movements social system compact and closely knitted, less splendid on the surface but stronger at the core—a hundred farms for every plantation, fifty homes for every palace, and a diversified industry that meets the complex needs of this complex age."[1] In Henry Grady's time, few people would have called Atlanta beautiful, and even fewer African Americans would call it brave. Atlanta was blessed with people who were Brave and Beautiful.

Even as Grady made his case, African Americans in Atlanta were asserting their own vision of a New South. The response of Atlanta leaders—black and white—in the aftermath of the Civil War laid the foundation for the modern Atlanta that possessed the physical infrastructure, human resources, and international reputation to host the world in the Centennial Olympic Games. Their policy choices and actions would bring truth to Grady's brash statement.

There is no good reason that Atlanta, Georgia, grew from a tiny railroad junction in the 1840s to become a metropolitan area of almost six million people in less than 175 years. Unlike Savannah and Charles-

---

[1] Henry Grady, "A Message from the South," *New York Times*, 23 December 1886, 2.

ton, elegant cities of the colonial era, Atlanta was not located on a navigable waterway; it was not a port city on the ocean, a lake, or a great river. Located in the interior of Georgia with its red clay soil, Atlanta was not a place that was fertile for crops to grow. The city lacked the mineral wealth that propelled the growth of Houston and Birmingham. How, then, did Atlanta emerge from a sleepy Southern town to become a large, modern city? The answer to this question may help a new generation of residents in Atlanta as well as people in other places. Over the course of many centuries, a few people have understood the most essential ingredient for city growth. In her classic book *The Economy of Cities*, Jane Jacobs quotes the sixth-century-BC Greek poet Alcaeus who said, "Not in well-fashioned houses, nor in walls, canals, and dockyards make the city, but in men able to use their opportunities."[2] While we might wish to change the gender to a more neutral term, the sentiment is correct: *people* make the city. This is the story of some of the people and their work that helped to shape the Atlanta area. It is told from the perspective of one of the city's most important public leaders, Andrew Young.

The New South

On September 2, 1864, the mayor of Atlanta and a delegation of citizens rode out to meet with Union soldiers to offer surrender to General William T. Sherman. The delegation consisted of carefully chosen Union loyalists and included one surprising choice, a slave named Bob Yancey. Like many slaves in the cities of the South, Yancey was permitted by his master to "hire out" his services. His master set him up in a barber shop, and he proved to be a good businessman. In return for a portion of his earnings paid to his owner each month, Yancey lived independently with his wife in a house that he owned. By 1861, he operated two shops employing nine barbers. Yancey also made loans to white merchants, and during the war he undertook the dangerous task of assisting

---

[2] Jane Jacobs, *The Economy of Cities* (New York: Vintage Books, 1969) 144.

Union prisoners held in the city.[3] Little is known of Yancey's life after the surrender of Atlanta. He changed his surname from that of his master to Webster and continued to operate his shops for a few years after the war's end. His inclusion in the party of civilians who surrendered Atlanta was part of an effort to present the city as different from other Southern places in its willingness to show loyalty to the Union cause.

Atlanta's white leaders were not blind to the difficulties that the regime of racial segregation and white supremacy imposed upon the aspirations of the city. Seeking to impress New Yorkers with Atlanta's sophistication in order to garner investment for industrial development, Henry Grady, managing editor of the *Atlanta Constitution*, in 1886 spoke of the mutual understanding that existed between whites and blacks in Atlanta:

> But what of the Negro? Have we solved the problem he presents or progressed in honor and equity towards the solution? Let the record speak to the point. No section shows a more prosperous laboring population than the Negroes of the South; none in fuller sympathy with the employing and land-owning class. He shares our school fund, has the fullest protection of our laws and the friendship of our people. Self-interest, as well as honor, demand that he should have this. Our future, our very existence depend upon our working out this problem in full and exact justice.[4]

Born in Athens, Georgia, Grady's father was a Confederate officer who died from his wounds in 1864, when his son was fourteen. Henry Grady finished college at the University of Georgia before turning to a career in journalism. In 1880, he became managing editor and part owner of the *Atlanta Constitution*. Grady used his position as an editorial writer to promote his political and economic views. Foremost among his ideas was what he called a vision for a New South with Atlanta as its center. The New South movement spread to other people and places, but Henry Grady in his writings and speeches became the idea's most prominent advocate. The first element of Grady's vision was for the industrial-

---

[3] Thomas G. Dyer, *Secret Yankees: The Union Circle in Confederate Atlanta* (Baltimore: Johns Hopkins University Press, 1999) 191.

[4] Grady, "A Message from the South."

ization of the South to provide factory jobs for those who wanted them. This program of industrialization depended on investment from the North, so the second part of Grady's New South vision was a reconciliation of the sections of the nation. Next, Grady wanted to improve the conditions of agriculture in the South to bring more prosperity to farmers. Among his recommendations for farmers were diversification of crops and less dependence on commercial fertilizer. Grady was a firm believer in white supremacy. As William Link points out, Grady sought to romanticize the relationship between owners and enslaved persons during the era of slavery, as well as appeal to the disposition toward white supremacy that prevailed in the North. Grady's version of the "cooperation" between the races needed for Southern economic progress did not include social and political equality for African Americans.[5] As Link writes, "The very concept of racial equality violated what Grady claimed was a national policy of American prejudice. To change that policy and that prejudice contradicted the 'universal verdict of racial history.'"[6]

Throughout the 1880s, Henry Grady worked to advance his ideas for a modernized South and to promote Atlanta as the ideal setting to make this vision of the New South a reality. Grady and other Atlanta leaders saw that their city had two advantages over the older coastal cities that were identified with the agrarian past. First, Atlanta was connected to the rest of the region and the nation by an expanding network of rail lines. Although the shipping and processing of cotton was the major economic activity of the city, there were other important commercial enterprises, such as the retail and wholesale trade that also depended on the railroads. A second advantage of Atlanta's white business leaders was a unified vision of their city as the center of the New South. Grady and his

---

[5] Harold E. Davis, *Henry Grady's New South: Atlanta, A Brave and Beautiful City* (Tuscaloosa: University of Alabama Press, 1990) 13–18, and Edward L. Ayers, *The Promise of the New South: Life after Reconstruction* (New York: Oxford University Press, 1992) 54.

[6] William A. Link, *Atlanta, Cradle of the New South: Race and Remembering in the Civil War's Aftermath* (University of North Carolina Press, Chapel Hill, 2013) 153.

newspaper described this vision as the "Atlanta Spirit" that was the "militant expression of Atlanta's personality—forceful, aggressive, intelligent, harmonious, with an abundance of that requisite indispensable in man or city—sleepless initiative."[7]

In December 1886, Henry Grady was invited to speak to a group of wealthy and powerful northerners at the New England Society in New York City. With General William Sherman in the audience, Grady spoke of how he had been a "careless man about fire," but "never was restoration swifter. From the ashes he left us in 1864 we have raised a brave and beautiful city." Grady's eloquence won applause from the audience and the New York newspapers.[8] The New England Society speech not only exemplified Grady's extraordinary talent as an orator, it also showcased Atlanta as the center of the New South movement. One biographer described Grady as promoting a pattern of urban imperialism in that he wanted Atlanta to advance even if other towns and cities in the region did not.[9]

Grady's strategy on race was helpful in establishing the narrative that Atlanta was somehow different. He emphasized that there were good feelings between the races and that progress in relations between whites and blacks had been made. In his speech he asked Northerners to trust Southern whites, whose affectionate relationships with black people were "close and cordial."[10] These views were less harsh than many other Southern whites, and cleverly appealed to the disposition of many of the Northern industrialists whose good will and investment Grady was courting.

---

[7] Don H. Doyle, *New Men, New Cities, New South: Atlanta, Nashville, Charleston, Mobile, 1860–1910* (Chapel Hill:
  University of North Carolina Press, 1990) 157–58.
[8] Link, *Atlanta, Cradle of the New South*, 138–42.
[9] Davis, *Grady's New South*, 17–18.
[10] Link, *Atlanta, Cradle of the New South*, 142.

We Are Rising

As Grady pitched his New South vision to a white audience, the Reverend Edward R. Carter, pastor of the Friendship Baptist Church, was developing a history of Atlanta's 'black side." Carter wrote,

> In beginning the history of the Black Side, or the Afro-American, in this the beautiful, enterprising city of Atlanta, because of the unfriendly relations existing between most of the whites and blacks, and because of the continual effort to debar and prevent the Brother in Black from entering into any lucrative business, I am inclined to use the words of the Apostle Paul: "For here we have no continued city, but seek one to come."

And seek they did. Reverend Carter was almost certainly referring to the Reverend Fredrick Ayer, Edmund Asa Ware, and other members of the American Missionary Association (AMA) when he wrote "there are among us white brothers who will do us any favor or show us unlimited courtesy."[11] Ayer and his wife came to Atlanta in 1865 under the auspices of the abolitionist AMA to serve the newly liberated African-American community. The AMA acquired a boxcar and had it shipped to Atlanta to serve as a school. The newly organized First Colored Baptist Church (later Friendship Baptist Church) and its pastor, Reverend Frank Quarles, possessed land. The historian of Atlanta University, Clarence Bacote, writes, "Since Ayer had a building and Friendship had land, an agreement was reached between Ayer and Quarles, whereby Ayer would set up a schoolhouse for 'Colored children of Atlanta on a portion of the same ground designed for a church edifice for the said church of which said Frank Quarles is pastor.'"[12] One of the first teachers in the newly opened Storrs School was a self-taught, newly freed slave named James Tate. He came to the city and opened a small grocery story

---

[11] Edward R. Carter, *The Black Side: A Partial History of the Business, Religious, and Educational Side of the Negro in Atlanta, Ga* (1894; repr., Freeport, NY: Books for Libraries Press, 1971) 11.

[12] Clarence A. Bacote, *The Story of Atlanta University: A Century of Service, 1865–1965* (Atlanta University, 1969), 4.

before joining with Frederick Ayer to begin teaching the children. The Storrs School was the product of the first of Atlanta's black and white coalitions. The work of the AMA expanded with additional school buildings, a teacher's dormitory, and an orphanage. A non-denominational church was founded and became the First Congregational Church of Atlanta. In Atlanta and across the state of Georgia, schools for African Americans were supported by the AMA, the Freedman's Bureau, and contributions from the meager resources of the newly freed African Americans themselves. Four years after the end of slavery, reports to the Freedman's Bureau indicated that "It is estimated that during the preceding year, Negroes provided between thirty and forty thousand dollars for current expenses of schools, in addition to large sums for the erection and repair of churches and schoolhouses." This is itself indicated the great interest that Negroes took in education.[13]

Reverend Carter's book, published in 1894, extolls the industry and accomplishment of Atlanta's African-American community. In answer to those who would question the capabilities of African Americans, he describes the fine homes, prosperous businesses, buildings, churches and educational institutions of "the Black Side." In nearly every biographical sketch of the leading black citizens of Atlanta, the role of the Storrs School and Atlanta University is a recurring theme.

The partnership between the white missionaries of the AMA and the leaders of Atlanta's African-American community emerging from slavery to freedom laid the foundation for the black-white partnership that would be a signature of Atlanta and its local government. In the close and long-term relationships with the Ayers, Edmund Ware, and other teachers from New England who came to Atlanta as an expression of faith believing that African Americans could master the same curriculum taught in New England's finest colleges, the students of Storrs School and later Atlanta University learned crucial lessons. Fruitful and sustained alliances could be made with white people, alliances that were beneficial to African Americans and advanced their own interests in at-

---

[13] Ibid., 15.

taining true equality. These were not the alliances of slavery—clever manipulations of owners aimed at sheer survival—but partnerships of free men and women based on a principal of brotherhood and equality. The Storrs School began with African Americans bringing value and resources to the alliance, rather than being passive recipients of Northern charity.

Atlanta University would form the nucleus of the largest concentration of historically black colleges in America. Within two decades of the chartering of Atlanta University, the AMA was joined by the Freedman's Aid Society of the Methodist Episcopal Church, establishing what became Clark College. In 1879, the precursor of Morehouse College, Atlanta Baptist Seminary, relocated to Atlanta from Augusta, and in 1881 the Atlanta Baptist Female Seminary (now Spelman College) was formed. Later that year, Morris Brown College was founded by the African Methodist Episcopal Church and began holding classes at Big Bethel AME.[14] Initially, these institutions were offering grammar- and high-school-level instruction to people who had been denied any opportunity for an education. That soon changed, as the students and academic institutions made rapid progress.

Under the leadership of Edmund A. Ware, Atlanta University graduated its first class of students with the Bachelor of Arts degree in 1876.[15] This achievement is extraordinary, given that few institutions in Georgia were able to confer college degrees. There was no other institution offering college-level courses and bachelors' degrees in Atlanta. The University of Georgia located in Athens (founded by Abraham Baldwin who, like Ware, was a Congregationalist from Yale) held its first classes in 1801.[16] Mercer University, located in Macon, graduated its first class

---

[14] Herman Skip Mason, Jr., ed., *Going against the Wind: A Pictorial History of African-Americans in Atlanta* (Atlanta: Longstreet Press 1992) 10, 26.

[15] Bacote, *The Story of Atlanta University*, 37.

[16] Larry B. Dendy, "University of Georgia," *New Georgia Encyclopedia*, http://www.georgiaencyclopedia.org/articles/education/university-georgia (15 December 2015).

in 1841.[17] Georgia Tech would be established for white men in 1888 (women would not be accepted until 1952 and blacks in 1961).[18] Agnes Scott College began as Decatur Female Seminary in 1889.[19] Emory College, founded in Oxford, Georgia, in 1835, would not move to Atlanta until 1914.

In the absence of public education for African Americans, Atlanta University had won an annual state appropriation of $8,000 beginning in 1870.[20] As Reconstruction began to wane and the doctrine of separation of the races began to take hold, Atlanta University was challenged for offering education to African Americans and whites in the same classrooms. The governor, John Gordon, was a former Confederate general who objected to white students attending classes alongside African-American students. The white students were the children of the AMA teachers and pastors. The minister of First Congregational Church, Evarts Kent, stated in the *Atlanta Constitution* that his children attended Atlanta University because the school provided "technical and intellectual training more thorough and varied than that of any other school in the city; because in practice it accords with the most enlightened public sentiment in the country."[21] Atlanta University lost the state appropriation in 1887. Legislation was offered that threatened fines and time in the state chain gang for teachers who taught black and white students together. Despite the loss of funds to educate African Americans, the black community supported the decision not to accede to the demand to ex-

---

[17] J. C. Bryant, "Mercer University," *New Georgia Encyclopedia*, http://www.georgiaencyclopedia.org/articles/education/mercer-university (11 May 2013).

[18] Marla Edwards and John D. Toon, "Georgia Institute of Technology (Georgia Tech)," *New Georgia Encyclopedia*, http://www.georgiaencyclopedia.org/articles/education/georgia-institute-technology-georgia-tech (7 April 2015).

[19] Jennifer Owen, "Agnes Scott College," *New Georgia Encyclopedia*, http://www.georgiaencyclopedia.org/articles/education/agnes-scott-college (8 November 2013).

[20] Bacote, *The Story of Atlanta University*, 87.

[21] Evarts Kent, "Why a White Youth Goes to a Colored University," *Atlanta Constitution*, 20 July 1887, 4.

clude white students from Atlanta University. An appeal to the Congregational Churches of New England raised more than $18,000 to protect the principle of universal human brotherhood upon which Atlanta University was founded.[22]

The state funds taken from Atlanta University were eventually used to establish the first state college for African Americans in 1891, a segregated institution with African-American students and teachers known as Savannah State University. The first president of Savannah State was Richard R. Wright, a member of the first graduating class of Atlanta University. On the campus of what is now Clark Atlanta University, a monument stands to this foundational partnership between blacks and whites in Atlanta. Upon the death of Edmund Asa Ware in 1885, the graduates of Atlanta University would not accept placing his remains in a segregated cemetery. Instead, they raised the funds to bury his remains on the campus and brought a boulder from Massachusetts inscribed with the message "…in grateful memory of their former teacher and friend and the unselfish life he lived and the noble work he wrought that they, their children, and their children's children might be blessed."[23]

Cast Down Your Buckets

Extraordinary progress took place in Atlanta's African-American community under the protection of the Union army, the Freedman's Bureau, and the federal government's program of Reconstruction. The Tilden Hayes Compromise of 1876 brought to an end the shelter and support of these policies. Federal troops were withdrawn from the South, and the fate of African Americans was returned to the judgment of those who had rebelled against the Union—the former slaveholders.

While Henry Grady, Samuel Inman, and other white leaders of Atlanta looked for strategies to invigorate the economy out of the ashes of the Civil War, African Americans searched for strategies to build a community out of the legacies of slavery and segregation. The two came

---

[22] Link, *Atlanta: Cradle of the New South*, 131–34.
[23] Bacote, *The Story of Atlanta University*, 84, 100.

together in the Atlanta Exposition of 1895. Emulating Chicago's successful Columbian Exposition of 1893, Atlanta's white leaders began to plan a comparable exposition in Atlanta to showcase the city and foster trade. In the public-private partnership approach that would be a hallmark of Atlanta, the Atlanta City Council and Fulton County made their contributions, estimated at $175,000, and a group of business leaders formed the Exposition Company, which raised $134,000.[24] Whether an attempt to secure federal funds for the exposition, a response to calls for a separate black exposition, a result of the belief that Atlanta must always showcase racial tolerance, or a consequence of the success of "Freedman's Day" at the International Cotton States Exposition in 1881—it was decided to include a "Negro pavilion" in the fair. Booker T. Washington and two African-American ministers, Wesley J. Gaines and Abraham Grant, were part of the Atlanta delegation seeking funds from the Congress. Funds were appropriated for the Atlanta Exposition, and a Negro Building was included. In a recurring theme, African Americans accepted a segregated fair, but as the fair showcased the capabilities of Atlanta, the Negro Building was the first public exhibit to promote African-American achievement in the city and the region and showcased the work of black inventors, artists, businessmen, artisans and farmers.[25] "The Negro Building," declared the *Constitution*, was "built by negroes, under the supervision of negroes, and filled with exhibits showing the progress of the colored race."[26]

However, one of the most popular exhibits at the fair was an "Old Plantation" exhibit, complete with African Americans playing the role of happy slaves. At the time of the Negro Building exhibit, African Ameri-

---

[24] Harvey K. Newman, *Southern Hospitality: Tourism and the Growth of Atlanta* (Tuscaloosa: University of Alabama Press, 1999) 52.

[25] Link, *Atlanta, Cradle of the New South*, 157–63.

[26] *Atlanta Constitution*, "NEGRO PROGRESS: The Colored Building Was Formally Presented Yesterday. MANY SPLENDID SPEECHES Rev. J. W. E. Bowen's Oration Was a Magnificent Effort. THE EXERCISES WERE VERY INTERESTING Professor Davis's Ode Was Well Read, Speeches by Garland Penn and President Collier," 22 October 1895, 4.

cans were not welcome in any public accommodation serving whites. A new hotel had to be built for those who came to experience the Exposition and the Negro pavilion. Other African-American visitors had to stay with friends and relatives.[27]

In that context, it was a remarkable that Booker T. Washington addressed a general gathering as a keynote speaker at the exposition. Perhaps reading the signs of the times, he exhorted African Americans to cooperate with white Southerners and cease "agitation on the questions of social equality." Washington warned,

> Our greatest danger is, that in the great leap from slavery to freedom we may overlook the fact that the masses of us are to live by the productions of our hands, and fail to keep in mind that we shall prosper in proportion as we learn to dignify and glorify common labor and put brains and skill into the common occupations of life.... No race can prosper till it learns that there is as much dignity in tilling a field as in writing a poem. It is at the bottom of life we must begin and not the top. Nor should we permit our grievances to overshadow our opportunities.[28]

Ralph McGill would later observe, "Booker T. Washington, for reasons even now not fully comprehended (but likely pragmatic), participated in what was the establishment of a new caste system. Within the newly developing economy the Negro was fixed as a sharecropper, tenant, small landowner, or in the more menial jobs in the cities and towns. With few exceptions he was excluded from skilled employment."[29] McGill wrote with the advantage of hindsight. Initially, even W.E. B. DuBois, completing his PhD at Harvard, wrote to congratulate Washington: "Let me heartily congratulate you on your phenomenal success in

---

[27] Newman, *Southern Hospitality*, 55.

[28] Booker T. Washington, "Cast Down Your Buckets: The Atlanta Compromise Speech," PBS.org, *Rise and Fall of Jim Crow*, http://www.pbs.org/wnet/jimcrow/historical_docs/hist_doc_altantacomp5.html (accessed 29 September 2015).

[29] Ralph McGill, *The South and the Southerner* (Athens: University of Georgia Press 1992) 160.

Atlanta—it was a word fitly spoken."[30] The Atlanta Compromise Speech was delivered in a pivotal moment where cooperation seemed possible, at an Exposition where black achievement was celebrated, in a hall where a black contingent was present. Booker T. Washington extended an open hand to the white South. He could not have predicted the clenched fist that would come in return. As a result of this speech, Washington was heralded as the nation's most influential black leader.

The following year, the US Supreme Court would deal a devastating blow to the aspirations of African Americans to equality—the ruling in *Plessy v. Ferguson* that would establish constitutional protection for segregation in law and custom throughout America. Racial segregation would flourish under the full force of American law until 1954. By 1901, Booker T. Washington, who had been celebrated in Atlanta by a largely white audience, was roundly attacked when President Theodore Roosevelt received him for dinner in the White House. This breach of the doctrine of separation of the races and its context of white supremacy would not be tolerated by Southern politicians and newspaper editors who attacked the Republican president. The *Constitution* wrote, "We people of the South have been born and raised so that we cannot accept the negro as our social equal and we cannot respect any man who does."[31] In South Carolina, Senator "Pitchfork Ben" Tillman was even more inflammatory in his rhetoric: "The action of President Roosevelt in entertaining that nigger will necessitate our killing a thousand niggers in the South before they will learn their place again."[32] The violent suppression of African Americans to assert white supremacy and keep blacks in their place predicted by Tillman was not long in coming to the region.

---

[30] W. E. B. DuBois, *The Souls of Black Folk* (New York: Vintage Books 1990) 62.

[31] Deborah Davis, *Guest of Honor: Booker T. Washington, Theodore Roosevelt, and the White House Dinner that Shocked a Nation* (New York: Atria Books, 2012).

[32] Ibid., 227.

Jim Crow and the doctrine of white supremacy and separation of the races spread throughout the South, including Atlanta. Within a short time, laws would govern how black citizens walked on sidewalks, where they could ride on public transportation, and where and whether they could sit in theaters and ballparks. Businesses were required to post signs indicating which race was served. African Americans were denied entrance to the new public library, the city parks, and the zoo.[33] Newly arrived at Atlanta University with his PhD from Harvard University, W. E. B. DuBois was led to write, "To-day, it makes little difference to Atlanta, to the South, what the Negro thinks or dreams or wills."[34]

The Atlanta Riot

The nadir of relations between black and white in Atlanta was unquestionably the Race Riot of 1906. Mass violence of white Americans against African Americans was a recurring tragedy throughout the South, born of the sickness of racism and the demand of the Southern economy that African Americans be readily available as laborers who could be underpaid and poorly treated. As Isabel Wilkerson describes in her book on the great migration, "Blacks who had had enough were often prevented from leaving and had to resort to tactics to conceal their plans to leave—buying train tickets in towns where they were not known or leaving their homes under cover of darkness."[35] African Americans were 40 percent of Atlanta's population in 1900. W. E. B. DuBois, as a professor of sociology at Atlanta University, reported in "The Negro in Business" that there were sixty-one businesses in the city owned by African Americans.[36] Thus, Atlanta was a reasonable place for Booker T. Washington to choose as the site for the Seventh Annual Convention of the Negro Business League in 1906. The convention met at Big Bethel AME

---

[33] Newman, *Southern Hospitality*, 65.

[34] DuBois, *Souls of Black Folk*, 62.

[35] Isabel Wilkerson, *The Warmth of Other Suns: The Epic Story of America's Great Migration* (New York: Vintage Books, 2011) 163.

[36] W. E. B. DuBois, "The Negro in Business," in *Fourth Annual Conference on the Condition of the Negro* (Atlanta: Atlanta University, 1899) 70–71.

Church and was greeted by Atlanta's mayor and the president of the white Chamber of Commerce.[37] DuBois chastised residents of Atlanta, writing,

> Atlanta must not lead the South to dream of material prosperity as the touchstone of all success.... For every social ill, the panacea of Wealth has been urged,—wealth to overcome the remains of slave feudalism; wealth to raise the "cracker" Third Estate; wealth to employ the black serfs, and the prospect of wealth to keep them working; wealth as the aim of politics.[38]

In fact, the common goal of economic expansion would be the lever that African Americans would use to broker partnerships with white Atlanta. Despite the laws of segregation, the prospect of a thousand convention visitors to Atlanta brought financial support from the white business community, kind words from the mayor, and dinner for the visiting business leaders in the otherwise segregated Piedmont Park. The "Atlanta Way" was taking shape.

One month later, beginning in the saloon district on Decatur Street, white mobs attacked African Americans throughout Atlanta. Scholars believe the riot was caused by the toxic soup of a racialized political campaign, the growing black population in Atlanta, and the race-baiting of the newspapers to sell papers. The day of the riot, the newspapers reported four instances of black men raping white women. There was never any substantiation of a single one of these inflammatory newspaper stories. Nevertheless, between twenty-five and forty African Americans were killed, and black-owned businesses were destroyed in violence that raged across the city from Saturday evening, 22 September, until Tuesday, 25 September.[39]

Ever resilient, Atlanta cleaned itself up—company was coming. A convention of the National Association of Retail Druggists came to At-

---

[37] Newman, *Southern Hospitality*, 66.

[38] DuBois, *Souls of Black Folk*, 61.

[39] Gregory Mixon and Clifford Kuhn, "Atlanta Race Riot of 1906," *New Georgia Encyclopedia*, http://www.georgiaencyclopedia.org/articles/history-archaeology/atlanta-race-riot-1906 (29 October 2015).

lanta in October for its first convention in the South.[40] Drugstores were the primary outlet for Atlanta's most profitable homegrown business— the Coca-Cola Company under the ownership of Asa Candler.

At the First Congregational Church, founded by white missionaries from Yale, its first African-American leader, Henry Proctor, a graduate of Yale Divinity School, expressed a similar resolve: "Now is not the time to think of leaving Atlanta. This riot gives us our opportunity. It is over; the whole city is forever sobered by it. Out of it will come a better understanding between the two races and a glorious progress for us. This is our appointed time if we can but show ourselves worthy of it."[41] With this faith and resolve, Reverend Henry Proctor reached out to the minister of First Presbyterian Church, Reverend Plato Durham, who would later serve as dean of the Candler School of Theology, Emory University, to discuss healing the city from the effects of the riot. Along with other black and white Christian clergy, they formed the Committee on Church Cooperation. In their statement of purpose, the ministers affirmed,

> We, a group of Christians, deeply interested in the welfare of our community, irrespective of race or class distinction, and frankly facing the many evidences of racial unrest, which in some places have already culminated in terrible tragedies, would call the people of our beloved community to a calm consideration of our situation....[42]

Out of the ashes of the violence and destruction of the Atlanta Riot, African-American leaders reached out to white leaders and found ways to move forward.

---

[40] Newman, *Southern Hospitality*, 69.

[41] Bruce Barton, "The Church that Saved a City: How Atlanta Found Itself after the Race Riots," *The Congregationalist and the Christian World* 99/4 (5 November 1914): 586.

[42] Moses N. Moore, "From Atlanta to Brooklyn: The Social Gospel Ministry and Legacy of Henry H. Proctor," American Theological Library Association, *Union Seminary Quarterly Review* 62 (2010): 58.

Reverend Proctor and others led the way to rebuild the black-owned businesses destroyed in the Atlanta Riot along the Auburn Avenue corridor. When Congregational minister and writer Bruce Barton visited the church in 1914, he was amazed at the church Procter had built in the aftermath of the riot and the wealth and industry of his parishioners. Barton quoted Alonzo Herndon, the founder of Atlanta Life Insurance Company, on the influence of Proctor: "one Sunday I dropped into that First Congregational Church.... It gave me an entirely new outlook on life, a new respect for myself and my own possibilities. I said to myself, 'I am going to attend this church and I'm going to amount to something in this city.'"[43] Herndon was born during slavery in Walton County, Georgia, and came to Atlanta in 1883. Within six months of arriving, Herndon bought a half interest in the barber shop in which he was working. By the turn of the century, he owned three barber shops in Atlanta, including a grand shop on Peachtree Street outfitted with crystal chandeliers and gold fixtures. Herndon dressed the staff in tuxedoes and served an all-white clientele. Herndon invested his profits in real estate and during the early twentieth century became the wealthiest African American in Atlanta. [44] At the time of Barton's visit, Atlanta Life Insurance Company operated in five states and owned "a modern office building entirely devoted to Negroes. In it are doctors and lawyers, architects and real estate dealers; hair dressers and jobbers; dentists and assorted businessmen."[45] These represented the growing number of educated and well-to-do African Americans in Atlanta.

In African-American communities, "Cast down your buckets where you are," is the most quoted segment of Booker T. Washington's Atlanta Compromise speech. The phrase refers to the effect of the Amazon River that provides fresh water far out into the ocean. His meaning to white and black Southerners is that the people around them are the ones they

---

[43] Barton, "The Church that Saved a City," 586.
[44] Alexa B. Henderson, "Alonzo Herndon (1858–1927)," *New Georgia Encyclopedia*, http://www.georgiaencyclopedia.org/articles/business-economy/alonzo-herndon-1858-1927 (6 January 2016).
[45] Barton, "The Church that Saved a City," 586.

need to survive, even thrive. Blacks need not leave the South, and whites need not bring immigrants to provide labor. Washington sought to inspire a "blotting out of sectional differences and racial animosities and suspicions."[46] He encouraged former slaves to stay among the former slave owners and seek honest work and prove worthy of greater rights. Washington also sought to remind white Southerners of the invaluable role of black labor in the growth of the South. He acknowledged segregation of the races, saying, "In all things that are purely social we can be as separate as the fingers, yet as one hand in all things essential to mutual progress." In a speech he gave to the National Unitarian Association earlier that year, Washington demonstrated a sincere belief that white Southerners could be convinced that blacks deserved to be treated fairly, saying, "Let a colored man spend $10,000 a year in hauling freight on a rail road where there are competing lines: do you think the rail roads will put this man into a Jim Crow car? Not at all. Rather than lose his patronage they will put on a Pullman Palace Car for him. The American dollar has not an ounce of sentiment in it."[47]

Born a slave and educated at Hampton University, Washington had a different, perhaps more painfully pragmatic vision than DuBois and Proctor, each born free and educated among the America's white elite at Harvard and Yale. Atlanta's black community would embrace both visions, it would seek education and property, and it would also heed the call to "Cast down your buckets, where you are."

The Pause That Refreshes

Like Atlanta itself, the success of Coca-Cola® is a result of brilliant marketing and represents a cornerstone of the "Atlanta Way." The breadth of the company's business interests and its engagement in the global marketplace served to counter the Southern provincial values that

---

[46] Washington, "Cast Down Your Buckets: The Atlanta Compromise Speech."

[47] Louis R. Harlan, ed., *The Booker T. Washington Papers*, vol. 3 (Urbana: University of Illinois Press, 1974) 478.

might otherwise have gone unchecked. Henry Grady was interested in how Atlanta looked to the Northern business interests. Robert Woodruff would be interested in how Atlanta looked to the world.

Coca-Cola® began in 1886 as a soda fountain drink sold in Jacob's Pharmacy, located at Five Points on Peachtree Street. Asa Candler bought the rights and the formula, and by the turn of the century the drink was being sold in pharmacy soda fountains and in glass bottles across the South. Ernest Woodruff purchased the Coca-Cola® Company from Asa Candler and his family in 1919. In doing so, he set the stage for his control of the company and made his son, Robert, president in 1923. Robert had proved to be a successful truck salesman while working for the White Motor Company with his offices in New York City. He returned to Atlanta, taking a $50,000 a year pay cut to serve as president of the Coca-Cola® Company. Under Woodruff's leadership, Coca-Cola® expanded across the country and into Canada, Mexico, and Europe. Its impact on Atlanta was enormous. The fortune and prestige of local banks, law firms, and numerous Atlanta families grew with the expansion and success of the Coca-Cola® Company. Even as he built the fortunes of the company, Robert Woodruff set an example of personal generosity and philanthropy. Rather than fire Jim Key, older black man who cared for Asa Candler's horses at the company, Woodruff gave him the title of "staff vice president" and kept him on the payroll. During the Great Depression, no one was fired from the Coca-Cola® Company, and when a black man who worked on his Baker County, Georgia, hunting land was lynched in 1933, Woodruff sent Pinkerton detectives to find the killer.[48] Robert Woodruff was paternalistic, even kind in his treatment of African Americans in his employ. The rules of segregation permitted blacks to be valued and well-treated as servants, but it would be several decades before a graduate of any of the colleges in the Atlanta University complex would be recruited to a white collar job in the Coca-Cola® Company.

---

[48] Frederick Allen, *The Secret Formula: How Brilliant Marketing and Relentless Salesmanship Made Coca-Cola the Best-Known Product in the World* (New York: HarperBusiness, 1994) 154, 157, 282.

During the 1920s, Atlanta leaders set their sights on becoming a city of national importance. The Chamber of Commerce under the leadership of Ivan Allen, Sr., promoted investment in the city through a nationwide advertising campaign known as "Forward Atlanta." As a result of their efforts, many national corporations built plants and regional headquarters in Atlanta. In spite of a variety of strategies to market the city, Atlanta was a regional commercial town, whose growth was limited by the poverty of the South, the Great Depression, and World War II.[49]

Gone with the Wind

Even before Coca-Cola® became the world's most well-known brand and CNN was piped into every home with a cable connection, Margaret Mitchell's book *Gone with the Wind* defined the city of Atlanta to the world. Her work remains one of the best-selling books of all time, and the Technicolor film that debuted in 1939 established Atlanta in the national imagination, a place, like Scarlett O'Hara, "self-willed and vigorous." As Mitchell wrote, "[Atlantans] were proud of the place, proud of its growth, proud of themselves for making it grow."[50] A native of Atlanta who grew up on Peachtree Street, Mitchell, like Atlanta, was out of step with the romanticized image of the Old South represented by Ashley Wilkes in *Gone with the Wind*. Her heroine, Scarlett O'Hara, like Atlanta itself, operated with a value system of "economic individualism, industrialism, and urbanism represented by Scarlett's dynamic pragmatism."[51] Scarlett would do anything for a dollar: purchase convict labor for her saw mill, steal her sister's fiancé, defy social conventions regarding women, and do business with Union officers. Mitchell believed that the myths and legends of the Old South would give white Southerners the strength to persevere in the new era of uncertainty. This was myth-

---

[49] Newman, *Southern Hospitality*, 101–102.

[50] Margaret Mitchell, *Gone with the Wind* (New York: MacMillan, 1936) 142–43.

[51] Elizabeth I. Hanson, *Margaret Mitchell* (Boston: Twayne Publishers, 1991) 51.

making on a grand scale, and it set Atlanta apart, glorifying the "Atlanta Spirit" as it pertained to commerce and a business-friendly climate.

Atlanta's mayor, William Hartsfield, was determined to have the premiere of the motion picture version of *Gone with the Wind* in Atlanta, even sending magnolias to the producer, David O. Selznick.[52] In addition to national attention, the city reaped nearly $1 million in hotel charges from the increase in visitors to the city that year. Despite her global fame, Margaret Mitchell continued to live modestly in the city and quietly supported worthy causes.

City Too Busy to Hate

There were many false starts on the promise of a "New South." According to Atlanta's best known newspaper columnist, Ralph McGill, industry that came South prior to World War II was seeking low wages and adding little to the share of national investment income in the South.[53]

McGill was a Tennessee farm boy who attended Vanderbilt University, served in the US Marine Corps, and came to Atlanta in 1929 to work on the *Atlanta Constitution*. Eventually he became its editor and published a syndicated column read throughout the South.

McGill wrote as a son of South and loved its regional flavor. For his time, he was a liberal who promoted the idea that the South must have education and industry. He sought to paint the Klan as harmful to the South, writing, "The Ku Klux elements may not understand it, but they are not a good advertisement for a region which wishes to attract industry, to educate its children, and to move into the future with the rest of the nation." Often in his columns, McGill denounced the Ku Klux Klan in even stronger terms calling them "a rat-souled gang," "anti-Christian," and "un-American." As early as the 1940s, McGill denounced the "anti-Negro set" and rejected the notion that love of the South was synonymous with the oppression and terrorization of black people. He wrote,

---

[52] Newman, *Southern Hospitality*, 116.
[53] McGill, *South and the Southerner*, 206.

It seems to me that the Southerner who loves his region must love it enough to fight for it. He must love it enough vigorously to denounce and oppose all those who seek to say the American Dream of justice and opportunity for all Americans is not a Southern dream, too. The person who loves the South must love it enough to refuse to see it exploited by those who seek to say the lynchings and mob violence are a part of the South. They must love it enough to say that the Negro may have full justice and economic opportunity without any harm to the South's true traditions.

Ralph McGill's columns appealed to the best of the South and in calling out the Klan, he distinguished what he termed the "criminal element" in the South from his readers, the "decent people." He exhorted his readers to obey the rule of law and find a new self-image. His columns chastised white Southerners who maintain "'good niggers' don't want to vote, or to educate their children or have the same rights." Ralph McGill wrote in another column, "Southern honor and pride cry out to us—asking that the South do what is right and decent.... Is it really so difficult to allow all qualified persons to vote, to use the parks, to go to school? Are we so weak and afraid we cannot trust ourselves to do what is right—to answer honor instead of shame?"[54] Ralph McGill provided the intellectual underpinning of the response among Atlanta's white elite to the demands and aspirations of Atlanta's black elite.

The end of World War II revitalized America and Atlanta was no exception. The experience of fighting for democracy abroad renewed determination in the African-American community to expand democracy at home. Many white Southerners, having seen segregation through the lens of Europe and the Holocaust, returned home with a different perspective.

The city enjoyed remarkable continuity in political leadership throughout the post-war era with a single person, William B. Hartsfield, serving as mayor from 1942 until 1961. Hartsfield had a love affair with the airplane and anticipated that Atlanta would need to prepare for the

---

[54] Ralph McGill, *Best of McGill: Selected Columns* (Atlanta: Cherokee Publishing Company, 1980) 100, 104, 105, 107, 108, 121, 127, 128.

advent of the aviation age. As an alderman, he arranged the purchase of Asa Candler's racetrack to serve as Atlanta's municipal airport. As a result of Hartsfield's prescience, by 1948, Atlanta had a modern airport for passengers, regular service, and runways able to accommodate the latest aircraft.[55]

In 1946, the US Supreme Court ruled that African Americans could vote in the previously all-white Georgia primary elections. A delegation of Atlanta's black leaders met with Mayor Hartsfield shortly after that decision and requested that the mayor desegregate the city's police force. Hartsfield declined, but he issued a challenge to the group that if they could register 15,000 African-American voters, he would change his mind about the police department. After a massive voter registration drive in the black community, almost 18,000 African Americans registered in less than two months.[56] The black leaders returned to visit Hartsfield to remind him of his pledge. The mayor hired eight black police officers that year, but more importantly, began a political coalition of the mayor, white businessmen, and black community leaders. This coalition led to Hartsfield's reelection as often as he sought the office and established a governing coalition that shared a vision of economic growth and expansion for the city.[57] The alliance allowed Hartsfield to begin a process of gradually negotiated desegregation in the city. In contrast to other cities in the region, Atlanta's gradual but peaceful desegregation promoted an image that supported Mayor Hartsfield's claim that Atlanta was the "city too busy to hate."

Atlanta was an oasis in Georgia for African Americans who aspired to leave behind the sharecropper cabins of rural Georgia, to pursue an education, and to live with some degree of dignity. Yet, Atlanta was the capital of Georgia, and the politics of the state were a constant reminder

---

[55] Harold H. Martin, "William Berry Hartsfield: Mayor of Atlanta (Athens: University of Georgia Press, 2010) 68–69.

[56] Clarence Albert Bacote, "The Negro in Atlanta Politics," *Phylon: The Atlanta University Review* 16/4 (Fourth Quarter 1955): 348.

[57] Clarence N. Stone, *Regime Politics: Governing Atlanta, 1946–1988* (Lawrence: University Press of Kansas, 1989) 31.

that outside the bustling streets of Auburn Avenue and Hunter Street and the leafy green quadrangles of the Atlanta University Schools, segregation reigned. Henrietta Antonin remembers the voice of Georgia's governor when she was a teenager at the segregated Booker T. Washington High School:

> [T]hey were not afraid to use the "N" word—nigger, nigger, nigger, nigger—that's all you heard. We didn't accept it, but we had no choice; we had no voice. They wanted Washington High School Glee Club to sing at the Governor's Mansion.... I was not excited because I remembered that he [Governor Herman Talmadge] said "blood would run down the streams of Georgia like water before we integrate," and his term for African Americans was "nigger."

Henrietta Antonin was a soloist for the Glee Club, and the adults pressured her to go and sing for the governor. The buses carrying the students from Washington High School were not allowed inside the gate, and students had to walk to the outside of the governor's mansion in a cold rain. They watched as white students were allowed to sing on the grand porch of the mansion, then were invited into the mansion for refreshments. Antonin remembers,

> We were all excited... when it was time for us to sing, they told us..."you can't go on the porch, you stand in the yard." So we had to stand in the yard, in the rain and sing...even in the rain, we still did a fabulous job. When we finished, I remember Betty Talmadge saying, "Well, let me see the little soloist...let's give her a hand." They gave me a hand. Then they said, "Well, thank you very much."

The Washington High students watched as the governor and his party turned around and entered the mansion, leaving them in the rain. Antonin continues, "The kids thought they were going to be invited in for cocoa and cookies and fruitcake.... I went [back to the bus] with tears in my eyes."[58]

[58] Henrietta Antonin (retired executive vice president, Atlanta Life Insurance Company), interview by authors, 15 July 2011, audio, Special Collections and Archives, University Library, Georgia State University.

Nevertheless, the underpinnings of segregation were cracking. With its landmark 1954 decision in *Brown v. the Board of Education*, the Supreme Court reversed the ruling in *Plessy v. Ferguson* that had affirmed the idea of separate but equal. The brave citizens of Montgomery, Alabama, led by a young minister from Atlanta, Martin Luther King, Jr., successfully integrated the bus system following a year-long boycott. The decades-long battle of the NAACP to remove the constitutional support for segregation had been won, opening the door for new opportunities.

A new generation of progressive white business leaders was coming of age in Atlanta. After their exposure in the military and in schools outside the South, the scions of prominent Atlanta families saw with fresh eyes the caste system that dominated the South. Some were disturbed by what they saw. Cecil Alexander was the product of one of Atlanta's oldest Jewish families; his forebears had moved from Charleston to the young town of Atlanta in 1848. Cecil attended Yale and Harvard, but it was his service in World War II that opened his eyes to the impact of segregation on the South. He recounts his evolution "from a gentleman racist to an advocate for civil rights," explaining, "I was in the Marine Corps in World War II. I was a dive bomber pilot. It hit me that I was coming back to a country entirely different from the African Americans who were coming back. That I had all these doors open to me just didn't seem right."[59]

Alexander was not alone in his understanding that the South would have to change. Ivan Allen, Sr., the leader of the Forward Atlanta campaign of the 1920s, told his namesake,

> We've kept the nigger not in a second class but in a third- or fourth-class position, and as a result we've impoverished him and we've impoverished this section of the country.... [H]ere we are advocating human decency and freedom all over the world, and we find ourselves with dirty skirts at home. It's time for some major changes. Your generation

---

[59] Cecil Alexander (architect and civic leader), interview by authors, 30 June 2011, audio, Special Collections and Archives, University Library, Georgia State University.

is going to be confronted with it, and it will be the greatest agony that any generation ever went through.[60]

Since the Civil War, Atlanta developed a group of well-educated African Americans and an enterprising white business community that aspired to represent a "New South" without the stigma of racial hatred. As Henry Grady said in 1886, "Our future, our very existence, depends upon our working out this problem in full and exact justice."[61]

---

[60] Ivan Allen, Jr., and Paul Hemphill, *Mayor: Notes on the Sixties* (New York: Simon and Shuster, 1971) 13–14.
[61] Grady, "A Message from the South."

Henry Grady
(Georgia State University Archives)

Henry Proctor
(Library of Congress)

Students at Atlanta University, above *(Library of Congress)*
Cecil Alexander and William Hartsfield, below *(Cecil Alexander Collection)*

Cecil Alexander and Robert Woodruff
(Cecil Alexander Collection)

2

Fighting for Civil Rights

On February 1, 1960, four African-American students attending North Carolina A&T University sat down at the lunch counter in a Woolworth's store in downtown Greensboro. They captured the attention of the nation. Students trained in non-violence at Fisk University and American Baptist Seminary began their own sit-ins in Nashville. John Lewis was one of the Nashville students and recalled, "You would see these young people sit down in a restaurant and someone would come in and pull them off the stool or spit on them or put out a lighted cigarette on them. They would continue to sit and sit."[1]

Soon, the student demonstrators were joined by others from the six historically black colleges and universities in Atlanta who wanted to play a part in history. Julian Bond and Lonnie King from Morehouse College began discussing the Greensboro sit-ins at the Yates and Milton drugstore. Ruby Doris Smith and Carolyn Long (from Clark College) and Roslyn Pope and Marian Wright (from Spelman College) soon joined them for regular meetings.[2] Carolyn Long Banks recalled, "We saw the North Carolina A&T kids being beat up at the Woolworth counters. We talked about it and said we cannot just sit and do nothing. So…we planned it out step by step, that we were not going to be boisterous; we were going to be a non-violent movement."[3]

---

[1] John Lewis (5th District U.S. congressman), video interview, 26 November 2013.

[2] Harry G. Lefever, *Undaunted by the Fight: Spelman College and the Civil Rights Movement 1957–1967* (Macon: Mercer University Press, 2005) 24–27.

[3] Carolyn Long Banks (former student activist and Atlanta City Council member), interview by authors, 1 August 2011, audio, Special Collections and Archives, University Library, Georgia State University.

Not all of those who took part in the student movement to desegregate Atlanta were from the Atlanta University Center institutions. As the demonstrations began, some white college students from Emory, Agnes Scott College, and Georgia Tech joined the movement. The peaceful protest movement in Atlanta went nationwide when students such as Julian Bond from Morehouse and Marian Wright Edelman from Spelman helped to organize a group known as the Student Non-Violent Coordinating Committee (SNCC). Edelman would later become an attorney, founder and head of the Children's Defense Fund and Chair of the Spelman College Board of Trustees.[4] SNCC was formed in North Carolina in 1960 but moved its offices to Atlanta later that year in order to become the student-led nonviolent direct action group affiliated with Dr. King's Southern Christian Leadership Conference (SCLC). The SNCC attracted both black and white student leaders, many of whom came to Atlanta to work on initiatives such as the sit-ins, the "freedom rides," and voter registration drives. One of these white students was Tom Houck, who participated in the early civil rights and anti-war demonstrations sponsored by SNCC.[5] Another student, John Lewis, was a veteran of the Nashville Sit in Movement and the Freedom Rides that ended discrimination in intercity buses. He came to Atlanta in came to Atlanta in 1963 after studying at the American Baptist Seminary and Fisk University in Nashville. Lewis became head of the Student Non-Violent Coordinating Committee, was a speaker at the March on Washington, and participated in such civil rights protests such as the March from Selma to Montgomery, Alabama, in 1965. On that march, Lewis led the procession across the Edmund Pettus Bridge where he and others were beaten in what came to be known as "Bloody Sunday." The national news coverage of these events included violence against the peaceful demonstrators by the Alabama State Patrol troopers that galvanized support for the Voting Rights Act. John Lewis remained as the leader of SNCC until the fol-

---

[4] Guy-Sheftall and Stewart, *Spelman*, 79.

[5] Tom Houck (owner of tomhouck.com), retired civil rights leader and journalist), interview by authors, 17 July 2012, audio, Special Collections and Archives, University Library, Georgia State University.

lowing year when subsequent leaders changed the name to drop the word Nonviolent and substitute "National," reflecting a new focus on black power.[6]

At their home in their integrated, middle-class neighborhood in Queens, New York, Jean and Andrew Young saw the story of the Nashville student sit-ins on television and were moved by the dignity, courage, and persistence of the students. Andrew Young recalled, "We were sitting down in front of the fireplace, very comfortable and successful. And here comes John Lewis and Diane Nash and James Bevel talking about sitting-in, and we watched that Nashville sit-in story, and before it was over, Jean said 'It's time for us to go home,' and I said 'We are home.' She said, 'No, our home is back South.'" Jean was right and they returned to the South. The move to Atlanta was a return to a South that many well-educated African Americans had left to seek more opportunity and a less restrictive racial climate. Young was born in New Orleans and first visited Atlanta at the age of fourteen when he attended a High Y conference at the Butler Street YMCA. The city that Young experienced as a teen has been described as "conservative, old-fashioned, and segregated."[7] When Young saw the Klan parading down Auburn Avenue, he observed later, "It was the first time I had seen the Klan. I called my mother, and she said 'Come home. Catch the next bus or train home.'" He stayed for the conclusion of the conference before returning to New Orleans. However, the image of the Klan remained with the impressionable teen, who was destined for a life that would bring him back to Georgia and to the struggle for civil rights.

Following in his father's footsteps, Young ventured north to Washington, DC, for his undergraduate education at Howard University.

---

[6] Irene V. Holliman, "Student Nonviolent Coordinating Committee (SNCC)," *New Georgia Encyclopedia*, http://www.georgiaencyclopedia.org/ articles/history-archaeology/student-nonviolent-coordinating-committee-sncc (11 December 2015).

[7] The Reverend Austin Ford (retired director, Emmaus House, and Episcopal priest), interview by authors, 11 July 2011, audio, Special Collections and Archives, University Library, Georgia State University.

Howard had been founded during Reconstruction to educate the "freed-men," African Americans newly freed from slavery by the Civil War and free African Americans now released from the risk of enslavement. Young's father had attended Howard for his degree in dentistry and graduated in 1921. In the 1950s, Howard was a center for black excellence and vibrated with the hope of new opportunities for African Americans in the wake of the fight for democracy in Europe and the Pacific. Like his father, Young joined the Alpha Phi Alpha fraternity; however, he rebelled against following his father into dentistry, instead attending graduate school at the Hartford Theological Seminary in Connecticut. Young had decided he would be a man of God...and of the people. He said, when reflecting on his decision, "God had put me on this earth for a purpose. And if I could do the best I could one day at a time and not worry about the future, 'let the days own trouble be sufficient unto the day thereof.'"

Young met Jean Childs in Marion, Alabama, when he was directed by the leadership of the Congregational Church to serve the First Congregational Church of Marion for the summer and lead a youth program in the small town. The Childs and the Youngs were beneficiaries of the American Missionary Association and their commitment to create schools and churches across the South for African Americans in the aftermath of the Civil War. As happened with Atlanta's Storrs School, one of Jean's ancestors provided land for a school, and the AMA sent the teachers, founding what became Lincoln Normal.[8] One of Jean's schoolmates at Lincoln was Coretta Scott, who would later marry Martin Luther King, Jr. Andrew's parents were educated at Dillard University in New Orleans and were leaders in the Central Congregational Church, each institution founded with the support of the AMA. Jean, a student at Manchester College, was home for the summer when the two met. They married in June 1954 after her graduation from college, the same year that the US Supreme Court issued the decision in *Brown v. The Board of*

---

[8] Andrea Young, *Life Lessons My Mother Taught Me* (New York: Tarcher/Putnam, 2000) 116.

Education of Topeka, Kansas and struck down segregation in public schools. The *Brown* decision was the result of an intellectual legal strategy developed at Howard University Law School and implemented by Thurgood Marshall and the NAACP. The decision opened the door for change, but segregation still had a vice-like grip on the region. It was a dangerous time for those who were agents of change.

In 1956 Andrew and Jean Young went to serve a cluster of Congregational churches in Thomasville, Georgia, and Jean taught in the segregated elementary school near the Bethany Congregational Church. John Wesley Dobbs, of the Atlanta Negro Voters League, asked Andrew to spearhead a voter registration drive. This drive was part of Dobbs's organization's effort to push the ballot as a way to uplift blacks in Atlanta and throughout the state. The Klan in Thomasville was not happy about registering African Americans so that they could vote in larger numbers. The KKK threatened to attack Young and his wife, Jean, at their home. Having grown up in a small southern town, Jean Young was an expert riflewoman. Andrew recalls his conversation with Jean when they were faced with the likelihood of a Klan attack on their home:

> I need to negotiate from a position of strength. If they come here, I'm going to go down and talk with them. I want you to sit in the window with a rifle and point it at the person I am talking to. Then I can negotiate from a position of strength. And she said "No, I cannot do that." I said "Why not?" She said "I cannot point a gun at another human being." I said "That is the Ku Klux Klan." She said that "If you do not realize that under that sheet is the heart of a child of God, you got no business calling yourself a preacher."

Jean won the argument, and it was decided they should spend the night with church members William and Lucille Morris. The next day, Andrew discovered that Morris and two other African-American business leaders had met with white business leaders and threatened a boycott if the Klan was allowed to march in Thomasville. There were no more Klan marches, and the voter registration drive went on as planned. Andrew learned an invaluable lesson about the power of the business community in setting the tone for race relations.

A year after the Klan incident, Andrew received an offer to serve in the youth division for the prestigious National Council of Churches (NCC). Young remembered,

> In Thomasville I observed the challenges facing America in microcosm, from the level of family, church, and household. As an executive with the NCC, I was able to gain a global and national perspective on these same challenges. I traveled across the United States and met business leaders and young people who would become influential religious leaders in their communities. I traveled to Europe and met religious leaders from Eastern Europe, Latin America, and Africa. I met leaders of African liberation movements on the early days of the evolution...to independent nations. I learned about the emerging forces of communications known as television, and how to shape information to meet its demands.[9]

Inspired by the student sit-ins, Andrew and Jean moved to Atlanta, where he administered the Dorchester Citizenship Education Project from the offices of the Southern Christian Leadership Conference with its founding president, Martin Luther King, Jr. Following the success of the Montgomery bus boycott, Dr. King had become an important national—even international—figure. The growing movements for nonviolent social action that were inspired by Montgomery's example created a tremendous demand for Dr. King's time and attention. African Americans around the country wanted Dr. King's help to end segregation in their own communities. Dr. King's secretary, Dora McDonald, commented that she was overwhelmed by all the mail they were receiving and asked if Young could help. "So she gave me a stack of mail about a foot high, and I took it home with me and wrote answers to it. Dr. King sort of liked the approach that I took," observed Young.

Andrew and Jean Young, meanwhile, discovered the power of the buck within Atlanta's African-American community as they settled into their new hometown where black people were beginning to exercise their financial muscle. Young recalls, "We got a mortgage in three days in At-

---

[9] Andrew Young, *An Easy Burden: Civil Rights and the Transformation of America* (New York: Harper Collins, 1996) 95, 123.

lanta, and it had taken me three months to get a mortgage in New York. And so I immediately saw the difference in a city where black people have access to financial institutions and where they had worked out respectful arrangements between blacks and whites." Jean and Andrew found a three-bedroom brick bungalow in the Mozley Park neighborhood on the west side of Atlanta with quiet, tree-lined streets and easy access to public parks, swimming pools, and tennis courts. Their African-American neighbors were teachers, nurses, and small business owners. Jean and Andrew opened their home to the young people who were the front lines of the civil rights movement—black and white.

Jean Young's Congregational heritage led her to become active in the First Congregational Church, one of the oldest and most influential churches in Atlanta. Soon she was teaching Sunday school, taking her three daughters in their color-coordinated dresses her mother made and patent-leather Mary Jane shoes to the tan brick sanctuary built by Henry Proctor. It was Jean Young who began to put down roots in Atlanta as she volunteered with the Sunday school in the First Congregational Church, voter registration drives, and the March of Dimes. She taught second grade in the Atlanta public schools and hosted neighborhood children for reading workshops. While teaching at Whiteford Elementary School, Jean Young met Samuel Bacote, a fellow teacher whose father was scholar Clarence A. Bacote. Samuel Bacote's wife, Joyce, was a daughter of one of Atlanta's pioneering African-American businesswomen, Lottie Watkins.[10] The relationship between the Youngs and the Bacotes would be invaluable to the development of Andrew Young's political career in Atlanta.

With Atlanta as a home base, Andrew Young traveled the South, recruiting and training the natural leaders in Southern black communities in the Citizen Schools. The purpose of the Citizen School was to educate community leaders about the importance of voting and their rights as citizens. The United Church of Christ's American Missionary Association division (AMA) paid Young's salary and provided an old

---

[10] Young, *Life Lessons My Mother Taught Me*, 86–87.

AMA mission school—Dorchester Center—for a residential training center near Midway, Georgia. Along with former Charleston school teacher Septima Clark and Dorothy Cotton, a veteran of the civil rights campaigns in St. Petersburg, Virginia, Young gathered community leaders for a week-long residential training on their rights as citizens of the United States with workshops on African-American history, literacy, practical civics, non-violent protest philosophy, the laws supporting segregation, and the constitutional principles that empowered them with the rights of citizenship, including the right to vote.[11] Soon, Young was involved more directly with the work of Martin Luther King and the Southern Christian Leadership Conference. He helped plan strategy and negotiate settlements in the landmark campaigns that would create federal civil rights laws to accomplish the goals of desegregation.

While Andrew and Jean Young were relocating to Atlanta, the Atlanta Student Movement was in full force. At the urging of the Atlanta University Center presidents, leaders drafted a five-page manifesto titled "An Appeal for Human Rights." "They printed their demands in the *Atlanta Journal & Constitution*, and people all over the city saw what these young people were appealing to before they had their first sit-in," said John Lewis with admiration.[12] In very clear language, the appeal demanded an immediate end to racial segregation. Their "Appeal for Human Rights" clearly laid out the reasons for their protests:

> We, the students of the six affiliated institutions forming the Atlanta University Center—Clark, Morehouse, Morris Brown, and Spelman Colleges, Atlanta University, and the Interdenominational Theological Center—have joined our hearts, minds, and bodies in the cause of gaining those rights which are inherently ours as of the human race and as citizens these United States....
>
> We do not intend to wait placidly for those which are already legally and morally ours to be meted out to us at a time. Today's youth will not sit by submissively, while being denied all of the rights, privileges, and joys of life. We want to state clearly and unequivocally that

[11] Ibid., 144, 148.
[12] Lewis, video interview, 26 November 2013.

we cannot tolerate in a nation professing democracy and among people professing democracy, and among people professing Christianity, the discriminatory conditions under which the Negro is living today in Atlanta, Georgia—supposedly one the most progressive cities in the South.

Among the inequalities and injustices in Atlanta and in Georgia against which we protest, the following are outstanding examples:

(1) EDUCATION: In the Public School System, facilities for Negroes and whites are separate and unequal, Double sessions continue in about half of the Negro Public Schools, and many Negro children travel ten miles a day in order to reach a school that will admit them. On the University level, the state will pay a Negro to attend a school out of state rather than admit him to the University of Georgia, Georgia Tech, the Georgia Medical School, and other tax-supported public institutions. According to a recent publication, in the fiscal year 1958 a total of $31,632,057.18 was spent in the State institutions of higher education for white only. In the Negro State Colleges only $2,001,177.06 was spent. The publicly supported institutions of higher education are inter-racial now, except that they deny admission to Negro Americans.

(2) JOBS: Negroes are denied employment in the majority of city, state, and federal governmental jobs, except in the most menial capacities.

(3) HOUSING: While Negroes constitute 32% of the population of Atlanta, they are forced to live within 16% of the area the city. Statistics also show that the bulk of the Negro population is still:

a. locked into the more undesirable and overcrowded areas of the city;

b. paying a proportionally higher percentage of income for rental and purchase of generally lower quality property;

c. blocked by political and direct or indirect restrictions in its efforts to secure better housing.

(4) VOTING: Contrary to statements made in Congress by several Southern Senators, we know that in many counties in Georgia and other southern states, Negro college graduates are declared unqualified to vote and are not to register,

(5) HOSPITALS: Compared with facilities for other people in Atlanta and Georgia, those for Negroes are unequal and totally inadequate. Reports show that Atlanta's 14 general hospitals and 9 related institutions provide some 4,000 beds. Except for some 430 beds at Grady Hospital, Negroes are limited to the 250 beds in three private

Negro hospitals. Some of the hospitals barring Negroes were built with federal funds.

(6) MOVIES, CONCERTS, RESTAURANTS: Negroes are barred from most movies and segregated in the rest. Negroes must even sit in a segregated section of the Municipal Auditorium. If a Negro is hungry, his hunger must wait until he comes to a "colored" restaurant, and even his thirst must await its quenching at a "colored" water fountain.

(7) LAW ENFORCEMENT: There are grave inequalities in the area of law enforcement. Too often, Negroes are maltreated by officers of the law. An insufficient number of Negroes is employed in the law-enforcing agencies. They are seldom, if ever promoted. Of 830 policemen in Atlanta only 35 are Negroes.

We have briefly mentioned only a few situations in which we are discriminated against. We have understated rather than overstated the problems. These social evils are seriously plaguing Georgia, the South, the nation, and the world.[13][end block]

Dozens of brave and determined students demonstrating, peacefully, to protest segregated stores and lunch counters were arrested, fortunately without serious violence, thanks in part to Atlanta Police chief Herbert Jenkins. Unlike his counterparts in Birmingham, Montgomery, and other Southern cities, Jenkins demonstrated a remarkably enlightened leadership by insisting that his officers maintain close contact and open communication with the protestors. Morris Redding, later chief of police under Mayor Andrew Young, recounted,

> I could communicate with a lot of the students, and a lot of the young people that were involved in the civil rights movement, and we had good relationships, as well as Chief Jenkins. I know when we would tell him that students were going to march and what area they were going to march in, if he saw there would be a possibility of some kind of con-

[13] Atlanta Student Movement, 1960–2010, "An Appeal for Human Rights," http://www.atlantastudentmovement.org/An_Appeal_for_Human_Rights.html (26 December 2014).

flict, he would personally go and talk to the leaders and try to get them to change their routes.[14]

Student leader Lonnie King gave similar testimony to Jenkins's pragmatism: "Chief Jenkins was no liberal, but he was a law enforcement officer operating within a system where you can't afford to have black people beaten up and have that carried on the front page of the *New York Times* because that's not good for business. That's not good for Atlanta's image." The image suffered, though, from time to time. The Ku Klux Klan, angered by the protests, staged counter demonstrations downtown. The protests continued through much of 1960 and into 1961, but slowly a split developed between the younger, more militant students and the older, more established black leaders, who preferred a more moderate approach. According to Lonnie King, "[The older leaders] were basically trying to say that you need to let the NAACP do this. Let us older people do this. Yes, they did not try to say [the student protests were] bad, but they kept saying you are the wrong soldiers to do this."[15]

But the students didn't let up. At one point, 2000 of them were involved in the sit-ins. The Atlanta jails filled up with prisoners, and business downtown began to suffer. One store in particular, Rich's, became a focal point for the students. Remembered King, "It was the largest department store south of Chicago or New York. It had offices in Atlanta, Birmingham, Columbus, Georgia, and Knoxville, Tennessee. It was a juggernaut. The idea was, if we can bring down Rich's department store, the rest will fall like dominoes."[16] Carolyn Long Banks, then a student at Clark College, recalled, "So because there were two different eating places there, one for blacks and one for whites, it became even more important for us to sit-in at the Magnolia Room. We got to the doors, and they slammed the doors shut and we just sat there silently. They said

---

[14] Morris Redding (retired chief of police, City of Atlanta), interview by authors, 8 March 2013, audio, Special Collections and Archives, University Library, Georgia State University.

[15] Lonnie King (former student activist and civil rights leader), video interview, 9 December 2013.

[16] Ibid.

they would never change their policies, that we would never be welcome there."[17] As Ivan Allen reported in his memoir of the era, Rich's board of directors actually considered becoming an all-white store. Allen recalled, "That is how naïve we were on the race issue at that point, on the verge of the greatest civil-rights struggle in the history of the United States."[18] Allen met with retailers and restaurant owners and persuaded them to allow him to work out a settlement with Atlanta's African-American community. Working with Dr. Rufus Clement, attorney A. T. Walden, Dr. Benjamin Mays, and other leaders, Allen and Opie Shelton of Rich's negotiated a settlement. The settlement included a truce and cooling-off period. After five months, the shops and restaurants in Atlanta would be desegregated. Students were let out of jail, but many were suspicious that they had been sold out by the more established leaders.

It was Martin Luther King, Jr., who saved the agreement. He had been persuaded by the students to join their demonstrations. Upon being arrested during a demonstration with them, he was transferred to DeKalb County on an outstanding warrant for driving with an Alabama driver's license. In the middle of the night, he was transferred to Georgia's state prison at Reidsville in the back of a paddy wagon with a police dog. It took a call from presidential candidate John Kennedy to Coretta Scott King to speed his release. The news of Kennedy's phone call was published in papers across the country and with additional support from candidate Kennedy's brother, Robert, King was granted bail and freed. After he was freed from the state prison, King returned to Atlanta during a tense meeting at Wheat Street Baptist Church led by Dr. William Holmes Borders. Neither Borders nor King could calm the students. Ivan Allen describes the scene where King "took to the pulpit and stood before the crowd a full minute, searching every face in the audience. It became deathly quiet.... [He said,] 'If this contract is broken it will be a disaster and a disgrace. If anyone breaks this contract, let it be the white

---

[17] Banks, interview, 1 August 2011.
[18] Ivan Allen, Jr., and Paul Hemphill, *Mayor: Notes on the Sixties* (New York: Simon and Shuster, 1971) 36–37.

man.'"[19] Carolyn Long Banks fondly recalled what happened next: "I got a call from Mr. Rich himself, and he said, 'We would like to, we give in, would like to invite you to come and be the first to come and eat in the Magnolia Room.'"[20] The students had won an important victory.

She became the first black buyer for the store and credits Mr. Rich as a mentor. He also served as a mentor for other leaders in Atlanta such as Dr. Michael Mescon, the long-time Dean of the Georgia State University Business School. Mescon tells the story of how Mr. Rich taught him the importance of customer service that helped reinforce the bond between residents of the city and the department store.[21] Carolyn Long Banks continued her leadership in the city when she became the first African-American female to serve as a member of the Atlanta City Council.[22]

It wasn't until 1964, with the historic passage of the federal Civil Rights Act of 1964, that desegregation finally became the law of the land. By that time, civil rights battles were raging throughout the south, but Atlanta—conscious of its image and its business climate, and blessed with far-seeing leaders, black and white—chose a different path. John Lewis reflected on the era: "They wanted to maintain peace. They did not want to see a Birmingham or Selma, and I think that's what saved Atlanta and spared Atlanta. You did not see the racial violence; you did not see people using dogs and fire hoses. When you were arrested in this city, it was in a peaceful, orderly fashion."[23]

More change was coming. In 1962 the US Supreme Court ruled that the Georgia's county unit system was unconstitutional. That system had given the white-dominated rural counties much more power than

---

[19] Ibid., 21–41.
[20] Banks, interview, 1 August 2011.
[21] Michael H. Mescon (dean emeritus, Robinson College of Business Administration, Georgia State University), interview by authors, 18 January 2012, audio, Special Collections and Archives, University Library, Georgia State University.
[22] Banks interview.
[23] Lewis, video interview, 26 November 2013.

the increasingly black cities, like Atlanta. This had the effect of diluting the black vote in statewide elections and in the state legislature. The ruling opened the door for aspiring black politicians such as Leroy Johnson, who won election that year to the state Senate. One of his first moves was to desegregate the Capitol's all-white facilities. Johnson recalled his approach to desegregation, saying, "I did so by carrying my pages to restrooms where it says white only, to drinking water fountain where it says white only, and by going into the restaurant."[24] There was resistance, but he had done his job and the Capitol was integrated.

Next up for Johnson was the Commerce Club, the center of political and financial power in Atlanta, with a strict policy of segregation. Few club members were aware that many of the meetings between Ivan Allen, A. T. Walden, Dr. Clement, and other black leaders over the student demonstrations had taken place in private rooms of the club. Ironically, despite the settlement on public restaurants, the club intended to maintain its whites only practice. Senator Johnson, however, insisted on his right to dine with his colleagues in the Georgia State Senate. Journalist Maria Saporta recounted, "They tell him he can't come into the dining room. He says, 'Well, I was invited along with the other legislators.' He goes in, he sits down, they take away his plate, and he still stays here, you know, they take away his silverware and everything."[25] According to Johnson, he responded by informing the staff, "I intend to have lunch here. I suggest that you get in touch with the governor and explain to him that I will either eat here with the other Senators or I will call a press conference, which is not part of my makeup. I will call a press conference and I will expose this to the world."[26] He was served, but it was not until many years later that the Commerce Club invited its first black member.

In 1962, the Reverend Fred Shuttlesworth persuaded Martin Luther King and his SCLC staff, including Andrew Young, to support ef-

---

[24] Leroy Johnson (attorney and former state senator), interview by authors, 27 July 2011, audio, Special Collections and Archives, University Library, Georgia State University.

[25] Maria Saporta, (journalist) video interview, 18 October 2013.

[26] Leroy Johnson interview.

forts to desegregate Birmingham, Alabama. At a retreat at Dorchester Center, SCLC leaders, along with leaders from Birmingham's Alabama Christian Movement for Human Rights, planned a series of organized demonstrations designed to highlight the injustices of segregation. Martin Luther King, Jr., was arrested during the demonstrations and wrote his famous "Letter from a Birmingham Jail." The violence of the law enforcement officials in Birmingham was in marked contrast to the orderly approach to demonstrations in Atlanta. Ultimately, the world witnessed on television the violence of Police Commissioner Bull Connor against the peaceful, non-violent demonstrators. Andrew Young had maintained contact with white business leaders during the demonstrations. He wrote in *An Easy Burden*, his memoir of the civil rights movement, "Reconciliation was an essential part of our definition of a successful movement. We were trying to transform America, not triumph over white folk."[27]

In February 1963, following the signing of a voluntary agreement to desegregate Birmingham, President John Kennedy introduced legislation in the US Congress to ban segregation in all public accommodations:

> We are confronted primarily with a moral issue. It is as old as the scriptures and it is as clear as the American Constitution. The heart of the question is whether all Americans are afforded equal rights and equal opportunities, whether we are going to treat our fellow Americans as we want to be treated.... [O]ne hundred years of delay have passed since President Lincoln freed the slaves, yet their heirs, their grandsons, are not fully free. They are not yet free from the bonds of injustice. And this nation, for all its hopes and all its boasts, will not be fully free until all of its citizens are free.... Next week I will ask the Congress of the United States to act, to make a commitment it has not fully made in this century to the proposition that race has no place in American life or law.[28]

The bill forbade segregation and discrimination based on race, color, national origin and religion in transportation, education, and em-

---

[27] Young, *An Easy Burden*, 250.

[28] President John F. Kennedy, "Civil Rights Announcement," delivered 11 June 1963, available at http://www.pbs.org/wgbh/americanexperience/features/primary-resources/jfk-civilrights/ (2 February 2016).

ployment. It stated, "All persons shall be entitled to the full and equal enjoyment of the goods, services, facilities, and privileges, advantages, and accommodations of any place of public accommodation...without discrimination or segregation on the ground of race, color, religion, or national origin."[29] It was the milestone in the effort for equality that the students from the sit-ins in Atlanta, Greensboro, and Nashville; the adults in the citizenship schools in Dorchester; the demonstrators in Birmingham, and many others had been working toward. News of Kennedy's phone call helped to turn African-Americans voters, who still had some allegiance to the party of President Abraham Lincoln, to support for Kennedy. It was the beginning of collaboration between the Kennedys and the African-American struggle for equality that led the president's brother, Edward M. Kennedy, to become a champion of civil rights in the Senate.

In summer 1963, however, African Americans were still seeking the right to eat a hamburger sitting down and to sleep in a hotel. Atlanta's mayor, Ivan Allen, was asked to live up to Atlanta's slogan of "A city too busy to hate," and testify in favor of the bill submitted to Congress by President Kennedy. The president called Allen personally to request his testimony. Allen understood that segregation was the "step-child of slavery" and that voluntary efforts, such as had happened in Atlanta and Birmingham were incomplete and insufficient. Allen recalled, "Other than a handful of liberals, [Robert] Woodruff was about the only white person in Atlanta who told me I should go to Washington and support the bill."[30] Even many African-American leaders were concerned for Al-

---

[29] "An act to enforce the constitutional right to vote, to confer jurisdiction upon the district courts of the United States, to provide injunctive relief against discrimination in public accommodations, to authorize the Attorney General to institute suits to protect constitutional rights in public facilities and public education, to extend the Commission on Civil Rights, to prevent discrimination in federally assisted programs, to establish a Commission on Equal Employment Opportunity, and for other purposes," 2 July 1964; Enrolled Acts and Resolutions of Congress, 1789–; General Records of the United States Government; Record Group 11; National Archives, Washington DC.

[30] Allen and Hemphill, *Mayor*, 104–106.

len's future as mayor if he supported the civil rights bill. Andrew Young recalled, "Interestingly enough, the black community did not want him to testify because if he testified, he would build up so much white resistance that he could not be re-elected as mayor. It was Mrs. Louise Allen who encouraged him and said 'Ivan if you really want to do this and don't do it you will always regret it.'"

In his book *Mayor: Notes on the Sixties*, Allen recounted his experience testifying before Senator Strom Thurmond and other Southern senators in support of Kennedy's bill. He described the letters of condemnation and the disapproval of friends and even family. He wrote,

> I have to be honest with myself that up until the time I had to make a decision whether to go to Washington or not go, my liberalism on the race issue had been based to a large degree on pragmatism: it was simply good business for Atlanta to be an open city, a fair city, a 'city too busy to hate,' a city trying to raise the level of its poorest citizens and get them off the relief rolls...at this point I had finally crossed over and made my commitment on a very personal basis.[31]

It would take another year to overcome the Senate filibuster on the civil rights bill. In the meantime, there was more violence and suffering. Four little girls were killed in a church bombing in Birmingham. Dr. King became the voice of the civil rights movement and the conscience of the nation with his speech at the 1963 March on Washington for Jobs and Freedom, where he famously said, "I have a dream that one day this nation will rise up, live out the true meaning of its creed: 'We hold these truths to be self-evident, that all men are created equal.'"[32] On November 22, 1964, the bright, shining President Kennedy was assassinated. The "Master of the Senate," Vice President Lyndon Baines Johnson, picked up the fallen baton and the commitment to racial equality.

Andrew Young was called to St. Augustine, Florida, America's oldest city, to work with activists there, led by a dentist, Dr. William Hayling. In St. Augustine, the behind-the-scenes negotiator found himself

---

[31] Ibid., 116.
[32] Martin Luther King, Jr., "I Have a Dream..." 1963, http://www.archives.gov/press/exhibits/dream-speech.pdf.

on the front lines, leading demonstrations and receiving a brutal beating at the hands of a Klan-inspired gang. The brutality in St. Augustine once again galvanized the nation. As Young recalls, "We will never know if the Senate filibuster would have been defeated if St. Augustine hadn't provided a vivid reminder of the injustices the bill was designed to address." President Lyndon Johnson signed the Civil Rights Act of 1964 on July 2 in an extraordinary televised ceremony in the Capitol Rotunda. Andrew Young recalled with admiration, "He made the strongest civil rights speech ever made by an American president. He had personally seen to the passage of the legislation in the Senate, where he had been majority leader, twisting arms and calling in favors to defeat the Southern filibuster."[33]

Nobel Prize Dinner

In 1964, an announcement from Oslo, Norway, shook the entire South, indeed, the entire nation, as Martin Luther King, Jr., was awarded the Nobel Peace Prize. When he won the award, King saw the Nobel Prize as a burden of responsibility. America's civil rights movement was validated by the rest of the world, but in Atlanta, resistance remained. According to Tom Johnson, retired head of Atlanta-based Cable News Network (CNN), "There were those who still believed that Martin was a threat to America rather than an asset, see, and they believed that."[34] Mayor Ivan Allen; Dr. Benjamin Mays, president of Morehouse College; Rabbi Jacob Rothschild; and Archbishop Paul John Hallinan were leaders in the effort to host the integrated dinner to honor Dr. King for his achievement. Allen sought the support of Robert Woodruff, the legendary head of the Coca-Cola Company, and Paul Austin, Coca-Cola's

---

[33] Young, *An Easy Burden*, 297–98.

[34] Wyatt Thomas (Tom) Johnson (retired president of CNN), interview by authors, 17 November 2011, audio, Special Collections and Archives, University Library, Georgia State University.

chairman.[35] Laura Jones Hardman, local civic leader and daughter of Woodruff Foundation president Boisfeuillet Jones, recalled the incident:

> I can tell you when Mr. Woodruff speaks people listen and that was one instance that made a big difference. He did it very quietly. Woodruff had the trust and the respect of others, and he had a sense of right and wrong, and I think because he did so much not out of self-interest but out of a real concern for the community. People listened to him and respected him and minded him as they did because they all went to the dinner.[36]

Bill Clement added, "Woodruff told other white business leaders that Coca-Cola® didn't need Atlanta, we can operate anywhere else. We want you to attend this dinner, and the dinner was sold out in two hours."[37] But, if many whites were reluctant to attend the dinner, blacks were somewhat afraid. More than forty years later, Azira Hill recalled how fearful she felt for her husband Jesse Hill and herself as they prepared to attend the first black-tie integrated event in the city's history. Mrs. Hill was also worried about what to wear to the event. Stores in Atlanta clung to the Jim Crow past and were reluctant to allow blacks to try on clothing. So, Azira Hill avoided the pain of segregated stores by buying the cloth and making the dress she wore to the dinner in Dr. King's honor.[38]

There were other white business leaders who helped make the Nobel Peace Prize dinner a success. One who worked behind the scenes to make sure the event was held in grand style was Cecil Alexander. An

---

[35] Gary M. Pomerantz, *Where Peachtree Meets Sweet Auburn* (New York: Penguin Books, 1996) 337.

[36] Laura Jones Hardman (civic leader and trustee of Emory University), interview by authors, 7 May 2012, audio, Special Collections and Archives, University Library, Georgia State University.

[37] William A. (Bill) Clement (former president and CEO, Atlanta Life Financial Group), interview by authors, 22 July 2011, audio, Special Collections and Archives, University Library, Georgia State University.

[38] Azira Hill (civic leader and wife of Jesse Hill), interview by authors, 8 July 2011, audio, Special Collections and Archives, University Library, Georgia State University.

architect and principal in one of the city's major firms, Alexander was, in his own words, a "gentleman racist" while growing up in Atlanta. He went on to explain that there were in the segregated city many whites who were racists, but they were not very genteel about their prejudices. During the 1950s he worked with the mayoral administration of Bill Hartsfield to improve housing opportunities for blacks. As a civic leader, Alexander worked to improve race relations in Atlanta, and he saw the dinner honoring Dr. King as a part of that effort. Throughout the remainder of his life, Cecil Alexander was proud of the letter Dr. King wrote to him, thanking him for his help in organizing the dinner at the Dinkler Plaza Hotel.[39] The significance of the event was later captured in the play and film *Driving Miss Daisy*, written by Atlanta-born Alfred Uhry.

The Nobel Peace Prize tribute dinner indicates how the leadership of the city's business community worked and is an example of the "Atlanta Way." Progressive whites and well- educated blacks joined together to make the event a success. While there were some white business leaders who thought about boycotting the dinner, there was no unfavorable publicity surrounding this threat. The leadership of Robert Woodruff was decisive as more than 1,500 people attended. At the event, blacks, whites, Jews, and gentiles joined hands and raised their voices in signing the anthem of the civil rights movement, "We Shall Overcome," led by Rabbi Jacob Rothschild and his wife, Janice. For a Southern city in the tumultuous decade of the 1960s, this became a night to celebrate and remember. It made Atlanta look different from other cities in the region, and it was part of a process of achieving racial moderation. Clarence Stone called this pattern "civic cooperation," and the ability of the Atlanta's leaders to reach across racial lines was a key to how the city got things done.[40]

---

[39] Cecil Alexander (architect and civic leader), interview by authors, 30 June 2011, audio, Special Collections and Archives, University Library, Georgia State University.

[40] Clarence N. Stone, *Regime Politics: Governing Atlanta, 1946–1988* (Lawrence: University Press of Kansas, 1989) 95.

Another key to the relatively peaceful desegregation in Atlanta was the courageous action of the students who attended the colleges and universities of the Atlanta University Center. From the publication of their demands in the "Appeal for Human Rights" to their willingness to endure arrest, the students protested in a well-organized and peaceful way. The students used two-way radios to coordinate their peaceful sit-ins and picketing in downtown Atlanta. Their demonstrations brought large numbers of arrests under Georgia's trespass law, as well as counter-demonstrations by robed Klan members. Mayor Bill Hartsfield reacted to the demonstrations and counter-demonstrations in typical Atlanta-booster fashion. Hartsfield announced to the press, "Well, at least in the field of lunch counter demonstrations, Atlanta can claim two firsts. With the help of the Ku Klux Klan, it can be the first to claim integrated picketing. And now we have radio-directed picketing. At least we are handling our problems in a progressive way."[41] This kind of publicity, in contrast to the violence in other Southern cities, made Atlanta seem more progressive in dealing with issues of race than may have been the actual case.

Violence in cities was not limited to the South. During summer 1965, rioting erupted in the Watts neighborhood in Los Angeles. African-American neighborhoods in many cities were places of overcrowding, poverty, and unemployment. Tensions were raised due the effects of expressway construction and urban renewal programs that contributed to the overcrowding in many places, including Atlanta. The following summer rioting spread to other cities such as San Francisco, Chicago, Cleveland, and Detroit. National Guard troops clashed with demonstrators in these and other cities, and shooting and property damage were widespread. While many of the same tensions simmered in Atlanta during the summers of 1965 and 1966, the city was spared the worst of the violence that took place elsewhere.

Leadership within the civil rights movement in Atlanta was chang-

---

[41] Jack L. Walker, "Protest and Negotiation: A Case Study of Negro Leadership in Atlanta," in *Atlanta, Georgia, 1960–1961: Sit-Ins and Student Activism*, ed. David J. Garrow (Brooklyn, NY: Carlson Publishers, 1989) 69–82.

ing. The student arm of the SCLC was known as the Student Non-
Violent Coordinating Committee (SNCC). Initially led by John Lewis,
the organization changed early in 1966 with the more militant black
power advocate, Stokely Carmichael, becoming the head of SNCC. In
the morning of 6 September 1966, Carmichael and a group of supporters
confronted Mayor Ivan Allen, Jr., in his office at city hall. The mayor
diffused the confrontation, but later in the afternoon a white police officer shot a black man suspected of car theft who resisted arrest and attempted to flee. The suspect was wounded in the hip and leg before being taken to Grady Hospital for treatment. Rumors spread through black
neighborhoods, especially in the area near Atlanta-Fulton County Stadium known as Summerhill, that the suspect had been handcuffed and
murdered. Stokely Carmichael used the unrest to protest police brutality
directed against blacks. At 4:30 p.m., a call came into City Hall reporting
rioting in the Summerhill neighborhood. The mayor, accompanied by
police captain Morris Redding and Detective George Royal, went to the
scene where they saw several overturned cars and a crowd of people.
Mayor Allen tried to calm the crowd, urging them to return to their
homes, but the group refused to disperse. In an act of real courage, Allen
climbed on top of the police car that had brought him to the scene. As
he pleaded for calm, the crowd shook the car until Allen fell off the roof
and was caught by Redding and Royal. As more police and African-
American ministers such as "Daddy" Martin Luther King, Sr., arrived,
the crowd began to disperse with little more disruption. The next day,
the mayor's courage received praise from many since he had managed to
calm what became known as the Summerhill Riot. Ralph McGill wrote
in the *Constitution*, "No other mayor of any city experiencing the trauma
of riots has so behaved. Even the more angry and bitter could not fail to
respect him." White voters in other parts of Georgia did not respect
Mayor Allen's racial moderation as three weeks later they elected segregationist Lester Maddox as governor of the state.[42]

---

[42] Pomerantz, *Where Peachtree Meets Sweet Auburn*, 345–50.

The riot in Summerhill spurred the mayor and Board of Aldermen to focus on the conditions in many of the city's poor black neighborhoods. In November 1966, Mayor Allen and the Board created the biracial Community Relations Commission (CRC) to deal with neighborhood grievances and other issues. Much of the work of getting the CRC approved and organized fell to vice mayor Sam Massell. During the first three years, the commission was distrusted by many whites and blacks in the city. The CRC's work was limited to an advisory role of bringing problems to the fore and exposing them to the public.[43] Searching for someone new to lead the CRC and build trust between blacks and whites, newly elected mayor Sam Massell turned to civil rights leader Andrew Young and appointed him chairman of the commission.[44] This appointment was the beginning of Young's transition, in his words, "from a rabble rouser to a public official."

The commission was useful in focusing attention on issues such as education, housing, and employment in Atlanta. The CRC held public hearings in a number of Atlanta neighborhoods to enhance racial harmony and to prevent future disorders, but the actions of the commission were not sufficient to prevent another outbreak of violence in the Dixie Hills neighborhood in northwest Atlanta during June 1967. The area had the same problems of poor housing and lack of recreation facilities that were common in many of the city's black neighborhoods. The CRC reports for the year noted that the problems in Dixie Hills and elsewhere were the result of the need for fundamental city services rather than the result of "civil rights or discrimination." People needed adequate housing, safe streets and sidewalks, streetlights, recreation improved public transportation, sufficient sewers and sanitary services, an end to police brutality, and increased police patrolling. Apparently the combination of the disturbances and the work of the CRC helped focus the attention of

---

[43] William Henry Boone, Jr., "The Atlanta Community Relations Commission," master's thesis, Atlanta University, 1969, 16–22.

[44] Sam Massell, Jr., (former Atlanta mayor and president of Buckhead Coalition) video interview, 5 August 2013.

mayors Ivan Allen and his successor, Sam Massell, on the need for improved municipal services to low-income areas.[45]

Federal policy changes in response to the rioting were also affecting Atlanta. President Lyndon Johnson declared a "war on poverty" aimed at creating the Great Society. Johnson proposed several new initiatives that extended federal aid directly to the nation's cities; among the most important was the creation of the federal Office of Economic Opportunity. This program recognized that previous federal policies such as the Urban Renewal Program were top-down in their approach to aiding urban areas and resulted in slum clearance that contributed to overcrowding in central cities. The new Office of Economic Opportunity mandated citizen participation in decision-making at the local level. Mayor Allen responded by creating an agency known as Equal Opportunity Atlanta (EOA). As part of its effort, EOA established neighborhood service centers to assist with employment, education, and other social services within the communities in which the programs were needed. The program faced the challenges of overcoming decades of neglect, but it did provide neighborhood residents with a voice in how the program was to operate. The executive director of EOA was Bill Allison, an African American who was able to establish a level of trust with the citizens' advisory groups and the EOA board, which consisted of civic leaders such as Andrew Young of the Community Relations Commission, business leaders, and neighborhood leaders. The participating citizens formed a network that became active in local politics, and many became part of the Neighborhood Planning Units that were required under the new city charter that took effect in 1974 when Maynard Jackson became mayor.[46] Another key leader providing support behind the scenes from Atlanta's businessmen was Boisfeuillet Jones. He had gone to school with Ivan Allen, Jr., graduated from Emory University, and served as a civic leader in

---

[45] Ronald H. Bayor, *Race and the Shaping of Twentieth-Century Atlanta* (Chapel Hill: University of North Carolina Press, 1996) 141–43.

[46] William Allison (former executive director, Economic Opportunity Atlanta), interview by authors, 28 August 2012, audio, Special Collections and Archives, University Library, Georgia State University.

many organizations. Jones worked briefly in the Kennedy administration in Washington as an assistant secretary in the US Department of Health, Education, and Welfare. He knew how to get things done by working quietly with others to "enable collaboration" in ways that were key to the "Atlanta Way." Jones brought his experience and connections to his role as chair of the board of EOA.[47] Among the benefits of the EOA board was its diverse membership where low-income neighborhood residents met face-to-face with business leaders. Some of the women residents became important figures in political block clubs, neighborhood associations, and other civic affairs. Women such as Mary Sanford, Susie La-Bord, Lillian Shepard, and Dorothy Bolden learned much from their EOA board experience and continued to be community leaders in the city. Mary Sanford became president of the Perry Homes Tenant Association and active with the Atlanta Housing Authority and MARTA planning committees. Her efforts helped the MARTA referendum to pass and the Proctor Creek rapid rail line to be built. Boisfeuillet Jones was also well connected to the city's philanthropy community and served as director of the Woodruff Foundation and several others. In spite of his low profile, Boisfeuillet Jones was recognized by Emory and the city of Atlanta with buildings named in his honor. He established the credibility of the EOA and established the pattern of generous support for local needs by the head of the Coca-Cola Company, Robert Woodruff.

Mayor Allen, Robert Woodruff, and Boisfeuillet Jones were to play key roles in 1968 when the tragedy of the assignation of Atlanta's leader of the civil rights movement, Martin Luther King, Jr. As Andrew Young recalls, King and most of the staff of the SCLC arrived in Memphis to assist striking sanitation workers. On the evening of April 3, 1968, King, speaking to a crowded church, gave one of his most memorable speeches. He placed the struggle for economic justice by the striking city workers within the broader efforts to win civil and human rights for all. In his words and actions, King had moved beyond just the struggle for civil rights and was concerned with economic justice and opposing the war in

---

[47] Hardman, interview, 7 July 2012.

Vietnam. In his speech that evening in Memphis, King said God has "allowed me to go up to the mountaintop and I've looked over. I've *seen* the Promised Land. I may not get there with you. But I want you to know tonight, that we as a people will get to the Promised Land.... I'm not fearing any man. Mine eyes have *seen* the glory of the coming of the Lord." Andrew Young remembers that the audience and the SCLC staff were awed and shaken by the power of King's speech. King's words foreshadowed the assassin's bullet that killed him as he stood on the balcony of the Lorraine Motel the next afternoon while Young and the other staff members watched.[48] King's death sparked rioting in cities across the United States. Many city leaders imposed curfews and called out National Guard troops. President Lyndon Johnson went on national television to appeal for calm in the aftermath of the assassination.

In Atlanta, Mayor Allen and his wife, Louise, drove as soon as they heard the news to King's home to assist Coretta Scott King. They took her to the airport, but when news arrived that her husband was dead, Mrs. King returned home to be with her children. When Allen returned home, he telephoned President Johnson to let him know that in King's hometown the streets remained mostly peaceful. A few moments later, Allen's phone rang. It was the president of Coca-Cola, Robert Woodruff, calling from Washington, DC. Woodruff had been with President Johnson when the news arrived that King had been shot. According to Allen, Woodruff said, "I want to give you a little advice." Usually Woodruff only gave advice to the mayor when it had been solicited. At this moment, Woodruff said, "You've got to start looking ahead, Ivan.... The minute they bring King's body back tomorrow—between then and the time of the funeral—Atlanta, Georgia, is going to be the center of the universe. I want you to do whatever is right and necessary, and whatever the city can't pay for will be taken care of. Just do it right."[49]

Woodruff correctly anticipated that the funeral for Dr. King would be like one for a head of state. Thousands of mourners from all walks of

---

[48] Young, *An Easy Burden*, 463.
[49] Pomerantz, *Where Peachtree Meets Sweet Auburn*, 356.

life crowded into the city—everyone from Vice President Hubert
Humphrey, mayors John Lindsay of New York City, Carl Stokes of
Cleveland, Joseph Alioto of San Francisco, and at least 150,000 others
participated in the procession that began at Ebenezer Baptist Church
where Dr. King and his father had served as co-pastors. The coffin, made
of African mahogany, was placed on a farm wagon pulled by two Alabama mules. The long procession moved from Ebenezer Church to the
quadrangle at Morehouse College for an outdoor service. The crowd
marched past the state capitol building, where the segregationist governor, Lester Maddox, had surrounded the building with heavily armed
state troopers while Maddox, convinced that the crowd intended to
storm the building, watched the funeral procession from inside his office.
Mayor Allen marched with the crowd, and no violence took place. Andrew Young remembers the sermon given by fellow SCLC leader, Ralph
Abernathy, who preached from the story of Joseph, "Let us slay the
dreamer, and see what shall become of the dream." Abernathy called upon all the listeners to take up King's cause and to dedicate ourselves to
the fulfillment of his dream.[50] In spite of the crowds, the day was peaceful, prompting former mayor Bill Hartsfield to say, "There was nothing
to tarnish the good name which Atlanta has abroad."[51]

---

[50] Young, *An Easy Burden*, 478.
[51] Pomerantz, *Where Peachtree Meets Sweet Auburn*, 363.

Students picketing Rich's Department Store
(Woodruff Library Atlanta University)

AN APPEAL
FOR HUMAN RIGHTS

We, the students of the six affiliated institutions forming the Atlanta University Center — Clark, Morehouse, Morris Brown, and Spelman Colleges, Atlanta University, and the Interdenominational Theological Center—have joined our hearts, minds, and bodies in the cause of gaining those rights which are inherently ours as members of the human race and as citizens of these United States.

We pledge our unqualified support to those students in this nation who have recently been engaged in the significant movement to secure certain long-awaited rights and privileges. This protest, like the bus boycott in Montgomery, has shocked many people throughout the world. Why? Because they had not quite realized the unanimity of spirit and purpose which motivates the thinking and action of the great majority of the Negro people. The students who instigate and participate in these sit-down protests are dissatisfied, not only with the existing conditions, but with the snail-like speed at which they are being ameliorated. Every normal human being wants to walk the earth with dignity and abhors any and all proscriptions placed upon him because of race or color. In essence, this is the meaning of the sit-down protests that are sweeping this nation today.

We do not intend to wait placidly for those rights which are already legally and morally ours to be meted out to us one at a time. Today's youth will not sit by submissively, while being denied all of the rights, privileges, and joys of life. We want to state clearly and unequivocally that we cannot tolerate, in a nation professing democracy and among people professing Christianity, the discriminatory conditions under which the Negro is living today in Atlanta, Georgia—supposedly one of the most progressive cities in the South.

Among the inequalities and injustices in Atlanta and in Georgia against which we protest, the following are outstanding examples:

(1) Education:

In the Public School System, facilities for Negroes and whites are separate and unequal. Double sessions continue in about half of the Negro Public Schools, and many Negro children travel ten miles a day in order to reach a school that will admit them.
On the university level, the state will pay a Negro to attend a school out of state rather than admit him to the University of Georgia, Georgia Tech, the Georgia Medical School, and other tax-supported public institutions.

According to a recent publication, in the fiscal year 1958 a total of $31,632,057.18 was spent in the State institutions of higher education for white only. In the Negro State Colleges only $2,001,177.06 was spent. The publicly supported institutions of higher education are inter-racial now, except that they deny admission to Negro Americans.

(2) Jobs:

Negroes are denied employment in the majority of city, state, and federal governmental jobs, except in the most menial capacities.

(3) Housing:

While Negroes constitute 32% of the population of Atlanta, they are forced to live within 16% of the area of the city.

Statistics also show that the bulk of the Negro population is still:

a. locked into the more undesirable and overcrowded areas of the city;

b. paying a proportionally higher percentage of income for rental and purchase of generally lower quality property;

c. blocked by political and direct or indirect racial restrictions in its efforts to secure better housing.

(4) Voting:

Contrary to statements made in Congress recently by several Southern Senators, we know that in many counties in Georgia and other southern states, Negro college graduates are declared unqualified to vote and are not permitted to register.

(5) Hospitals:

Compared with facilities for other people in Atlanta and Georgia, these for Negroes are unequal and totally inadequate.

Reports show that Atlanta's 14 general hospitals and 9 related institutions provide some 4,000 beds. Except for some 430 beds at Grady Hospital, Negroes are limited to the 250 beds in three private Negro hospitals. Some of the hospitals barring Negroes were built with federal funds.

(6) Movies, Concerts, Restaurants:

Negroes are barred from most downtown movies and segregated in the rest.
Negroes must even sit in a segregated section of the Municipal Auditorium.
If a Negro is hungry, his hunger must wait until he comes to a "colored" restaurant, and even his thirst must await its quenching at a "colored" water fountain.

(7) Law Enforcement:

There are grave inequalities in the area of law enforcement. Too often, Negroes are maltreated by officers of the law. An insufficient number of Negroes is employed in the law-enforcing agencies. They are seldom, if ever promoted. Of 830 policemen in Atlanta only 35 are Negroes.

We have briefly mentioned only a few situations in which we are discriminated against. We have understated rather than overstated the problems. These social evils are seriously plaguing Georgia, the South, the nation, and the world.

We hold that:

(1) The practice of racial segregation is not in keeping with the ideals of Democracy and Christianity.
(2) Racial segregation is robbing not only the segregated but the segregator of his human dignity. Furthermore, the propagation of racial prejudice is unfair to the generations yet unborn.
(3) In times of war, the Negro has fought and died for his country; yet he still has not been accorded first-class citizenship.
(4) In spite of the fact that the Negro pays his share of taxes, he does not enjoy participation in city, county and state government at the level where laws are enacted.
(5) The social, economic, and political progress of Georgia is retarded by segregation and prejudices.
(6) America is fast losing the respect of other nations by the poor example which she sets in the area of race relations.

It is unfortunate that the Negro is being forced to fight, in any way, for what is due him and is freely accorded other Americans. It is unfortunate that even today some people should hold to the erroneous idea of racial superiority, despite the fact that the world is fast moving toward an integrated humanity.

The time has come for the people of Atlanta and Georgia to take a good look at what is really happening in this country, and to stop believing those who tell us that everything is fine and equal, and that the Negro is happy and satisfied.

It is to be regretted that there are those who still refuse to recognize the over-riding supremacy of the Federal Law.

Our churches which are ordained by God and claim to be the houses of all people, foster segregation of the races to the point of making Sunday the most segregated day of the week.

We, the students of the Atlanta University Center, are driven by past and present events to assert our feelings to the citizens of Atlanta and to the world.

We, therefore, call upon all people in authority—State, County, and City officials; all leaders in civic life—ministers, teachers, and business men; and all people of good will to assert themselves and abolish these injustices. We must say in all candor that we plan to use every legal and non-violent means at our disposal to secure full citizenship rights as members of this great Democracy of ours.

Willie Mays
President of Dormitory Council For the Students of Atlanta University

James Felder
President of Student Government Association For the Students of Clark College

Marion D. Bennett
President of Student Association For the Students of Interdenominational Theological Center

Don Clarke
President of Student Body For the Students of Morehouse College

Mary Ann Smith
Secretary of Student Government Association For the Students of Morris Brown College

Roslyn Pope
President of Student Government Association For the Students of Spelman College

An Appeal for Human Rights document
(Woodruff Library Atlanta University)

Herman Russell at home with Martin Luther King, Ralph Abernathy,
and Andrew Young *(Russell Collection)*

Ivan Allen, Jr. testifies before Senate Commerce Committee
(Ivan Allen, Jr. Digital Collection)

A
RECOGNITION DINNER

honoring

DR. MARTIN LUTHER KING, JR.
CITIZEN OF ATLANTA

Winner of the

1964 NOBEL PEACE PRIZE

Sponsored by
CITIZENS OF ATLANTA

JANUARY 27TH

DINKLER PLAZA HOTEL • ATLANTA, GEORGIA

7 O'CLOCK

Nobel Prize dinner program
(Cecil Alexander Collection)

334 Auburn Ave., N.E.
Atlanta, Georgia 30303
Telephone 522-1420

Southern Christian Leadership Conference

Martin Luther King Jr., *President*   Ralph Abernathy, *Treasurer*   Andrew J. Young, *Executive Director*

March 15, 1965

Mr. Cecil A. Alexander
70 Fairlie Street, N. W.
Atlanta, Georgia

Dear Mr. Alexander:

In the rush of events surrounding Selma in our Alabama voting project,
I neglected to express my deep gratitude for your sponsorship of the
dinner honoring me on January 26. Please accept this belated note of
appreciation.

I must confess that few events have warmed my heart as did this occasion.
It was a tribute not only to me but to the greatness of the City of Atlanta,
the South, the nation and its ability to rise above the conflict of former
generations and really experience that beloved community where all differences
are reconciled and all hearts in harmony with the principles of our great
Democracy and the tenants of our Judeo-Christian heritage.

Sincerely yours,

Martin Luther King, Jr.

Kg

Thank you letter from Dr. King
(Cecil Alexander Collection)

Rabbi Rothschild presents Dr. King with Commemorative Bowl
(Cecil Alexander Collection)

Andrew Young (second row, third from right) with SCLC colleagues and King family members, above *(Young Family Collection)*; below, Andrew Young, Willie Ricks, and Ivan Allen during negotiations *(Auburn Avenue Research Library, AARL, Andrew Young Papers)*

3

Political Action—The Ballot

Mayors can learn many lessons from their predecessors. Andrew Young recalls learning about mistakes made by Atlanta's longest-serving mayor, William B. Hartsfield. During Hartsfield's first year in office in 1937, he attempted to reform local law enforcement, which resulted in a crackdown on illegal gambling and vigorous enforcement of traffic laws to catch speeders. His opponent in the next election used these two issues against Hartsfield as he sought re-election in 1940. As Andrew Young summarized it, Hartsfield lost the only mayoral election of his life because of his crackdown on the "bug," an illegal lottery operation, and for having traffic lights put up along Peachtree Street. When he became mayor, Young remembered these lessons and said, "I took the preacher's notion that God respects your right to go to hell if you insist on it. While we respect that right, as a city we need to tax you on the way to hell."[1] The willingness to learn these lessons from the past and move forward is an important part of the "Atlanta Way."

Hartsfield reclaimed the mayor's office in a special election in 1942 and remained in office until he decided not to seek re-election in 1962. No one is ever likely to repeat the length of time Hartsfield served as mayor due to the new charter imposing term limits. Over his long tenure as mayor, Hartsfield faced a variety of challenges and managed to forge a coalition of black and white voters that served the city well. Without a lot of public conflict, this coalition established the city's reputation as a place of moderation in comparison to other Southern municipalities. Hartsfield also worked closely with white business leaders such as Robert Woodruff of the Coca-Cola Company. From 1956 onward, Hartsfield

---

[1] Andrew Young, audio interview, 22 November 2011, Special Collections and Archives, University Library, Georgia State University.

proclaimed that Atlanta was a "city too busy to hate," as its residents were more focused on business than racial violence. In the period prior to the civil rights movement of the 1960s, the city's black residents were fortunate to have leaders who made a difference in their lives. Within a segregated society there were African-American teachers, ministers, business, and civic leaders who helped shape the political climate in Atlanta. One of the great African-American community leaders was John Wesley Dobbs. Throughout his long life (1882–1961), Dobbs supported the advancement of his race in the city where he became known as the unofficial "mayor" of Atlanta's major African-American street of commerce and culture, Auburn Avenue. In speeches to audiences of all types, Dobbs developed a five-point program for black uplift: religion, education, money, political security and culture. He often abbreviated these to the "three B's" the *book*, or education at one of Atlanta's historically black colleges; the *ballot*, or voter registration and showing up to the polls; and the *buck*, getting good jobs, creating new companies and providing a network for African-American businesses that would help forge a path to economic independence.[2] The three B's not only shaped Dobbs' life in the city, but they powerfully influenced many others in Atlanta. Dobbs himself took the three B's seriously. He raised six daughters, all of whom knew the importance of the book and graduated from Spelman College. Other members of Dobbs' family always remembered the three B's. In an interview, William Clement, a financial services executive and Dobbs' grandson, quoted the saying as did another grandson, Maynard Jackson, who put the idea of the book into action as a graduate of Morehouse College and North Carolina Central School of Law. Jackson used the ballot to be elected mayor of Atlanta three times.[3] He also knew the importance of the buck as Jackson was the founder of several business firms. Jackson's grandfather, John Wesley Dobbs traveled around the state as a

---

[2] Gary M. Pomerantz, *Where Peachtree Meets Sweet Auburn* (New York: Penguin Books, 1996) 147.

[3] William A. (Bill) Clement (former president and CEO, Atlanta Life Financial Group), interview by authors, 22 July 2011, audio, Special Collections and Archives, University Library, Georgia State University.

co-founder of the Atlanta Negro Voters League and Grand Master of the Prince Hall Masons of Georgia. Everywhere he spoke, Dobbs mentioned his three B's as the keys to change for his race. These elements—books, ballots, and bucks—would become cornerstones of making Atlanta a different city from others.

Before retirement, Atlanta native Julius Hollis was an entrepreneur and business owner. Hollis exemplifies how the three B's helped him to succeed. In an interview he commented, "Atlanta had all the building blocks in place. Let's look at the black community; it had a vibrant black middle class who were business owners, who were homeowners." Hollis was a student at Morehouse College when he began working in political campaigns for Andrew Young and Maynard Jackson. Hollis was part of a talented group of young African Americans who not only helped to win elections, but also learned valuable skills working for Atlanta city government before moving on to other opportunities.[4] The three B's not only influenced people like him but also became in many ways the path to leadership for African Americans in Atlanta.

At the center of this leadership was the group of black institutions of higher education that included Atlanta University, Clark College, Morris Brown College, Spelman College, and Morehouse College. These schools served as magnets, drawing talented faculty and students to Atlanta from elsewhere, and produced graduates who were the backbone of the city's African-American community. One of these leaders was Dr. Clarence A. Bacote, whose pivotal role in the political life of the city took place largely hidden from public view. Born and raised in Kansas City, Missouri, Bacote received his undergraduate degree from the University of Kansas and doctorate from the University of Chicago. In 1930, he became a professor of history at Atlanta University and a political activist in the city for the next forty-seven years. Three years after his arrival, Bacote became the first director of the citizenship schools established by the NAACP in Atlanta. He chaired the successful voter registration

---

[4] Julius Hollis (founder and chair, Alliance for Digital Equality), interview by authors, 30 January 2012, audio, Special Collections and Archives, University Library, Georgia State University.

drive in 1947 that resulted in the decision by Mayor Hartsfield to hire eight African-American police officers. In 1952, Bacote managed the campaign of Atlanta University's president Rufus Clement, who was the first black person elected to the Atlanta School Board.[5]

Professor Bacote worked constantly behind the scenes to ensure the registration of blacks. He trained newly enfranchised citizens in how to cast a ballot, helped run campaigns, and analyzed voting patterns in the city.[6] His work in local elections was aided by a US Supreme Court decision in 1962 that abolished the old "county unit" system that governed elections in Georgia. This system gave each county in the state roughly equal power in state-wide elections, increasing rural control of the legislature and reducing the influence of urban counties like Fulton, the county that included Atlanta. The court ruling required representation in the legislature based on the formula of "one man, one vote." As a consequence, the legislature was required to reapportion districts in the Georgia General Assembly, creating a predominately African-American senate district in Atlanta. In 1962, Clarence Bacote worked tirelessly along with Morehouse College president Benjamin Mays and others to secure the election to the legislature of Leroy Johnson as the first black to serve in the General Assembly since Reconstruction. Johnson was a graduate of Morehouse with a law degree from North Carolina Central University. Once elected, Johnson's next challenge was to desegregate the state capitol. When he entered in January 1963, the drinking fountains and restrooms still had signs for white and "colored." Johnson refused to use the segregated facilities, and the signs eventually came down. When he entered the cafeteria for the first time to eat, the white patrons left the lunchroom. Senator Johnson quickly learned the ways of the General Assembly and recalled later that "race doesn't matter if others need your

---

[5] Louis Williams, "Clarence A. Bacote (1906–1981)," *New Georgia Encyclopedia*, http://www.georgiaencyclopedia.org/articles/history-archaeology/ clarence-bacote-1906-1981 (27 May 2014).

[6] Samuel Bacote (retired educator, business leader, and son of Clarence Bacote), interview by authors, 25 August 2011, audio, Special Collections and Archives, University Library, Georgia State University.

vote." He also observed that "in politics, you don't get what you deserve, but what you can negotiate." Johnson was important in desegregating institutions of the state that helped make Atlanta different by demonstrating the possibilities of blacks and whites working together.[7]

In 1965, Q. V. Williamson continued the "firsts" to become the first African-American member of the Atlanta Board of Aldermen since Reconstruction. Bacote played a major role in his campaign, as well as in the successful election of Grace Towns Hamilton as the first black female in the Georgia legislature. In a city-wide election three years later, Maynard Jackson, the grandson of John Wesley Dobbs, won election to the position of vice mayor. With this sequence of election successes, there was interest in selecting someone to run for the US Congress representing part of the city of Atlanta. Andrew Young was working as an organizer with the SCLC, so he thought his role might be able to manage a campaign for someone else. Young went to New York to meet with Harry Belafonte to arrange for him to do a fundraiser for a black congressional candidate from the Deep South. During the conversation Harry Belafonte mentioned that Young was running for Congress. According to Young, "I had not thought of running for congress until the day he [Belafonte] announced that I was running."[8] Rather than rely on the experience of locals like Clarence Bacote, Young was surrounded during this first congressional campaign in 1970 by "experts" from outside the region. The campaign manager was hired from Philadelphia, and "he recommended spending $300,000 on television ads and doing focus groups so we could try to listen to what people were saying they thought they wanted."[9] The 1970 campaign was really challenging in the sense that the district included a lot of white communities that a black candidate normally would not consider going to, and Young made a spe

[7] Leroy Johnson, interview, 27 July 2011.

[8] Andrew Young, audio interview, 11 May 2011, Special Collections and Archives, University Library, Georgia State University.

[9] Ibid.

cial point of going into those communities and asking people for their support. While it was difficult having a black civil rights leader asking white Southerners for their votes, Young campaigned in every precinct in the fifth congressional district.

In spite of his hard work campaigning, election night was a huge disappointment for Young; he lost the election by just over 20,000 votes. One definition of a leader is the ability to attract and inspire followers. By this measure, Andrew Young proved, even in defeat, that he had the ability to attract and inspire followers. Two of these were Carol and Paul Muldawer, whom Young met while he was campaigning during this first run for Congress. The Muldawers had invited their white north-Atlanta neighbors to come to their home and meet Andrew Young. The Muldawers supported Young in all his subsequent campaigns. In this campaign, Young also gained the support of Jesse Hill, president of the Atlanta Life Insurance Company. Young recalled that he was looking for a strategy to mobilize support from African-American churches when he received sage advice from Rev. Fred Bennette. Bennette had been mentored by Martin Luther King, Sr., and knew his way around Atlanta's black leadership. He recommended that Young ask Jesse Hill to convene a meeting of ministers. Young recalled,

> And I said, "But, he's not a preacher." Bennette said, "Boy, I don't know how you can be so smart and still be so stupid. Don't you know how all those preachers got their churches? They borrowed the money through Atlanta Life. And do you know who Atlanta Life is?" I said, "Yes, Jesse Hill." He said, "When the man who holds your mortgage tells you to come to a meeting, you come to a meeting."

Jesse Hill and the Muldawers became part of a group of blacks and whites who continued their loyalty to Andrew Young over the years and called themselves members of "Youngdom."[10]

After his defeat in the 1970 congressional campaign, Young received a call to come and sit down with Clarence Bacote. In the conver-

---

[10] Carol and Paul Muldawer (civic leader and architect), interview by authors, 27 July 2011, audio, Special Collections and Archives, University Library, Georgia State University.

sation, Professor Bacote "showed me on a map why I lost in 1970 and how I could win in the next election." As former state senator Leroy Johnson recalled, "Bacote would calculate each vote. He would then have a chart to see how many voted from precinct A, precinct B, and so on. People would depend on Bacote for his political analysis. He did it with pencil and paper on a handwritten map of the city, precinct by precinct. It was exactly what Barack Obama did in his election with computers."[11] Bacote told Young that if he concentrated on getting the votes in these key precincts, he could go to Congress. The challenge in the next election was to do better organizing, and Young's experience at SCLC was combined with the experience of locals who understood voting patterns in Atlanta.

As Young began planning for the next election he had the advantage of Bacote's advice and a Fifth Congressional District that had been reconfigured to include more black voters. Although the district was still majority white, Young's appointment as chair of the city's appointment as chair of the city's Community Relations Commission by Mayor Massell helped soften his image with some voters. Massell recalled,

> He was a champion in bringing people together and he still is; that's his strong suit. And he really does know how to talk to both sides. Well, in his case, maybe all three sides, he really does a champion job.... [He] gives me credit for [helping his political career] and if so, I'm proud of it because it did give him a forum or platform from which he could campaign and get exposure, publicly and in particular with a lot of leadership in the community, so it played a dual role.[12]

For the next run for Congress, Young put together a campaign staff that included some of the sharpest young minds from the Atlanta University Center. Among these was Julius Hollis, a student at Morehouse. According to Hollis, the Young campaign in 1972 was very sophisticated

---

[11] Leroy Johnson, interview, 27 July 2011.

[12] Sam Massell, Jr., (former Atlanta mayor and president of Buckhead Coalition) video interview, 5 August 2013.

and the beginning of the Atlanta political machine that has continued to win elections in the city.[13]

Perhaps the most important part of Young's 1972 campaign was the support of his wife, Jean, a respected educator in the city. She got very involved in this campaign and started recruiting her friends; she built what for years was called her "standing committee of the house." She had her own kitchen cabinet of women who would do projects with her. Jean Young also started the Women for Young, the first political organization in the campaign that focused exclusively on women. Women for Young sought to mobilize female voters and talk about the issues that were important to them.

The second campaign for congress was better organized. Young had the active support of the head of Atlanta Life, Jesse Hill, who not only provided financial support but also gave Young advice on every facet of the campaign. Young recalled, "I would get out of bed early in the morning around six, creep down to my study in the basement of the house, and wait for my first call of the day that would be from Jesse Hill. Then, after a day of meetings, fundraising, and campaign stops, the last phone call of the day at ten or eleven at night was from Mr. Hill." Other financial support for the congressional campaign came from an unlikely source, Charlie Loudermilk, a white conservative Republican businessman. Loudermilk tells the story that he first met Young when the SCLC was organizing the march from Selma to Montgomery, Alabama. Young needed tents and folding chairs that the SCLC rented from Loudermilk's company, Aaron Rents. From these initial dealings, Loudermilk felt that Young was a decent person and a remarkable leader. Out of this experience the two became unlikely friends.[14] Young forged a coalition of black and white voters that served him well in 1972 and beyond.

---

[13] Hollis, interview, 30 January 2012.

[14] Charlie Loudermilk (retired chairman, Aaron Rents), interview with Andrea Young, 17 August 2011, audio, Special Collections and Archives, University Library, Georgia State University.

On election day there was grass roots support from throughout the black community as church buses and taxicabs made sure that voters got to the polls. Young recalls, "In a pouring down rain we had a 74 percent turnout in the black community and we got 14 percent of the white vote."[15] The key to victory, as Clarence Bacote had told him, was high turnout in the black precincts and just enough support from progressive whites. Young was building trust among voters of both races, who would continue to turn out for him in the years ahead.

Once in office, Congressman Young had to deliver services for his constituents in Atlanta. Among the most pressing needs in Atlanta was the improvement of its transportation system. The city had just approved its rapid transit system known as MARTA and needed federal assistance for the construction of the rail line. Young got on the Banking Committee in the House of Representatives and helped to create a mass transit subcommittee. He introduced and passed legislation that secured federal funding for high density residential and commercial development around MARTA stations. Other transportation initiatives later helped Maynard Jackson, as Mayor of Atlanta, expand the Atlanta airport so that it grew from what had once been a modest municipal air field to one of the busiest airports in the world. These two transportation initiatives improved the accessibility of the city for convention visitors and tourists. For local residents, Congressman Young helped secure funding for the Chattahoochee Recreation Area, a string of parks and recreation facilities along the Chattahoochee River. According to Skip Mason, an Atlanta historian, Andrew Young had become a public leader, building on the purpose of the civil rights movement, not just to march and demonstrate, but to open doors to political office.[16]

---

[15] Andrew Young, video interview.

[16] Herman (Skip) Mason (historian and archivist, Morehouse College), interview by authors, 14 August 2012, audio, Special Collections and Archives, University Library, Georgia State University.

The 1970s has been described as "the coming of age of black political power in Atlanta."[17] The group of talented people Andrew Young brought together to secure his election to Congress in 1972 formed the nucleus of the coalition that worked to change Atlanta's politics the following year. Maynard Jackson, large, handsome, and eloquent, graduated from Morehouse College at eighteen and studied law at Boston University before finishing his degree at North Carolina Central University. He helped pay his way through law school by selling encyclopedias, an experience that gave him self-confidence and some success as a businessman. He returned to Atlanta and worked for the National Labor Relations Board before going into private law practice. In 1968, as a brash thirty-year-old, Maynard Jackson challenged the white incumbent US Senator Herman Talmadge. Even though Jackson lost the election, he managed to receive a majority of the votes cast in the city of Atlanta. The name recognition Jackson received from this Senate campaign and the votes of city residents convinced him to run for the office of vice mayor the following year. His opponent was a long-serving member of the city's Board of Aldermen, Milton Ferris. Senior members of Atlanta's established black leadership such as Senator Leroy Johnson, Jesse Hill, Martin Luther King, Sr., and others did not think Jackson was old enough or ready to run for city-wide office so instead focused their efforts on adding more African Americans to the Board of Aldermen. Jackson went ahead with his campaign and won the election with 58 percent of the vote.[18] Sam Massell, Jr., won the mayor's race after a runoff against the candidate favored by the Chamber of Commerce and other business leaders. Massell won the election in 1969 with 90 percent of the black vote and 10 percent of the white vote.[19] The city's electorate was changing rapidly,

---

[17] Tom Houck (retired civil rights leader and journalist), interview by authors, 17 July 2012, audio, Special Collections and Archives, University Library, Georgia State University.

[18] Pomerantz, *Where Peachtree Meets Sweet Auburn*, 388.

[19] Sam Massell, Jr., (former Atlanta mayor and president of Buckhead Coalition) interview with authors, 28 July 2011, audio, Special Collections and Archives, University Library, Georgia State University.

and the following year the US Census reported that for the first time in its history, Atlanta had a majority black population.[20]

Once in office, Mayor Massell attempted to repair the coalition of business leaders and elected public officials in the city. Business support was needed to lobby the state legislature for the right to try another referendum on the transit system. This time, the system would be financed with federal aid and a one-cent sales tax in exchange for a promise to lower bus fares to 15 cents for ten years. A citizen committee of one hundred members, including both blacks and whites, was formed to give citizens input in planning the rapid rail lines for the MARTA system. The referendum passed due to the promises of the 15-cent fare and a rapid rail line from downtown to one of the city's lowest income neighborhoods, Proctor Creek, in the northwest part of town. Another citizen committee reviewed the city's charter and made recommendations to the state legislature for revisions. The city's weak mayor system with a sixteen-member Board of Aldermen would be replaced with an eighteen-member city council and a strong mayor-led government in which the mayor could appoint heads of administrative departments. Knowing he would likely face a challenge from Vice Mayor Jackson in the next election, Massell also tried to increase diversity at city hall. He recommended appointment of African Americans to head the personnel and public works departments, a first for city government. When a vacancy occurred on the Board of Aldermen, the mayor appointed the first female to serve in this position.

These efforts to increase diversity were not enough to prevent Maynard Jackson from challenging Massell for the mayor's office in 1973. At the outset the candidates were civil toward one another. As polls showed the race tightening, one veteran of the Jackson campaign, Walter Huntley, recalled, "Sam Massell ran a campaign ad saying Atlanta was too young to die, and he showed tumbleweeds going down the

---

[20] U.S. Bureau of the Census, *Nineteenth Census of the United States, 1970,* vol. 1 (Washington, DC: Government Printing Office, 1972).

center of town. It was fear, fear of the unknown."[21] Maynard Jackson also changed his campaign staff just a few months before the election. According to Julius Hollis, a youthful veteran of Andrew Young's successful congressional campaign, "Maynard's campaign at the time was run by a couple of people in a traditional way. And so we decided in consultation with Maynard's political guru, the late David Franklin, to go over and run his campaign for the last three months the way we ran campaigns."[22] The team began using the same date-driven political strategy developed by Clarence Bacote that focused on voter precinct profiling and spreadsheets and once again proved that approach was successful. During the four years since Massell was elected in 1969, many whites had fled from the city to the suburbs and more blacks had moved into the city. Massell summed up his loss to Maynard Jackson by noting that in 1973, Massell's numbers were reversed with 90 percent of a smaller white population voting for the incumbent, and only 10 percent of the new majority black population supporting him.[23]

As the first mayor under the new city charter, Maynard Jackson had the power to name department heads, and the city council assumed the more traditional legislative functions of the local government. Mayor Jackson wanted to use his authority to expand the diversity among city employees and in the businesses that had contracts with the city. When he took office, less than .5 percent of the city's contracts went to minority firms. Jackson insisted that this number be raised to 25 percent either through minority hiring or joint venture contracts. He also wanted to name an African American as chief of the police department. White business leaders, who were accustomed to having more influence in City Hall's decisions, opposed both of Jackson's plans, so the new mayor's first two years were especially difficult for the long-standing partnership between business leaders and local government. Their conflicts over the

---

[21] Walter R. Huntley, Jr., (president, Huntley Partners) interview with Andrea Young, 18 February 2014, Special Collections and Archives, University Library, Georgia State University.

[22] Hollis, interview, 30 January 2012.

[23] Massell interview, 28 July 2011.

police chief, public safety, and minority hiring spread to the front pages of the newspapers.

Another rupture in the partnership was caused by a letter written to the mayor by Harold Brockey, the head of locally owned Rich's department store and chair of the downtown business group Central Atlanta Progress. In the letter that was leaked to the press and appeared in the *Constitution*, Brockey described the fear of crime among business leaders and reported that the mayor was perceived as anti-white. He added that the split between business and political leaders in Atlanta could lead to more white flight and disinvestment in downtown.[24] This was the first significant public conflict between business leaders and the mayor's office since the end of World War II. Both sides quickly attempted to repair the damage with Mayor Jackson and Harold Brockey sending a joint letter to major publications such as the *New York Times* and *Business Week* to correct the "mistaken impression" about city hall-business relations. The mayor also accompanied the president of the chamber of commerce on a tour of several cities to promote business relocation to Atlanta and "to paint a picture of harmony between the mayor and the city's business community." In a speech to a Chicago audience, Mayor Jackson said, "Atlanta can't prosper without city hall and business in bed together."[25]

In spite of the efforts to reestablish the relationship, public criticism of Atlanta's first African-American mayor continued the following year. In March, the *Constitution* published a seven-part series of articles on Atlanta as a "City in Crisis." The series began by looking back to the 1960s as a time of prosperity and goodwill. "Atlanta was Camelot," but today, "Camelot has faded." The head of C & S National Bank, Richard Kettel, was quoted as saying, "It has been traumatic having the black community with the political strength and the white community continuing to hold the purse strings." Later in the series, former mayor Mas-

---

[24] Claudia Townsend, "CAP Warns of Crime Fears," *Atlanta Constitution*, 21 September 1974, 1A and 11A.

[25] John Huey, "Jackson, Brockey Sending Corrections," *Atlanta Constitution*, 15 November 1974, 9A; Colleen Teasley, "Mayor, Currey Deny Rift, Seek Business in Chicago," 21 November 1974, 1A.

sell noted that during the late 1960s and early 1970s, many of the older white leaders such as Ivan Allen, Jr.; Mills B. Lane, of C & S National Bank; Robert Woodruff, of the Coca-Cola Company; Ralph McGill, the editor of the *Constitution*; and Opie Shelton, the executive director of the chamber of commerce, had all retired. With the changes in the city, the newspaper expressed regret that the present day decisions were made more complicated by race, the inexperience of a new generation of leaders, and problems such as corruption in the police department, the decline in retail activity, the proliferation of "porno" shops, and increases in crime and welfare. The series of articles ended with the question, "Where does the city go now to find a common ground?"[26]

In addition to his troubled relationship with business leaders, Mayor Jackson also had the task of implementing the new city charter that gave him administrative responsibility for city departments and mandated citizen participation in planning through a new organization of neighborhoods. Known as Neighborhood Planning Units (NPUs), the system mandated by the revised charter established a network of community planning districts required to develop comprehensive land-use plans that would become part of the city-wide plan. The city's neighborhoods had organized around a battle to stop the construction of an expressway, and many of the residents affected by the proposed highway became part of his winning political coalition. As the first black mayor in a Deep South city, Jackson also faced expectations among his African-American constituents that the city would become more representative of their interests. This meant that services would be more equitably divided, employees would be more diverse, and issues such as police brutality would be addressed. The leadership of the police department was in the hands of a chief who was a white officer appointed under the previous system of alderman. Mayor Jackson wanted to fire the chief, but he had four years remaining on his contract. Instead, after considerable conflict, Jackson created the position of Public Safety Commissioner (or "super chief" as

---

[26] Bill Shipp, Lewis Grizzard, Sharon Bailey, Frederick Allen, and Sam Hopkins, "City in Crisis," *Atlanta Constitution*, 23 March 1975, A-1, A-16, A-17; 30 March 1975, A-1, A-12, A-13.

the appointee was nicknamed), who would be the boss of the chief of police. The old chief was assigned a duty that included staying in his office with the door closed while the new commissioner ran the day-to-day affairs of the department. Eventually the city was able to buy out the old chief's contract, and he left city government.

The public disagreement between business leaders and the mayor regarding continued economic development efforts in Atlanta was healed following the Brockey letter of 1974 and the "City in Crisis" articles the following year. Both sides were able to agree that Atlanta needed to keep existing businesses in the city and to continue to attract new ones. Conflict continued, however, on another issue—crime. The *Constitution* continued to print articles publicizing the city's crime statistics as a serious problem and urging stronger police efforts to combat a level of violence it considered unacceptable. As a consequence of this debate, many whites read the in the newspaper about a city in a state of anarchy and crisis and concluded that Atlanta should be avoided. This type of publicity helped some whites justify their choice to flee the city and comforted those who lived in the suburbs that they were removed from the widely discussed problem of crime and the less often discussed topic of race.[27] An analysis of crime rates shows that the number of homicides in Atlanta actually declined during 1973, the year before Jackson became mayor, and 1974, and continued to decline further the following year. While the number of aggravated assaults in the city did rise slightly in both 1974 and 1975, the rate of increase in both years was less than the national average and lower than the rate of aggravated assaults in Atlanta's suburban areas. A careful analysis of the location of violent crime indicates that most homicides and assaults took place in pockets of low-income areas away from downtown. The image of crime in the streets of downtown seemed to be a false impression created among people fearful of racial change in Atlanta.[28] Despite the fear by many whites of black political leadership,

---

[27] Kevin M. Kruse, *White Flight: Atlanta and the Making of Modern Conservatism* (Princeton, NJ: Princeton University Press, 2005).

[28] Harvey K. Newman, "Hospitality and Violence: Contradictions in a Southern City," *Urban Affairs Review* 35/4 (March 2000): 551–56.

Maynard Jackson was popular among African Americans in the city, and he won re-election by an overwhelming majority in 1977.

The city's reputation continued to suffer as Maynard Jackson entered his second term as mayor. Beginning in June 1979, a series of baffling murders took place in the city. Black male children and teenagers began to disappear from the streets, their bodies later found in isolated places. By May 1981, the number of murders reached twenty-eight. When residents realized there was a serial killer of young African-American males in the city, fear and panic began to spread. Many blacks feared the Ku Klux Klan might be responsible for the murders. On October 13, 1980, the midst of the crisis, an explosion at the day care center of a public housing project killed four children and a teacher. The explosion was the result of a faulty boiler, but the need to demonstrate swift action brought about reconciliation between the mayor and white business leaders. Funds were raised, and the day care center was rebuilt almost overnight. Finally, the new public safety commissioner, Lee Brown, and a special task force on the missing and murdered children case arrested Wayne Williams, an African-American male. After a sensational trial, Williams was convicted of several of the murders, and the serial killings stopped. Gradually the city returned to normal, but publicity from the case caused considerable damage to Atlanta's image.

After two terms in office, Maynard Jackson had to step down per the new charter's term limits. Jackson remained so popular with black voters that he could win any office he sought. Among white business leaders, his brash style and policies requiring minority hiring or joint venture contracts left considerable resentment toward him. After Maynard Jackson left office and in the remaining years of his life, the city's first African-American mayor never received an offer to work for an Atlanta law or brokerage firm. Remembering his grandfather John Wesley Dobbs's words about the importance of the buck, Maynard Jackson eventually formed his own law firm and a brokerage specializing in municipal finance.

After winning his third term to Congress in 1976, Andrew Young prepared to return to Washington and continue his work there on behalf of his constituents. This election year also brought Georgia's former governor to the national stage as Jimmy Carter was elected president. Young supported someone else during the presidential campaign, but when Carter called to ask if Young would introduce him to members of the Congressional Black Caucus, he agreed. The caucus had met with all of the Democratic candidates for president, but few of them wanted to meet with Jimmy Carter, a white, one-term governor who was not well known outside the Deep South. Congressional representative Barbara Jordan of Houston reminded the group that it had met with Lloyd Benson, the former governor of Texas, so it should meet with Carter as well. When the other presidential candidates such as Governor Jerry Brown of California, Representative Morris Udall of Arizona, and Senator Birch Bayh of Indiana were in the room with the Black Caucus, they said they agreed with the entire agenda of the congressional group. But in a room full of black people, all the candidates were nervous. The last question posed to each candidate was always the same: *How many black people are on your staff?* All of the candidates said they had one, except for the most liberal candidate, who said he was looking for one. Young recalled,

> When Jimmy Carter came in, he was perfectly relaxed. He only knew one person in the room besides me, and he went around and kissed her on the cheek. Carter went to Barbara Jordan and praised her for how impressive she had been during [Nixon's] impeachment trial. He went around the room meeting people and, while he was at ease, Carter did not agree with anything on the Caucus' agenda. He was against busing, against quotas; Carter was against the whole liberal agenda until they asked him how many black people he had on his staff. Carter said he did not know, and Charlie Rangel jumped up and said, "What the hell are we talking to you for if you don't know?" I said, "Wait a minute, Charlie, he didn't say he didn't have any black people, he said he didn't know how many black people he had on his staff. His assistant is outside, may I get him?" His assistant was Ben Brown, who was a black state senator from Georgia. When Ben came in, I said, "Ben, how many black people do you have on your staff?" And he said, "Right now, we have twenty-seven." It was obvious to the members of the Black Caucus that the other candidates were talking a good game, but

Carter was acting on it. I ended up helping Carter's campaign all over the country where there were members of the Black Caucus.

After the election, President-elect Carter asked Andrew Young to serve as ambassador to the United Nations. Young recalls the conversation in which he said,

I want to continue in Congress where I could serve as sort of the inside man in congressional relations. I also told Carter that he should appoint Barbara Jordan to the UN. Carter answered that he was serious about human rights issues and that was the one contribution he wanted to make and he couldn't without me. Carter thought Barbara Jordan was a better candidate, except she was not with Martin Luther King, and the thing we need if we're going to advance human rights is the legacy of Martin Luther King, and I carry that legacy. That was how I ended up going to the United Nations.

Few people realized how important Andrew Young's experience at the UN would be for the city of Atlanta. This background provided personal relationships with leaders all over the world. When Young returned to the city as Maynard Jackson was completing his second term as mayor, people wanted him to run for the office. The thinking was that Young was another progressive, coalition-building politician who would be an ideal candidate. He was regarded as the person who could continue the "Atlanta Way" of bringing people together.

Young himself was hesitant to run for mayor, and part of the reason was financial. As he said, "I had three children in school, and I was broke. I also didn't see any future in being mayor of a city when everything about cities was changing. Everything that happened in previous administrations was the federal government putting money into cities. Ronald Reagan had been elected, and there was going to be no more money for cities." The former ambassador just did not think he could afford to be Atlanta's mayor—until something happened that made him realize he *had* to do it. As Young said,

A lady by the name of Miss Susie LaBord...walked into the meeting that was discussing who should run for mayor since I said I wasn't going to run. They asked me to attend the meeting, but she came in late, and she walked right up to me with her cane and she said, "Look here, boy—when you came here, you wasn't nothing." She said, "We made you somebody and now we need you and you turn your back on us? We done wasted our time on you!" And she walked out of the room, and nobody said a word, but the word was said, because everything good that had happened to me had happened because of people like Miss LaBord.

She was among the many community leaders involved in the initial organizing efforts of the Economic Opportunity Atlanta program and the city's neighborhood planning units.

Once he made the decision to run for mayor, Young faced the challenges of organizing and financing a campaign. For financing Young turned to Atlanta Life President, Jesse Hill, and Aaron Rents Chairman, Charlie Loudermilk. Young recalled,

> I worked with Jesse on everything because Jesse Hill was in everything, and you couldn't not work with Jesse Hill. We needed Charlie because I didn't want to run a black-versus-white campaign, and we needed someone prominent in the white community. And I said to Charlie, look, if I don't win it's no problem, but if I win and we can't pull this city back together it's a real problem. I said I need you with me and he understood that.

Candidate Young needed to build a coalition to win the mayoral election, and he was a master coalition builder. Atlanta attracted a lot of New South whites and people who did not want to be associated with the legacy of racism and segregation. These folks were willing to support a candidate who was qualified, and they would not allow prejudice to deter them from that support. Young was qualified, and he was able to draw white supporters, some of whom had supported his congressional races. He was a former lieutenant of Dr. King with his message of unity, and Young wanted to serve the whole community. One veteran of the campaign for mayor was Doug Gatlin, who went door to door on behalf of Andrew Young in the predominantly white Virginia-Highlands neighborhood. Gatlin recalls that Young's reputation as a congressman and UN ambassador made him a good candidate among liberal voters in the area.[29]

Andrew Young's diplomatic skills were also needed with the white business community that had scars after battling the Jackson administration for eight years. Architect Paul Muldawer observed, "When he began the campaign, most of them thought stereotypically that Andy was Maynard, and Andy got very little white support, just our little cadre of liberals."[30] Charlie Loudermilk provided an invaluable bridge between the campaign and the white business community. According to Young, "He really took a leading role in fundraising and in badgering his colleagues in the business community to realize that I was not the kind of person they thought I was." One of the fears of the white business leaders concerned the future of cities led by black mayors. When white business leaders looked at black mayors such as Carl Stokes of Cleveland, Richard Hatcher of Gary, and Kenneth Gibson of Newark, they felt that decline was the inevitable result of African-American political leadership. These places seemed to be drying up, and Atlanta's business leaders became convinced that people would not invest in cities with black mayors. Charlie Loudermilk worked to calm those fears, "I walked into Rotary Club and I said to a friend, 'I'm going to support Andy Young for Mayor.' He said, 'You can't do that, sit down and let me talk to you.' So I sat down and I said, 'Look, I want you to get your vice-presidents and your top people and let Andy come and tell you his vision for Atlanta and what he hopes to do for Atlanta.'"[31]

There was also the fear of change because the era of the "good old boy" network had changed. White business owners were no longer sure they had a friend in city hall. As Maynard Jackson's wife, Valerie, expressed it, "They lost the access they had been used to. Many of them could pick up the phone and call Hartsfield or call Ivan Allen, and just,

---

[29] Doug Gatlin (retired executive director, Faith and the City), interview by authors, 18 August 2011, audio, Special Collections and Archives, University Library, Georgia State University.

[30] Muldawer, interview, 27 July 2011.

[31] Loudermilk, interview, 17 August 2011.

you know, talk and deal. They couldn't do that with Maynard because they didn't know him."[32]

On election day, Young's black supporters gave him their votes against his opponent, a progressive long-time state legislator, Sydney Marcus. Young won with a 55 percent majority, but he knew there were relationships to build with the city's white business leaders. He recalled,

> I won my election on Tuesday. We counted the votes on Wednesday morning, and we got Charlie Loudermilk and Roberto Goizueta of Coca-Cola, and we invited all eighty-five CEOs together. We met at John Portman's Top of the Mart restaurant that Friday. I said I won without you, but if I mess up I just mess up a $50,000 a year job and I go off and get me another job somewhere else. But, if I'm not a good mayor, your businesses are going to suffer far more than I will. I need you to help me succeed so I can help your businesses succeed.

This was the beginning of a new partnership between city hall and business leaders in Atlanta. Young's way of bringing blacks from city hall together with business leaders was part of the public-private partnership that he called "public-purpose capitalism," allowing capitalism to work for everyone.

Not only did Young talk to business leaders in a new way, he also signaled by his actions how open the new administration was going to be to their concerns. The mayor made himself accessible to the business community. He gave everyone his phone number, and he assigned staff members to work as business liaisons. Young was less confrontational than his predecessor, and he also used his power to make appointments designed to quiet the fears of white city residents. Young selected a long-serving white police officer, Morris Redding, to become chief of police. Redding was a Korean War veteran from Thomaston who enrolled at Georgia State University on the GI Bill. As a foot patrol officer during the early 1960s, Redding walked a beat that included Auburn Avenue. He took the time to stop in the headquarters of the Southern Christian

---

[32] Valerie Jackson (radio host, philanthropist, and widow of Mayor Maynard Jackson), interview by authors, 18 November 2011, audio, Special Collections and Archives, University Library, Georgia State University.

Leadership Conference and talk to the leaders of the civil rights movement. Redding recalled,

> ...a lot of times when I was down there I'd stop by and talk to her [Dora McDonald, secretary to Martin Luther King, Jr.] like I used to stop by and talk to Mrs. King, and I'd go by and talk to Reverend Hosea [Williams] and Reverend Bennette. Rev. Bennette was a real good friend of mine and he would always tell me, he says, "You know if we have an issue, let's talk about it," and I think he and I were probably the liaisons that got along real good.[33]

Redding's ability to keep a dialogue going with the SCLC leaders and the student demonstrators from the Atlanta University Center made him someone Andrew Young trusted when he became mayor. Redding said he was surprised when newly elected Mayor Young called and asked him to become chief of police, but he promised to do a good job. Having worked under five mayors, he brought experience. Former chief Herbert Jenkins, who was chief under mayors Hartsfield and Allen, had mentored Redding when he was a young officer. Jenkins was not a liberal, but he enforced the law with fairness, often talking with demonstrators and making certain that officers sent to arrest students and other protestors did so without violence and confrontation. After he became chief, Redding appointed a young black officer named George Turner to serve on Mayor Young's security detail. When he gave him the opportunity, Redding told Turner, "It would be like getting a PhD in city government by working with Mayor Young. You'll find out how the government works, you'll understand more about budgets and you'll also understand the major problems of running a major city.' That was when I sent him [Turner] over there, and I was thrilled to death when he was appointed the chief by Mayor Reed [in 2010]."[34]

Within the police department Chief Herbert Jenkins gave an opportunity to a young officer, Morris Redding, who watched and learned and passed on the opportunity to another future chief, George Turner, in an excellent example of the "Atlanta Way"—leaders from one generation

---

[33] Redding, interview, 8 March 2013.
[34] Ibid.

mentoring the leaders from the next generation. In an interview, Chief Turner said he would not be head of the police department if it were not for Mayor Andrew Young because he learned about leadership watching him.[35]

With solid support from the business community, as well as African Americans, Andrew Young was easily reelected to the mayor's office in 1985. His political path in the city was set with the "peace luncheon" held immediately after his election four years earlier. Young was convinced that he could best govern with the cooperation of business leaders. He had learned that lesson from Maynard Jackson's experience, but he also knew that the *ballot* had to be combined with the *buck*. His experience with the civil rights movement had taught him that breaking down the walls of segregation in places such as Alabama was not accomplished through the ballot box, but also through economic pressure from boycotts. With Atlanta's pattern of biracial cooperation, Young believed "you never get progress through guilt. You make people change by making them feel more secure." When commenting on his partnership with business leaders as mayor, Young said, "Politics doesn't control the world; money does. And we ought not to be upset by that. We ought to begin to understand how money works and why money works." The Atlanta partnership was an exchange of power based on electoral control in exchange for a share of the city's economic growth. As he expressed it, the mayor's job "is to see that whites get some of the power and blacks get some of the money."[36] Young was interested in attracting investment in Atlanta that would benefit residents by providing jobs. At the same time, local businesses could grow and benefit the community. There were few other options because federal aid to cities had dried up under a presidential administration that was willing to let cities fail rather than to invest in them. Young saw that private sector investment was the only oth-

---

[35] George Turner (police chief, City of Atlanta), interview by authors, 17 February 2012, audio, Special Collections and Archives, University Library, Georgia State University.

[36] Clarence N. Stone, *Regime Politics: Governing Atlanta, 1946–1988* (Lawrence: University Press of Kansas, 1989) 136.

er choice. With his international background, Mayor Young traveled around the world looking for investors to come to Atlanta. When he was criticized for spending too much time overseas, Young responded to his critics by donning a reflective vest and going with a city crew to fix potholes in the street.

After eight years as mayor, Andrew Young stepped aside, and in a surprise move, Maynard Jackson decided to seek the office for a third term. The election pitted him against Michael Lomax, a former staff member in his administration and chair of the Fulton County Commission. Lomax was popular, but as one minister expressed it, "Michael is my friend, but Maynard Jackson is my friend and my mayor."[37] In a later interview, Lomax admitted that running against Jackson in 1989 was not a smart political move. It did establish his independence from his mentor and paved the way for Lomax to go on to a career as a university president and head of the United Negro College Fund.[38] Maynard Jackson won the election by a wide margin, and he returned to the mayor's office. Although Jackson approached the job with his characteristic energy, the challenges of the city were different from what they had been during his earlier years as mayor. Jackson did work closely with Andrew Young, Billy Payne, and others to begin the application process to bring the 1996 Centennial Olympic Games to Atlanta. Jackson was part of the large delegation from the city than went to Tokyo in 1990 when the selection was made. Jackson returned to Atlanta to lead the celebration that Atlanta had been named the site of the 1996 Games. Jackson had a grand vision that the Olympic preparation would present an opportunity to address the persistent poverty in the city by improving housing and job opportunities for Atlanta's poor. The inability to find funding for this initiative added to Jackson's frustration with the role of mayor. After heart surgery in 1992, Jackson announced the following year that he

---

[37] Robert A. Holmes, *Maynard Jackson, A Biography* (Miami: Barnhardt & Ashe Publishing, Inc., 2011) 232.

[38] Michael Lomax (president and CEO, United Negro College Fund), interview by authors, 11 January 2013, audio, Special Collections and Archives, University Library, Georgia State University.

would not seek an additional term. With an open seat, city council member Bill Campbell received an endorsement from Jackson and was elected mayor in 1993. As mayor he would preside over the Olympic Games at the opening ceremony in July 1996.

In one sense the next phase in the civil rights movement was for Andrew Young, Maynard Jackson, and others in Atlanta to enter the political process. In winning a seat in congress and the mayor's office, Young and Jackson fulfilled John Wesley Dobbs's words. The ballot had served to advance African-American leadership in the city. Jackson and Young built on the legacy of former mayors, but together they trans-formed the city's politics. Building on the voter coalition between blacks and whites that served to elect Bill Hartsfield, Ivan Allen, Jr., and Sam Massell, they organized black voters and appealed to progressive white voters, forming a coalition that has remained a fixture in city politics. Their elections took advantage of changing demographics in the city but used the sophisticated political analysis of talented people such as Clarence Bacote to win votes. They also made Atlanta an attractive city for talented African Americans who came to be part of their administrations. Others came to Atlanta for the economic opportunities promoted by their policies. The system of mentoring that passed down the lessons of political life in Atlanta was also important for the city. Shirley Franklin became Atlanta's first female African-American mayor when she was elected in 2001. She was among the talented group attracted to Atlanta. Franklin went to work for city government under Mayor Jackson in 1978 as director of the Bureau of Cultural Affairs. Recognizing her abilities, Mayor Young promoted Franklin to the position of chief administrative officer, and she was the first female to hold that position. She also served as the highest-ranking female in the Atlanta Committee for the Olympic Games (ACOG). She considers both Jackson and Young mentors who prepared her for a life of public service in Atlanta. Her successor, Kasim Reed, met Andrew Young when Reed was an undergraduate student at Howard University. Reed also considers Young a mentor and an important supporter in his election campaigns. This mentoring process has resulted in a continuation of strong political leadership and the long-standing partnership with business leaders to advance local policy making. These are important traditions in Atlanta's way of doing things.

The ballot was important in helping Atlanta's African Americans achieve a share of political power in the city. But, as Atlanta historian, Ron Bayor points out, the vote was not enough.[39] Vigorous policies for economic development were needed to add the *buck* to the *ballot*. As mayors, Jackson and Young did much to change the policy to bring more fairness to economic development policies in Atlanta. This process began with the building of transportation infrastructure under the leadership of mayors Massell and Jackson. Once again, these mayors had many lessons to learn from the experience of their predecessors.

---

[39] Ronald H. Bayor, *Race and the Shaping of Twentieth-Century Atlanta* (Chapel Hill: University of North Carolina Press, 1996) 52.

Senator Leroy Johnson (second from right) and Governor Carl Sanders
(Courtesy Leroy Johnson)

Senator Johnson (third from right) taking the oath as a member
of the Georgia Senate *(Courtesy Leroy Johnson)*

Maynard Jackson swearing in
(Jackson Papers Woodruff Library AU)

Andrea, Jean, Andrew, and Paula Young during Congressional campaign
(Young Family Collection)

Andrew Young addresses City Council meeting.
(AARL, Andrew Young Papers City Council, 431-12)

Groundbreaking includes Mickey Steinberg, Maynard Jackson, Sam Williams, John Portman, Andrew Young, and Jack Portman *(Courtesy Portman Archives)*

Jean and Andrew Young, Hank and Billye Aaron, and neighbors
at campaign event *(AARL, Andrew Young Papers)*

Jean, Lisa, Paula, and Andrew Young at Young for Congress event
(AARL, Andrew Young Papers)

Lisa, Jean, Andrea, Andrew, Daisy, Sonjia, and Walter Young
at First Congregational Church *(AARL, Andrew Young Papers)*

Maynard Jackson
(*AARL, Andrew Young Papers*)

Mayor Young's family Christmas 1987: Lisa and Douglas Alston, Paula, Bo, Andrea, Taylor Stanley, Andrew and Jean Young, (seated) Daisy Young, and Idella Childs
(Young Family Collection)

From the second on the left, Ralph Abernathy, Coretta King, Harry Belafonte, John Lindsey, Andrew Young at New York Campaign Fundraiser

Rosalynn and Jimmy Carter, Jean and Andrew Young, Thurgood Marshall as Young
gives oath as U.N. Ambassador *(Young Family Collection)*

Shirley and David Franklin with Andrew Young
(AARL, Andrew Young Papers)

Shirley Franklin, Reginald Eaves, Andrew Young Mayoral Campaign event
(Sue Ross©sjr)

"Think Young" button
(Young Family Collection)

4

Atlanta's Lifeblood—Transportation

In describing the importance of transportation in the history of Atlanta, George Berry, former commissioner of aviation for the city, said, "Transportation is to Atlanta what sunshine is to Miami and gambling is to Las Vegas."[1] His comment captures how Atlanta's public and private sector leaders have made transportation the life-blood of the city. Atlanta began as the rail center of Georgia and continues as the home of the world's busiest airport.

In 1837, the governor of Georgia sent the survey team to locate the endpoint of the state's first railroad. Within a few years of Atlanta's founding, the downtown was intersected by rail lines heading north to Chattanooga, south to Macon, and east to Augusta. The triangle formed by the rail lines affected roads in downtown as streets were laid out parallel to the railroad tracks.[2] The owners of the railroad began building hotels. Other business investments followed so that most of the early settlers depended on the rail lines for their livelihoods. The construction of the rail lines also brought remarkable growth to the small settlement as it expanded from a mere handful of people in 1840 to more than 2,500 residents a decade later.[3] Even the three names of the city—Terminus, Marthasville, and Atlanta—reflected the importance of the rail lines to the young town. "Terminus" reflected the town's location as the end point of the Western and Atlantic Railroad; "Marthasville" was in honor

---

[1] George Berry (former commissioner of aviation, City of Atlanta), interview by authors, 26 July 2011, audio, Special Collections and Archives, Georgia State University.

[2] Edward Young Clarke, *Illustrated History of Atlanta* (1877; repr., Atlanta: Cherokee Publishing Company, 1971) 23–31.

[3] US Bureau of the Census, *Seventh Census of the United States, 1850*, vol. 1 (Washington, DC: Beverly Tucker, 1854).

of Governor Wilson Lumpkin's daughter. As governor, Lumpkin had commissioned the initial rail line ending in the town. "Atlanta" is a feminine form of the word "Atlantic," from the name of the initial railroad line to Chattanooga.[4] The early rail lines formed the basis of a network of "rivers of steel" that enabled business leaders to make Atlanta grow as the rail hub and major commercial center for the southeast.

During the Civil War, the rail lines made Atlanta a strategic hub for munitions manufacturing and troop transport. The railroads also made Atlanta the target of General William T. Sherman and his troops as they moved south from Chattanooga. After a brief siege, the Confederate troops withdrew, leaving the mayor and city leaders to surrender the town. Sherman occupied Atlanta and issued a proclamation for all civilians to evacuate. Before leaving the city, Sherman ordered his soldiers to burn the rail stations and all other buildings of potential importance to the Confederacy before he began his march through the state toward Savannah.[5]

In spring 1865, some residents returned to Atlanta and began rebuilding the rail lines that were destroyed. Following the end of the war, federal troops made Atlanta the administrative headquarters for the reconstruction of the city and state. The city's rail connections were strategically important for exercising command and control over the state. When Georgia voters ratified a new state constitution in 1868, Atlanta became the state capital. This event increased the importance of Atlanta as one of the most prominent cities in Georgia, and whetted the appetite of civic leaders to make the city a leader within the region. These Atlanta leaders used the rail lines to attract attendance at a series of three expositions in 1881, 1887, and 1895, as well as the city's first national convention in 1885.[6] By the end of the nineteenth century, Atlanta achieved its

---

[4] Franklin M. Garrett, *Atlanta and Environs: A Chronicle of Its People and Events*, 2 vols. (Athens: University of Georgia Press, 1969) 1:150, 188–89, 225.

[5] Clarke, *Illustrated History of Atlanta*, 51–56.

[6] Harvey K. Newman, *Southern Hospitality: Tourism and the Growth of Atlanta* (Tuscaloosa: University of Alabama Press, 1999) 37–59.

goal of being a city of regional importance thanks to its leadership and the rail lines.

Atlanta's town limits were initially a half-mile radius from the center point where the surveyor's stake marked the end point of the Western and Atlantic Railroad. As the town grew, leaders moved the limits of the radius outward to a mile. During this time, people could generally walk from one place to another with little inconvenience except from the red clay streets that turned to mud following rain. In 1874, the owners of an amusement park and health spa known as the Ponce de Leon Springs built a trolley line out to the springs. Horses or mules pulled the trolley cars at first, later giving way to electric streetcars. Enterprising owners of these lines began selling lots for suburban residential development along the streetcar lines because people visiting the park were good prospects to purchase the housing lots. City dwellers could now live further from their work within the compact circle around the railroad tracks that was Atlanta's initial settlement pattern. The sprawling new streetcar suburbs contributed to the city's outward expansion as other lines were added and the city annexed the new residential areas in 1903 and 1910.[7]

Streetcars had a significant impact on the city, but a new twentieth-century technology, the automobile, would have a stronger influence on transportation within and around Atlanta. In 1909, civic leaders hosted the meeting of the National Association of Automobile Manufacturers. This was the first time that the group had met outside the cities of New York and Chicago. The event propelled the city into the automobile age. Local sales of cars increased along with dealerships to sell them and, eventually, assembly plants. Atlanta became the regional hub for both the sales and production of automobiles. This led to the demand for paved streets and the expansion of automobile-related businesses. The first paved federal highway, which opened in 1929, connected the Great Lakes with the Florida Keys and passed through Atlanta. This national

---

[7] Garrett, *Atlanta and Environs*, 2:557–59.

highway was the first of a network of federal roads leading into the city that contributed to truck and automobile traffic.[8]

Long lines of cars and trucks had to wait for the large number of trains that still came into the intersecting network of railroad lines in downtown. This congestion reached a peak during the 1920s, resulting in calls for action to reduce the problem. City leaders solved the problem by building bridges called viaducts spanning the downtown railroad tracks. Eventually the stores and other commercial buildings along the viaducts opened second-floor entrances that became the new street level, leaving the old rail lines "underground" in the center of the city. The old storefronts and warehouses were neglected until the 1960s, when the area under the viaducts reopened as a popular tourist attraction known as Underground Atlanta.

Among the many attractions built in the city for the 1909 meeting of the National Association of Automobile Manufacturers, few would become more important than the racetrack for cars constructed south of town by the owner of the Coca-Cola Company, Asa G. Candler. Following the auto show, the family continued to maintain the race track until 1925, when a young member of the city's Board of Aldermen, William B. Hartsfield, encouraged the city to lease the property for use as Atlanta's first airport. Hartsfield became enthralled with aviation when he was a boy watching a barnstorming tour perform stunts with an airplane. As an alderman and later as mayor, Hartsfield worked to make Atlanta a regional hub for this new form of transportation, just as earlier leaders had pushed the city to become the rail and highway center of the South. In 1926 the federal government authorized an airmail route from New York to Miami. Atlanta's municipal rival, Birmingham, seemed a natural choice for the route because early low-flying airplanes could fly down the Shenandoah Valley to Birmingham and on to Tampa and Miami. Hartsfield anticipated that the designation of the federal airmail route could determine which city would become the regional center for

---

[8] Howard L. Preston, *Automobile Age Atlanta: The Making of a Southern Metropolis, 1900–1935* (Athens: University of Georgia Press, 1979) 24–44, 147–48.

aviation. He arranged for city officials to be on hand to greet the arriving assistant postmaster general, who was in charge of making the decision. Hartsfield had the city provide eight motorcycles as a police escort for a motorcade down Peachtree Street, followed by a lavish dinner at a private club with the mayor, governor, and business leaders. The federal official was also given a deluxe hotel suite for his overnight stay. Hartsfield proclaimed, "No East Indian potentate ever got the attention he did." A week later, the federal government designated Atlanta as a stop on the airmail route.[9] In 1929, Hartsfield persuaded the city to purchase the racetrack property as its municipal airport, and Atlanta became a regional leader in both airmail and airline passenger service.[10] At the same time, air travel languished in nearby Birmingham, giving rise to the saying that in order to get to heaven from the Alabama city you had to change planes in Atlanta.

The 1920s also saw the formation of a corporation that would advance the transportation business in Atlanta. In 1924 a crop-dusting operation known as Huff Daland Dusters began in Macon, Georgia, and moved to the delta country of Louisiana the following year. Four years later a former federal agricultural service extension agent, C. E. Woolman, bought the company that was headquartered in Monroe, Louisiana, and renamed it Delta Air Service. While Delta continued to provide crop-dusting service to fight the infestation of the boll weevil, it began passenger service in 1929 to Dallas, Jackson, Meridian, and Birmingham. The following year, Delta began passenger service to Atlanta. Under Woolman's leadership, the company gained financial stability after the federal government awarded Delta an airmail contract to provide service from Dallas to Charleston, South Carolina, by way of Atlanta. The air-

---

[9] William B. Hartsfield, "Airport Materials," Atlanta History Center archive collection.

[10] Frederick Allen, *Atlanta Rising: The Invention of an International City, 1946–1996* (Atlanta: Longstreet Press, 1996) 22–24.

line grew slowly within the region and in 1941 moved its corporate headquarters to Atlanta.[11]

Delta's main competitor in Atlanta was Eastern Airlines, which began operations in Philadelphia in the late 1920s. Eastern Airlines delivered airmail, initially (and later, passengers), along the east coast between New York and Florida through Atlanta. Thanks to its profitable routes and airmail contracts, Eastern emerged during the 1930s as one of the four largest airlines in the US. (The others were United, TWA, and American.[12]) During the early years of air travel in Atlanta, the airline companies built hangars that served the needs of airplanes as well as passengers. In 1932, the city entered a partnership with American Airlines to finance construction of the first dedicated airport terminal building. When the terminal was finished, the city of Atlanta lacked funds to provide furniture for the new building and had to buy the chairs and side tables with money from sight-seeing flights over Stone Mountain. This frugal approach to financing the airport led two of the most ardent boosters of aviation in the city to remark "Atlanta was establishing a reputation as an easy and inexpensive—and therefore desirable—airport at which to operate. Conversely, it perpetuated its financial plight and dependence on outside revenue." For the next few years, most of the financing for the expansion of runways and facilities at the airport came from the federal government's Works Progress Administration and the Army.[13]

Delta replaced American Airlines for airmail delivery routed through the city. This established the competition between Eastern and

---

[11] Jamil Zainaldin, "Delta Airlines," *New Georgia Encyclopedia*, http://www.georgiaencyclopedia.org/articles/business-economy/delta-air-lines (23 October 2015).

[12] Jamil Zainaldin, "Eastern Airlines," *New Georgia Encyclopedia*, http://www.georgiaencyclopedia.org/articles/business-economy/eastern-air-lines (27 October 2015).

[13] Betsey Braden and Paul Hagan, *A Dream Takes Flight: Hartsfield International Airport and Aviation in Atlanta* (Atlanta and Athens: Atlanta Historical Society and University of Georgia Press, 1989) 80.

Delta in both passenger service as well as mail routes. Both airlines survived the years during World War II by serving the needs of the armed forces. The training of pilots and mechanics and the transport of service personnel provided contracts for the airlines. Soon after the war ended, Mayor Hartsfield led an initiative to issue $3 million in general obligation bonds that would be matched by federal government funds for expansion of the airport. By 1948, the city had outgrown existing passenger facilities at the airport and used a surplus prefabricated federal building as a new terminal. This structure, described by Andrew Young as a "Quonset hut," served the city's airport until 1961.[14]

Mayor Hartsfield also led the city toward a new expressway system for automobiles. In the late 1940s, the city hired a planner to begin designing a pair of expressways going north-south and east-west that met in downtown. In advance of the federal interstate highway act, the city began construction of the two expressways during the early 1950s. Hartsfield also took advantage of available federal funds and began designating land near downtown as areas for urban renewal. By 1956 both the highway construction and the demolition of properties designated as "slums" were underway to reshape a downtown area that both white political and business leaders agreed was deteriorating. During the next ten years, these two public policies to build expressways and remove slums displaced more than 67,000 Atlanta residents, of whom more than 90 percent were African American.[15] The program for urban renewal was nicknamed "Negro removal" with some justification, and the two public policies resulted in severe overcrowding among low-income black neighborhoods and citizens' distrust of government programs. The already crowded neighborhoods that remained for poor black residents became more crowded as houses were torn down to make way for new roads designed to speed the commutes of residents from the city's largely white suburbs.

---

[14] James L. Townsend and Paul Hagan, eds., *Atlanta International Airport: A Commemorative Book* (Atlanta: National Graphics, 1980) 5.

[15] Eric Hill Associates, *City of Atlanta, Georgia, Report on Relocation of Individuals, Families and Businesses* (Atlanta: Community Improvement Program, 1966) 142.

African Americans also felt their neighborhoods were sacrificed for the improvements of downtown businesses. Only one-third of the families relocated received any financial assistance for the loss of their homes. They were forced to give up the familiar surroundings of their old neighborhoods with the proximity to downtown jobs, shopping, health care, and access to other social services. Mayor Hartsfield and downtown business leaders got their way, and the north-south expressway known as the downtown connector (I-85 and I-75) and the east-west expressway that became Interstate 20 were begun through the downtown area connecting to the suburbs.

The decision to build the expressways helped to fuel the population growth of the Atlanta area. As construction of the downtown connector began during the 1950s, the city of Atlanta's population grew from 331,314 in 1950 to 487,455 ten years later. The metropolitan area contained only 671,797 in 1950 but reached more than a million in 1960 as Interstate 85 extended from downtown Atlanta to Gwinnett County. The network of interstate highways grew over the next twenty years to include I-20 east and west, I-75 to the northwest and southeast, I-85 to the northeast and southwest, and the I-285 perimeter highway, so that by 1980 the metropolitan population reached more than two million. Atlanta's population peaked at 496,973 in 1970 and shrank by 50,000 over the next decade as whites became a minority in the central city and many fled to the suburbs. The completion of the network of interstates caused the number of counties within the metropolitan area to grow from five in 1958 to eighteen thirty years later. The City's inability to annex surrounding territory prevented Atlanta from capturing the rapid growth of population in the suburbanizing metropolitan area.[16]

After twenty-three years in office, Hartsfield decided against seeking another term as mayor in 1961. As he was leaving office, the city dedicated a new airport terminal building that would be named in his honor. The mayor wanted Atlanta to have an airport terminal large

---

[16] Paul M. Hirsch, "Atlanta: The City, Metropolitan Region and the Atlanta M. S. A." (Atlanta: Department of Urban Studies, c. 1983) 3–5.

enough to make a strong impression on visitors, so the architect designed an eight-story international-style office building above the terminal facility. The facility required the largest bond debt ever issued to construct the $20 million terminal. The airport opened with forty-eight gates, which enabled it to handle 6 million passengers per year.[17] New runways were longer to accommodate jet aircraft, and the gates at the new terminal were equipped with "jetways" to allow passengers to step directly from the waiting area onto the plane through an air-conditioned passage. In most airports, passengers still had to go outside and up steps into the airplane, so the new airport provided Atlanta-bound passengers the latest in comfort. After the dedication of the new airport terminal, the editor of the *Atlanta Journal* wrote, "When jets came in we could handle them. Now we can handle the passengers they bring.... In Atlanta we can't rest. We have to keep planning and working in order to maintain our present position and move ahead."[18] The city's leadership at both the airlines and the city were trying to keep Atlanta among the leaders in the aviation business—a process that always requires a close public-private partnership.

In fall 1961, with an open seat in the campaign for mayor for the first time in more than twenty years, the winner was Ivan Allen, Jr., the president of the Chamber of Commerce and son of a successful business and civic leader. His opponent was a segregationist restaurant owner named Lester Maddox, but Allen put together the long-standing coalition of downtown business leaders and African Americans. Part of Allen's campaign for the mayor's office was a six-point program for growth and economic development that included mass transit for the city. Mayor Allen promoted the transit system as a cure for the city's growing highway congestion and as a symbol of Atlanta's growth as a place of national importance. After all, a rapid transit system would put Atlanta into a category of major cities such as New York and Chicago, and it would set Atlanta apart from regional cities that did not have rail transit. The state

---

[17] Braden and Hagan, *A Dream Takes Flight*, 133–37.
[18] *Atlanta Journal*, "Now for Tomorrow," editorial, 3 May 1961, 28.

government obliged by creating the Metropolitan Atlanta Rapid Transit Authority (MARTA), which began planning for a takeover of the existing private bus system and the construction of rapid rail lines. In 1968, Atlanta area citizens prepared to vote on the proposed MARTA system. Opposition to the proposal came from prominent members of Atlanta's black community such as insurance executive Jesse Hill and Reverend Samuel Williams, the pastor of one of the city's oldest and most influential Baptist churches. Their objections to the proposal focused on the lack of rail service that the proposed MARTA rail system would provide to the city's African-American neighborhoods. Mayor Allen appointed the members of the MARTA board, most of whom were white downtown business leaders with the exception of one black banker. Leaders of the city's black community vowed to oppose the referendum if the rail lines were not redrawn and assurances made that MARTA would provide fair employment practices throughout the system. There was also fear the construction of the rapid rail lines would sacrifice more black neighborhoods as the urban renewal and expressway construction had done. Without African-American support, the result was a defeat in the vote to create the MARTA system.[19] Mayor Allen's leadership had failed to involve blacks in the planning for the rail system and in the preparations for the referendum.

After eight years in office and the defeat of the transportation referendum, Mayor Allen decided not to seek reelection in 1969. White business leaders rallied around his opponent, but city alderman Sam Massell put together a coalition of liberal whites and African Americans who helped him with the mayoral election. He began to build relations with business leaders through informal meetings and proposed another referendum on the mass transit system. As an effort to secure unified business support for the MARTA system, a white banker named Mills Lane, the head of the Citizens and Southern Bank, met with black real estate businessman Bill Callaway. At the urging of Callaway, the two agreed to en-

---

[19] Ronald H. Bayor, *Race and the Shaping of Twentieth-Century Atlanta* (Chapel Hill: University of North Carolina Press, 1996) 191–93.

large the conversation and create an informal biracial group of business leaders called the Atlanta Action Forum. Meeting were held once per month on Saturday mornings and focused initially on the need to move the transit referendum forward.[20] In future years the Action Forum would continue to meet and address major issues facing the city.

At the state level, a new governor named Jimmy Carter urged legislative support for the MARTA referendum and the one-cent sales tax that would support the proposed transit system. This meant that the new mass transit system would need financing from the fare box, the local one-cent sales tax, and the federal government. It would place MARTA in a unique position as the only urban mass transit system in the US that received no dedicated funding from its state government. Massell promised that with the sales tax MARTA would lower fares and keep them at 15 cents per ride for ten years. The mayor recalled that he wanted a free fare, but this was opposed by the chairman of the Fulton County Commission, who wanted a 25-cent fare. The two compromised on a 15-cent fare with free transfers. This was a reduction from the old transit system fare of 60 cents plus 5-cent transfer fees.

> I wanted a free fare, and Charlie Brown, who was chairman then of the Fulton County Commission said no—people would sleep on it if it was free. So, he wanted 25 cents, and we compromised on 15 cents. And I was able to go right into the neighborhoods with a blackboard and chalk, and I did physically and show them that where they were actually paying 60 cents and a nickel transferred each way, a $1.30 a day that it would only cost them 15 cents each way."[21]

Massell also learned from the mistakes of his predecessor by adding Jesse Hill to the MARTA board and making sure that staffing at the new agency included minorities at all levels. Mayor Massell also reached

---

[20] Mike Trotter (attorney and secretary to the Atlanta Action Forum), interview by authors, 25 October 2011, audio, Special Collections and Archives, University Library, Georgia State University.

[21] Sam Massell, Jr., (former Atlanta mayor and president of Buckhead Coalition) interview with authors, 28 July 2011, audio, Special Collections and Archives, University Library, Georgia State University.

out to the community in planning for the transit lines that would be built. He created a Committee of One Hundred that included a diverse group of citizens such as public housing tenant association president Mary Sanford. She insisted that a rapid rail line be planned for the northwest part of the city known as Proctor Creek. Former MARTA counsel, Bill Ide, recalled that the promise for the Proctor Creek rail line included in the final proposal helped the referendum pass in Fulton County by the narrow margin of 471 votes due to the support of black voters from the area.[22] Only two metropolitan area counties, Fulton and DeKalb, approved the system while two largely white suburban counties rejected the proposal. Massell still believes that MARTA should be free: "You know I walked on the sidewalks free. Drive my automobile in the streets free…. [W]e pay taxes for all of these things and the government provides them, and the government should be providing mass transit mobility."[23]

Few people understand the role a member of the US Congress can play in the district the member represents. For Andrew Young that role involved transportation in the city. As he said,

> I was elected and went to Congress in 1973. In the House of Representatives, I was on the Banking Committee and the Mass Transit Subcommittee. We had just passed MARTA here in Atlanta. In talking with Paul Muldawer, we discussed how we might plan the access and utilization of the area around the stations. I think we have a half-mile radius around the stations that I introduced legislation that created a public-private corporation that would help plan the use around the MARTA station area. It turned out to be pretty helpful because that is what we used to get the planning grant for the area around Underground Atlanta. It also helped with the area around the IBM building [One Atlantic Center] and the Arts Center Station. And, where the Lenox Square Station is was a little black community known as Johnsontown. It really was just little shacks but was valued at $15 to $30

---

[22] R. William (Bill) Ide (attorney, McKenna Long & Aldridge, and former counsel, MARTA), interview by authors, 11 November 2011, audio, Special Collections and Archives, University Library, Georgia State University.
[23] Ibid.

thousand, which was not enough to relocate people. So, we factored in the air rights, and instead of basing the appraisal on the existing land use, we did it on the future use for high-rise buildings, and that enabled us to give them money for relocation by adding $100 thousand to everybody's appraisal. For example, if you were appraised at $20 thousand, you got $120 thousand. The average person ended up, if you add the two churches that were in Johnsontown, with close to $150 thousand, and that enabled them to move and relocate. It also enabled the Lenox Square office and apartment buildings just north of the MARTA station to be built. It also let us take the MARTA rail line all the way to the airport. It meant that we could apply for federal grants to pay for the planning for each of these stations. We could plan for the design and use of an area of a half of a mile around each station. This was a one-sentence amendment that I slipped in as a member of Congress. Nobody knew what it meant, and nobody cared about it, so it just went on through, but it was important to MARTA and to Atlanta.[24]

With the population in Atlanta changing from majority white to black and with strong African-American political leadership from then-vice mayor Maynard Jackson, Sam Massell was limited to one term as mayor (1970–1974). His most impressive achievement was the success of the MARTA referendum and the implementation of a program of minority contracting in the construction of the transit system. This requirement of 25 percent minority contracts would form the basis of the minority business development program used by his successor, Mayor Jackson, as Atlanta built a new airport. The city's black and white business leaders created the Atlanta Action Forum that would provide a setting for problems to be addressed behind closed doors. The Action Forum initially included eighteen members and was always balanced with an equal number of blacks and whites. Only one elected public official, city council member Q. V. Williamson, was included since it was felt his position in the black business community was so significant that his participation was essential. Other elected officials were not included as members, although they were frequently consulted by the Action Forum members. After the first few meetings, the group began calling them-

---

[24] Young, interview, 2 August 2011.

selves the Atlanta Forum, but banker Mills B. Lane reminded the participants that they did not want to just talk, but also to act, so he suggested the name the Atlanta Action Forum.[25]

The members of the Action Forum soon recognized the need for objective analysis of complex issues facing the city and turned to an existing policy research organization called Research Atlanta. The task of Research Atlanta was to provide actionable research that was fair and helpful in framing public discussion of important issues facing Atlanta. With corporate support from many of the city's leading businesses, the biracial board raised funds to support Research Atlanta and hired as executive director a young Georgia Tech graduate, Sam Williams, who had worked in the Ivan Allen administration.[26] The Action Forum never issued any press releases or publicly mentioned their meetings. Architect and developer John Portman was one of the original members of the Action Forum. In describing how the Atlanta Action Forum worked, Portman quoted long-time Atlanta leader Robert Woodruff: "[I]f we think what is in the best interest of the city and we keep that in the forefront, then everybody wins. If we start selfishly thinking about what's in my best interest, then everybody loses."[27] The kind of quiet, consensus-building conversations the Action Forum promoted became a crucial aspect of the way Atlanta's leaders got things done.

The election of Maynard Jackson gave the Action Forum a number of issues to consider. One of the top issues early in 1974 when Jackson took office was the airport. The terminal opened by Hartsfield in 1971 had become the second-busiest airport in the US behind Chicago's

---

[25] Michael H. Trotter, *The History of the Atlanta Action Forum* (Atlanta: n.p., 1992) 3–4.

[26] Michael H. Trotter, *Research Atlanta: The Early Years* (Atlanta: n.p., 1987) 7–8; Sam Williams (initial executive director, Research Atlanta, and retired president and CEO, Metro Atlanta Chamber of Commerce), interview by authors, 8 December 2011, audio, Special Collections and Archives, University Library, Georgia State University.

[27] John Portman (founder and chairman, John Portman & Associates), interview by authors, 15 September 2011, audio, Special Collections and Archives, University Library, Georgia State University.

O'Hare Airport and was stretched far beyond its designed capacity. Planning for a second Atlanta airport was already underway with land purchased by the city in two locations on the north side of the metropolitan area. The airport overcrowding stirred a debate over the options of expanding the existing facility or building a second facility on one of the northside properties. During the early 1970s, the second airport debate divided representatives of the city, the airlines, the Federal Aviation Administration, and business leaders. This was a moment when Atlanta's business leadership needed to demonstrate unity, and the Action Forum provided a place for the discussions. According to John Portman, some business leaders wanted to keep the airport close to downtown, and Hartsfield International Airport was only seven miles from the center of the city. There was also the issue of connectivity because 70 percent of the passengers arriving in Atlanta were on connecting flights— meaning that fewer than 30 percent of the passengers began or ended their flights in Atlanta. A second airport would divert flights and passengers from the existing airport to a location requiring a long commute to change planes.[28] Mayor Jackson added the issue of race as another dimension to the discussion of a second airport. There was powerful symbolism in expanding the airport on the city's south side where employment opportunities and economic development were closer to neighborhoods where black voters lived. Jackson's proposal was to build a new terminal next to the existing one on the southern edge of the city.[29] As Action Forum participant John Portman recalls, the group agreed that they "wanted to keep the airport close to the heart of the city. Most airports in the world have gotten farther and farther out and they're very inconvenient and expensive. The cab rides to town in some cities are unbelievable."[30] In October 1974, the Action Forum met and supported the mid-field ter-

---

[28] Townsend and Hagan, *Atlanta International Airport*, 3–5.

[29] Adolph Reed, Jr., "A Critique of Neo-Progressivism in Theorizing about Local Development Policy: A Case from Atlanta," in Clarence N. Stone and Heywood T. Sanders, eds., *The Politics of Urban Development* (Lawrence: University Press of Kansas, 1987) 208–11.

[30] Portman, interview, 15 September 2011.

minal at the existing Atlanta airport, indicating their unity with the new mayor on this issue.[31]

In retrospect, the agreement to maintain one airport was vital to the continued growth of airport traffic. The same geographical characteristics that led to the positioning of rail lines and highways also favored the airport—so long as it maintained itself as a hub. George Berry recalled that the planning director at the time insisted that the airport and terminal be designed to handle connecting planes and passengers. They were using the Dallas-Fort Worth airport as a model in doing the planning for Atlanta, but the Texas airport was not built for connecting flights. Atlanta's airport serves as a hub for connecting flights so the terminal needed to be built like a high-rise building laid on its side. Berry said if you look at the terminal from the air, you see the five, and soon to be six, concourses in the terminal and then you have the elevator—the people mover—running between them.[32]

Atlanta's innovative airport design was the work of a public servant who was cognizant of the particular nature of the airport's strengths. The terminal was divided into two parallel sections so that ground transportation could bring passengers either to Delta side or to Eastern Airlines's ticketing and baggage claim areas. An underground people-mover system moved passengers from the terminal to the airline concourses. The initial design of the new airport included four concourses, but the facility was designed to expand to a capacity of 75 million passengers per year.[33]

The total cost for the new terminal would be around $400 million. Mayor Jackson wanted minorities to share in the economic development opportunity presented by the changes at the airport, so he announced that 25 percent of the contracts for all work done at the airport would have to go to women or black-owned businesses. To white business owners accustomed to having contracts with the city that did not require a lot of formal bidding procedures, this new minority participation require-

---

[31] Trotter, *History of the Atlanta Action Forum*, 7.
[32] Berry, interview, 26 July 2011.
[33] Braden and Hagan, *A Dream Takes Flight*, 182–84.

ment seemed likely to delay construction. In the words of the mayor's wife, Valerie Jackson, the white business owners

> really, really objected to it. Maynard put the project on hold for more than a year because they were fussing and fighting and didn't want to give him that percentage of minority participation. There was even an attempt to wrestle the airport from underneath the city and put it under the purview and authority of the state. But Maynard stood strong, and after about two years of delay the construction process on the new airport terminal began.[34]

While white business leaders objected to the minority participation requirement for contracts to build the airport, there were other challenges to overcome as well. One of the obstacles faced by Mayor Jackson was an interstate highway. Realizing that he needed assistance, the mayor called newly elected US Congressman Andrew Young. As Young tells the story,

> Maynard Jackson called me up and said that the new midfield airport project had a roadblock and needed to have Interstate 85 moved a mile to the west in order to build the new terminal and runways. There was not enough space near the existing airport to expand. Bill Coleman was the US secretary of transportation. We met with him, and Coleman said it makes sense to me, but if it lacks political support, then, I am going to be criticized for tearing up a roadway just to make room for an airport. He said he would be run out of town. We said we did not think so because Senator Talmadge was chair of the Senate finance committee. Coleman said if Talmadge would agree to it, I will put it in the budget. When we went to see Talmadge—the group included Wyche Fowler, Maynard Jackson, Bill Coleman, and myself. Talmadge sat chewing his tobacco with his feet propped on his desk, but he said, "That is very reasonable, gentlemen; I think we can handle that." I think Bill Coleman thought Talmadge was joking with us and did not believe it would be that easy. We learned later that Senator Talmadge owned part of the land where the road was going to be moved. He went out and bought more of the land where the new highway was supposed

---

[34] Valerie Jackson, interview, 18 November 2011. William T. Coleman was appointed by President Gerald Ford. He also served as President of the NAACP Legal Defense Fund.

to go. He sold it back to the government and relocated most of the highway on his land. He did not have to buy it all because he already had some of the land down there, and the new interstate was going across his property, so he did not mind that. It never became a controversy. There was not a single newspaper article about it, nobody complained since it was such a win for the city to expand its airport. It only took one meeting, and when Bill Coleman agreed, he put it in his budget, and when Talmadge said he would get it passed, that was that.[35]

Leadership at the local level and in Congress did not move mountains, but literally moved a highway in order to move the airport project forward.

Atlanta's business leaders eventually accepted the minority joint venture rules in order to reach a consensus about the airport, and once they started work, as Valerie Jackson expressed it, "they built it on time and under budget. The airport became his jewel, his crown jewel."[36] On September 18, 1980, the city held the dedication ceremony for Hartsfield International Airport, named in honor of the former mayor and boasting trans-Atlantic flights. Mayor Jackson was overjoyed not only that the project opened on schedule and within budget but also that he reached his goal of 25 percent minority participation. He called it an historic occasion that reflected great management and the achievement of important social goals. Jackson proclaimed, "We have proven it can be done. Right and excellence can walk hand in hand." He touted the economic impact the new facility would have on the metropolitan area and spoke about the partnership between government and business.[37]

By the time he left office in 1982, Maynard Jackson had changed the opportunity structure for minorities doing business with the city of Atlanta. The new airport terminal positioned the city to become one of the top facilities of its kind in the world. Minority contracting with the city was less than one percent in 1974; when Mayor Jackson left office 25

---

[35] Young, interview, 21 November 2011.

[36] Jackson, interview, 18 November 2011.

[37] Robert A. Holmes, *Maynard Jackson, A Biography* (Miami: Barnhardt & Ashe Publishing, Inc., 2011) 173.

percent of all contracts had joint ventures or minority participation. His style in working with white business leaders was aggressive and blunt. As Sam Williams put it, "Maynard broke a lot of china."[38] His successor as mayor, Andrew Young, was less confrontational, but still determined to lead the city forward in making transportation improvements and providing opportunity for minority contractors. In doing so, Mayor Young restored the close cooperation with the business community that had guided Atlanta decision-making for many decades.

The airport continued to demand attention. From the moment the new midfield terminal opened in 1980, the number of takeoffs and landings increased as the Atlanta hub attracted more flights. In 1984, Mayor Young dedicated the completion of a new, 9,000-foot fourth runway project at the airport and began an extension of the major departure runway to almost 12,000 feet. This increased runway length was needed to accommodate the new class of jumbo jets used in international service. The two major runway projects required $187 million in financing from revenue bonds that make the airport virtually self-sustaining as rental fees, landing fees, and a percentage of concession revenues are used to repay the interest and debt on the bonds. Unlike earlier periods of growth at the airport, there was neither federal nor state money for Atlanta's airport. These improvements at the airport enabled the total number of aircraft operations at Hartsfield Airport to increase from 571,562 in 1982 to 778,779 in 1988. During the same period, the number of passengers rose from 34,702,494 to 45,900,098. The number of flights and passengers made Hartsfield Atlanta International Airport the busiest in the world, a title it continues to hold.[39] When Maynard Jackson set a minority participation of 25 percent for all work on the airport, white business leaders initially balked and agreed only reluctantly; when Mayor Young raised the minority participation requirement to 35 percent, he did not face the same resistance from business leaders.

---

[38] Williams, interview, 8 December 2011.

[39] Nehl Horton, *The Young Years: A Report on the Administration of the Honorable Andrew Young, Mayor of the City of Atlanta, 1982–1989* (Atlanta: n.p., 1989) 222–23.

Other transportation issues also required the attention of the Young administration. Two proposed highway projects in the city were the subjects of longstanding controversy that required all of former Ambassador Young's diplomatic skills to resolve. The first was the extension of Georgia Highway 400 south from the perimeter highway to link with Interstate 85. Conflict between affected neighborhoods and transportation planners at the city and state levels had delayed this extension for more than twenty years. The other conflict between the neighborhoods and the city and state involved a proposed expressway initially known as Interstate 485 that would have linked the downtown expressway with the Stone Mountain Freeway. Both these projects involved running highways through well-to-do white neighborhoods that were well organized and able to block the proposals for many years. Andrew Young was able to secure support from the city council and agreement from neighborhood groups to end litigation, permitting the state to begin construction. The Interstate 485 project became the much less intrusive Freedom Parkway that combined new residential construction along the right of way with a linear park space surrounding the Presidential Library of Jimmy Carter.

Existing interstate highways also needed attention from Mayor Young. In 1988, Atlanta was set to host the Democratic National Convention, an event that would put the city in an international spotlight. As Young recalled,

> Later on when I was mayor, we needed money to expand the downtown connector, our interstate highways that run through the downtown portion of the city. I went to the state commissioner of the Department of Transportation, Tom Moreland, to ask for the money. Moreland said some congressman from New Jersey had frozen interstate highway funds. The congressman's name was Jim Howard. I used the fact that we were going after the Democratic National Convention to get Jim Howard to give us highway money. Back in 1972, when I went to Congress, Jim Howard had been reapportioned out of his district in New Jersey. He had a blue-collar, white district and had been elected in the 1964 Democratic landslide victory under Lyndon Johnson. That district in New Jersey had never had a Democratic representative in Congress before Jim Howard. When they re-drew the lines

after 1970, they made his district one-third black, one-third Republican, and one-third blue-collar white. They figured that was a way to get rid of him. I went up there to campaign for him on a couple of weekends and met with the preachers. I got all of them together and explained to the preachers that he was a good Democrat, and we should get out the vote and vote for him. I think John Lewis went up there with me because I think it was the labor unions that arranged to fly us up there. We got him reelected, and he had no trouble winning reelection after that. So, by the time 1984 came around, I was mayor and he was chairman of the House Transportation Committee. We went up there and told him what we were trying to do for the Democratic National Convention, and that we desperately needed this highway money. We brought him down to the city with his wife, and the Ritz Carlton Hotel was brand new. We took him up in a police helicopter and showed him what our transportation needs were. He went back and cut loose $900 million for us to go to work expanding these expressways. That fit right into our efforts to plan for the 1988 Democratic National Convention.

The Convention was a way to focus on the growth, development, and changes in the South. The Democrats had sort of written off the South by then, and that was part of my reason for wanting them here in Atlanta. Plus, we are a convention city, and we had more hotel rooms within walking distance than almost any city in the country. We were planning for a city of Atlanta with a million people. For that growth, we needed roads. I had been on the Banking Committee in the House, and I had learned that there was a lot of surplus capital around the world. The Swiss banks were charging people interest to keep their money. So, we went on a series of trade missions to the money centers of the world, urging people to invest in Atlanta. We emphasized that you don't have to pay anybody under the table; we guarantee you honest and efficient service, and you can bring your money in and take it out as you please. Whenever an investor would come into town, I insisted that they come into the mayor's office. I would look over their plans, and if they looked good, I would assign one person from my staff to work with them, to walk them through the clearances such as the environmental clearances, and all the building permits and things like that. We assigned one person to work with each project and that turned out to be pretty efficient. The other thing we did was to give each investor my home telephone number and my direct office line to the phone that rang on my desk, so if you are not getting good service or if you have any complaints, call me personally and let me deal with it. I always said that in front of the staff person, and I only got one call in eight years. We were very successful in bringing in international investment in the city.

We also expanded the airport to build the T concourse as an international concourse. This attracted more international airlines such as Japan Air, which also built the Nikko Hotel in Buckhead. This investment at the airport led to more airlines, and more hotels built by Swiss Air, Lufthansa, and others, which led to more businesses being located in the city. While I was mayor, we got three hundred Japanese companies to locate businesses in Atlanta, and we did the same thing in Germany, in Switzerland, in Scandinavia. I suspect that most of that was surplus Arab money that was sitting in banks around the world. The money came from holding companies that were holding Saudi and Kuwaiti investments, but it was a global effort. We got 1100 companies in my eight years as mayor, with more than $70 billion invested in the metropolitan area, creating over a million new jobs. Almost all of that investment was based on our transportation connections to the world through the airport.[40]

Andrew Young's international vision for Atlanta was important for the city's development. The long-time head of the downtown business organization known as Central Atlanta Progress, A. J. Robinson, watched parts of the city's skyline go up from his dorm room at Emory University. Robinson spent a year teaching in China before joining the Portman Company to work on international projects in Asia. He recalls Andrew Young's terms as mayor as something of a boom time with the level of international investment in Atlanta. Robinson cites the mayor's vision as a force in working with business leaders in the city to connect with other places around the world.[41]

Transportation is a critical public good that is essential for business growth, but it requires public support. The partnership between business and government is nowhere more evident than in the development of the

---

[40] Young, interview, 22 November 2011.

[41] A. J. Robinson (president, Central Atlanta Progress), interview with authors, 9 February 2012, audio, Special Collections and Archives, University Library, Georgia State University.

airport. The "Atlanta Way" is also seen in the way decisions were made about highways, mass transit, and even the taxi cab industry. The city was fortunate to have a dialogue among black and white business leaders in the Atlanta Action Forum. This produced a unified voice from business leaders that was used to engage public officials. The results smoothed the way for the passage of the MARTA referendum and the construction of the new midfield terminal at the airport. With these transportation improvements in place, Atlanta moved up as a convention city and a place in which to do business. The city also gained a reputation as a place of opportunity for African Americans through the minority contracting requirements of the Jackson and Young administrations. African Americans were able to benefit from transportation initiatives through contracting, improved services, and, in the case of MARTA, lower fares. Negotiating this support from African-American voters allowed the city to use bond-financing and even the regressive sales tax to expand the city's economic base.

The city's leaders acted on their knowledge that transportation is the life blood of Atlanta. Expanding Atlanta's transportation infrastructure was not without pain and controversy. The result of the collaboration of diverse leaders was that Atlanta maneuvered the transition from its beginning as a the terminus of a railroad line to a multi-modal local, interstate, and international transportation network of planes, trains, automobiles, trucks, and mass transit.

Atlanta Airfield, 1964
(Courtesy Hartsfield-Jackson Airport)

Atlanta Terminal, ca. 1940, the Quonset Hut
(Courtesy Hartsfield-Jackson Airport)

Atlanta Terminal, ca. 1960
(Courtesy Hartsfield-Jackson Airport)

Atlanta Terminal, ca. 1980
(Courtesy Hartsfield-Jackson Airport)

Atlanta airport tower construction, 2005
(Courtesy Hartsfield-Jackson Airport)

Marta train and the Atlanta skyline
(Courtesy MARTA)

Chapter 5

Minority Business Development—The Buck

Maynard Jackson's election as mayor in 1973 brought into the office a political leader committed to changing the conditions of poverty that had long affected many Atlanta residents. Decades of segregation, racial discrimination, and lack of employment opportunities contributed to the problem of poverty that affected Atlanta and other cities. Jackson's supporters had high expectations that the mayor would pay more attention to their needs than previous administrations had. As Mayor Jackson would learn, there were limits to the power of a political leader to make changes in such a long-term, multi-faceted problem. Internal factors within the city and larger issues made this task frustrating and difficult even for the most determined of mayors.

Patterns of segregation by custom and law dramatically restricted employment opportunities for blacks for much of the city's past. Both public and private policy decisions were designed to keep African Americans "in their place"—in subordinate jobs with low wages and few opportunities for advancement. The presence of the group of black colleges known collectively as the Atlanta University Center provided an educated elite, some of whom gained wealth through their entrepreneurial activities within the African-American community.[1] In spite of the success of this small group, most of Atlanta's black residents were relegated to

---

[1] For a discussion of Atlanta's prominent African-American community see Edward R. Carter, *The Black Side: A Partial History of the Business, Religious, and Educational Side of the Negro in Atlanta, Ga* (1894; repr., Freeport, NY: Books for Libraries Press, 1971) and Allison Dorsey, *To Build Our Lives Together: Community Formation in Black Atlanta, 1875–1906* (Athens and London: University of Georgia Press, 2004).

unskilled and semiskilled manual labor or domestic and personal services.[2]

Opportunities for advancement were limited because unions denied entry into membership and local ordinances restricted jobs during the first half of the twentieth century. For example, the white barbers' union resented the success of some black barbers, so the whites pressed the city council for legislation that would deny black barbers the right to serve white customers. White customers accustomed to patronizing shops owned by blacks thought this restriction was excessive, so the ordinance was passed denying blacks the right to cut the hair of white women, girls, and children under the age of fourteen.[3]

Limited educational opportunities and restricted career paths were two main obstacles for African Americans in Atlanta. While white youth could attend property tax-supported high schools in the city starting in 1875, it was another fifty years before political pressure from the African-American community resulted in the construction of Booker T. Washington High School for blacks. Despite the rhetoric of "separate but equal," the facilities, books, and pay for teachers in African-American schools were nowhere near the same standard as that provided by the school board to white schools.

Despite restrictions on employment and education, blacks formed their own community within the restrictions of racial segregation in Atlanta. Contemporary observers such as W. E. B. DuBois noted how the legacy of slavery and the imposition of segregation limited business opportunities for blacks in Atlanta.[4] Yet, as Carter described, there was a "black side" of town where business leaders emerged to provide goods and services within the segregated African-American community.[5] Atlanta's black community was based on the business, fraternal, religious,

---

[2] Bayor, *Race and the Shaping of Atlanta*, 94.
[3] Ibid., 97.
[4] W. E. B. DuBois, "The Negro in Business," *Fourth Annual Conference on the Condition of the Negro* (Atlanta: Atlanta University, 1899) 68.
[5] Carter, *The Black Side*, 201–203.

and educational institutions that developed in the city during the late nineteenth and early twentieth century.[6] Black Atlanta evolved significant institutions of higher education in the Atlanta University Center (AUC) with scholars like W. E. B. Du-Bois educated at Fisk and Harvard; Dr. Benjamin Mays, who earned his doctorate from the University of Chicago. The AUC also included theological seminaries that provided Atlanta's black congregations with a college-educated clergy. Leaders of the black community included physicians, lawyers and business leaders with graduate degrees from leading universities in the North. The sophistication of this leadership group would impress white leaders when circumstances required negotiation and interaction.

Segregation by custom and law guided relations between blacks and whites in Atlanta despite efforts by black leaders to create equality within the system of separation. The simple act of purchasing clothes was so demeaning that Mrs. Azira Hill recalled that she preferring to make clothes for herself and her daughters rather than shop under the conditions that confronted black customers in downtown stores.[7] Movie theaters, lunch counters, stores, banks, churches excluded or limited access by black citizens, restricting the economic opportunities of African Americans. In 1960, inspired by the sit-ins in Greensboro, students at the AUC took the lead in accelerating the process of change. That year marked the beginning of the sit-in demonstrations by students enrolled in the city's six private African-American academic institutions. The courageous students not only risked arrest by demonstrating in downtown lunch counters and other businesses, they also published a manifesto called "An Appeal for Human Rights" that demanded their rights to full citizenship and for equal access to businesses and employment opportunities. As eloquent as the students' appeal was, there was little progress made, so the demonstrations continued with protests staged in

---

[6] Dorsey, *To Build Our Lives Together*, 2.

[7] Azira Hill (civic leader and wife of Jesse Hill), interview by authors, 8 July 2011, audio, Special Collections and Archives, University Library, Georgia State University.

Rich's downtown department store as well as sit-ins at eating places located in public or tax-supported businesses such as the rail and bus stations, city hall, the county courthouse, and the capitol. At a meeting held
to resolve the conflict, white downtown business leaders met with the
students, but insisted that there would be no end to segregation. The
students shifted their focus to demonstrations against stores that depended upon black customers, but did not hire African Americans in any capacity. These demonstrations lasted through the spring and summer of
1960. By early fall, the students had succeeded in changing the employment discrimination against blacks in two grocery stores. Behind the
scenes, the students received important moral, strategic and financial
support from their elders—education leaders like Dr. Benjamin Mays,
the President of Morehouse College, ministers like William Holmes
Borders and black business leaders like Atlanta Life's Jesse Hill. Jesse
Hill's wife, Azira, recalled that her home was repeatedly put up as security to post bail for students.[8] Jesse Hill was an important figure in the city,
who was always known for his civility and mutual respect for everyone.
Attorney Bill Ide recalled that Jesse Hill "out thought and out worked"
everyone else.[9] The resources of Atlanta Life Insurance Company were
used in a variety of ways as the company printed signs for the student
demonstrators, used their switchboard as the communication center for
the movement, and provided space for meetings at its downtown headquarters.[10] These older black leaders had their misgivings about the tim-
ing of the student's actions, but they had no doubt as to the rightness of
their cause. Dr. Mays had been an outspoken critic of segregation since
coming to Morehouse in the 1940's. The immorality of segregation and
the importance of resistance were regular features in Dr. Mays' chapel
sermons. He was known to say that he would not sit in the segregated

---

[8] Ibid.

[9] R. William (Bill) Ide (attorney, McKenna Long & Aldridge, and former
counsel, MARTA), interview by authors, 11 November 2011, audio, Special
Collections and Archives, University Library, Georgia State University.

[10] Antonin, interview, 15 July 2011.

balcony of a theater if Jesus Christ, himself was the speaker.[11] Dr. Mays was hardly in a position to discourage his Morehouse students such as Lonnie King and Julian Bond from their sit-ins and protests.

After this success the student leaders reached out to a well-known Morehouse graduate (also a former student of Dr. Mays) and invited Dr. Martin Luther King, Jr. to join them in protests against downtown businesses. King had tended to remain aloof from the Atlanta demonstrations, concentrating his attention on other parts of the South that he felt needed his leadership and organizational skills. But this time, King felt he was needed in his hometown. By October 20, 1960, King and fifty-seven students had been arrested for sit-ins at Rich's and other downtown businesses. As more students were arrested in the months that followed, they shifted tactics and refused to post bond in order to crowd the jail. By March the following year, a volunteer agreement was reached in which Dr. King and the students would suspend their protests in return for a promise to end segregation in downtown businesses no later than mid-October 1961. With King's leadership the agreement held and Atlanta's businesses voluntarily began desegregating rather than closing as had happened in other southern cities.[12]

Later, Dr. King would take the campaign for desegregation of public facilities to Birmingham and the March on Washington. The mayor of Atlanta, Ivan Allen, was unique among Southern political leaders in his willingness to testify in support of the legislation that became known as the Civil Rights Act of 1964. This is further evidence that relationships between white and black leaders in Atlanta achieved an effective approach to addressing problems for the larger good of the community by face-to-face meetings.

Having Martin Luther King leading the efforts to end segregation helped the progress of African Americans in their efforts to obtain their

---

[11] Benjamin Mays, *Born to Rebel: An Autobiography* (Athens: University of Georgia Press, 1987).

[12] Jack L. Walker, "Protest and Negotiation: A Case Study of Negro Leadership in Atlanta," in *Atlanta, Georgia, 1960–1961: Sit-Ins and Student Activism*, ed. David J. Garrow (Brooklyn, NY: Carlson Publishers, 1989) 69–90.

civil rights in Atlanta. This process of peaceful, nonviolent protest set Atlanta apart when the national Civil Rights Act took effect in 1964. Later, Maynard Jackson would use Dr. King's words to characterize the initial struggle leading up to this landmark legislation as working to "get free" and end segregation so that blacks and whites could both enjoy the full rights of citizenship without the barriers of segregation. Before the end of his life in 1968, King shifted the focus of his protests toward the struggle for economic opportunity in order to "stay free."[13]

The beginning of the new decade in 1970 brought many changes to Atlanta and its leadership. Andrew Young followed his tenure with Dr. King at the Southern Christian Leadership Conference with an unsuccessful run for Congress in the 5th Congressional District that included Atlanta. The close partnership between white business leaders and elected officials at city hall began to change with the election of Sam Massell as mayor and Maynard Jackson as vice-mayor. Once in office, Mayor Massell responded by appointing African Americans to several key posts in his administration. Massell is proud of having appointed the first African Americans to head departments in city government. "The first vacancy I had was head of personnel, ...what a wonderful place to appoint an African-American if I wanted to increase opportunities for Blacks... so I let it be known, I called in Daddy King and Jesse Hill."[14] One of Massell's appointments was Emma Darnell, who as Director of Intergovernmental Relations became the first female, as well as one of the first African Americans to serve as a department head. Darnell would go on to serve in the Jackson administration and become a long-serving member of the Fulton County Commission. In addition, Massell appointed Andrew Young to Chair the city's Community Relations Commission. Not only were there new faces at city hall, African Americans were a majority of Atlanta's population in 1970 as blacks moved into the city and many white residents left for the suburbs.

---

[13] Daniel Halpern (president, CEO, and co-founder of Jackmont Hospitality), interview by authors, 29 September 2011, audio, Special Collections and Archives, University Library, Georgia State University.

[14] Sam Massell, Jr., video interview, 5 August 2013.

Mayor Massell was not elected with the traditional business support that had characterized most mayors such as William Hartsfield and Ivan Allen, Jr. Instead, there was a new electoral coalition of African Americans and liberal whites. With the help of his vice mayor and this new electoral coalition, Massell was successful in winning support for a 1971 rapid transit referendum that created the Metropolitan Atlanta Rapid Transit Authority (MARTA). The effort to enact mass transit legislation had failed in a previous attempt, lacking support from the African-American community. To engage their support an agreement was negotiated to ensure the provision of affirmative action requirements in MARTA contracts and employment.[15] Andrew Young called this agreement the Atlanta "fairness formula" that gave everyone a part of the benefits. The agreement called for 25 percent minority contracting on MARTA projects, 30 percent of the transit agency management would be minorities, and 30 percent of the bus drivers would be minorities. This was an initial step that coincided with further modest gains in employment and contracting within city government during Massell's administration. This situation changed quickly when Maynard Jackson defeated Sam Massell in the 1973 election to become the city's first African-American mayor. As in other cities the presence of a black mayor would provide a significant boost in support for minority businesses in Atlanta.

Among the first actions of the city council following Mayor Jackson's inauguration was the passage of what was called the Finley Ordinance after its author, council member Morris Finley. Morris Finley was a long-time veteran of the city council and a businessman who owned a print shop on Auburn Avenue. The Finley Ordinance used the language of Title VII of the 1964 Civil Rights Act that prohibited discrimination in hiring based on race and President Richard Nixon's Executive Order XXXVII issued in 1969 that prohibited discrimination in hiring by the federal government. The intent of Atlanta's Finley Ordinance was to

---

[15] Clarence N. Stone, *Regime Politics: Governing Atlanta, 1946–1988* (Lawrence: University Press of Kansas, 1989) 98–100.

provide the same anti-discrimination protections for hiring by the city government so the legislation tracked the language of the two federal documents. Within the Jackson administration, African-American women were given opportunities for advancement. The new mayor hired Marva Brooks, who had recently graduated from Harvard Law School and begun working on Wall Street. Jackson was campaigning for mayor when he met Brooks and asked her to move to Atlanta to become special counsel under his administration. She went to work in February 1974 and served as special counsel for several months before being promoted to city attorney. Her job was to explain the Finley Ordinance to white business leaders and make then understand how serious the mayor was in his efforts to provide opportunities for minorities. As Marva Brooks explained, "It was to get those who were contracting with the city to tell the city who they had employed and to disclose the ethnicity, race, and gender of their employees."[16] The Finley Ordinance also created the city's Office of Contract Compliance and an Equal Employment Opportunity office, which both reported to Emma Darnell, who was named by Mayor Jackson as commissioner of the city's Division of Administrative Services. While Darnell was hired at city hall by Mayor Massell, she was promoted by Mayor Jackson. This was the first cabinet-level position for a female in city government. Mayor Jackson asked Commissioner Darnell to assess and report on the participation of minority businesses in city contracts. In an interview Darnell recalled there was much work to be done as almost no city contracts went to minorities when she took office.[17]

Commissioner Darnell reported to Mayor Jackson that minorities, both African Americans and women, were not receiving a fair share of

---

[16] Marva Brooks (former city attorney), interview by authors, 7 March 2012, audio, Special Collections and Archives, University Library, Georgia State University.

[17] Emma I. Darnell (former city commissioner of administrative services and vice chair, Fulton County Board of Commissioners), interview by authors, 31 January 2012, audio, Special Collections and Archives, University Library, Georgia State University.

the contracts to provide goods and services to the city. In the year of his election, Jackson found that only .3 percent of the contracts with the city of Atlanta were awarded to women or minority-owned firms. Another issue was the limited number of women and minorities in the workforce of the city government. Although blacks represented 51 percent of the city's population, in 1973, minorities represented only 42 percent of city employees, most of whom were concentrated in low-wage, low-skill positions such as custodians and garbage collectors. Females represented only 12 percent of the city's total workforce, and only 27 percent held management positions in 1973.[18] These were statistics that Mayor Jackson was determined to change.

The proposed midfield terminal and related projects at the airport would require almost a half-billion dollars in bond financing and be one of the largest construction projects in the city's history. This provided Mayor Jackson the opportunity to promote his goal of increasing minority participation in contracts with the city through hiring or joint venture agreements. Marva Brooks and Emma Darnell were most responsible for the airport project's minority business development (MBD) program. Mayor Jackson's leadership in this situation was important. He worked with the city council to establish the broad principle that there would be no racial, ethnic, or gender discrimination by those who did business with the city. The task for Darnell, Brooks, and others working for the mayor was to establish the policies and procedures to implement this objective.

Another important person in the implementation process was chief administrative officer (and later, aviation commissioner) George Berry. He recalls the consternation among the leaders of the construction industry, many of whom had been working on plans for the airport's midfield terminal for five years. Many of these businessmen went to Mayor Jackson and tried to talk him out of his policy, but Jackson held firm. The reply from business leaders was "Mr. Mayor, you can't be serious,"

---

[18] *The Jackson Years: On Managing Change, 1974–1982* (Atlanta: Friends of Maynard Jackson, 1982) 2.

but they quickly found out that he was serious. In meetings with his cabinet, Jackson would say "You tell them that weeds will grow if 20 percent does not go to minority firms."[19]

At various times, Darnell, Brooks, and Berry would meet individually and collectively with white business leaders to explain the mayor's policy. Berry recalls saying to construction business owners, "You may think the mayor's crazy, but make no mistake, he is deadly serious. So, your choice is, you can file suit and you can tie us up for years maybe, or you can say, having 20 percent go to minorities and having 80 percent of the five hundred million dollar construction program is better than having 100 percent of nothing. And, to their credit, they finally agreed that that was the case." Many of the white business leaders had serious doubts whether the minority business requirement could be done, but they cared that the future of the city that would suffer if the airport construction did not take place.[20]

Former deputy chief administrative officer under Mayor Jackson, Eugene Duffy, described Jackson's decision as incredibly bold. The airport construction was the largest project the city had ever undertaken, and it was critical to the city's economic future. MBD programs were new and untested. In addition, Jackson proposed joint ventures so that black contractors would be involved at every level of airport construction. This would include not only construction, but also design, engineering, finance, and legal expertise—in short 20 percent of the entire project.[21] Andrew Young described typical MBD programs in other cities as giving black subcontractors the dirtiest jobs with the lowest profit margins. Bill Clement described the implementation of Atlanta's joint venture programs:

---

[19] Berry, interview, 26 July 2011.

[20] Ibid.

[21] Eugene Duffy (former deputy chief administrative officer and member of the executive committee, Paradigm Asset Management), interview by authors, 4 October 2011, audio, Special Collections and Archives, University Library, Georgia State University.

So you would then put together a large firm like Holder Construction with H. J. Russell. At that particular time H. J. Russell was primary a sub-contractor in dry wall. And this was the opportunity to move from being a specialty, a niche construction firm, to being general contractor.... You have bond law firms that did the bond work on all of these massive bond deals that were used to finance the airport. So, it just opened up avenues for minority firms that had not existed before and maybe would not have existed if not been for the opportunity Maynard presented and the city of Atlanta presented through his joint venture program.[22]

In spite of private negotiations through the Atlanta Action Forum, many white leaders resisted the minority business development proposals that were imposed as a condition for continuing to do business with the city of Atlanta. The city attorney, Marva Brooks, described the conflict as the "Second Battle of Atlanta." At one point, Mayor Jackson stopped work on the project and threatened to continue to halt work at the airport rather than allow construction without minority participation. Engineers, architecture firms, and construction contractors had no blacks in skilled positions and were unwilling to form joint ventures with minority-owned firms. Commissioner Emma Darnell emerged as the combative spokesman for the city, but no one doubted that the aggressive push to implement the policy was driven by the insistence of Mayor Jackson. The airport project was an expensive public works project, and the Jackson administration was determined to correct the longstanding policies of discrimination that had kept minorities from full participation in the economic growth of the city.

One administrative obstacle emerged to threaten the mayor's MBD program at the airport. As Aviation Commissioner George Berry recalled, the Federal Aviation Administration (FAA) had a rule that any contract involving federal dollars had to be competitively bid and the low bid accepted. He said,

---

[22] William A. (Bill) Clement (former president and CEO, Atlanta Life Financial Group), interview by authors, 22 July 2011, audio, Special Collections and Archives, University Library, Georgia State University.

So, we devised a pre-qualification system, and told the contractors that you have to become pre-qualified to bid, and as part of the pre-qualification process you have to tell us how you are going to reach the 20 percent goal. Then, we had a bidding process between those people who had pre-qualified, so we met the FAA's requirement. And then, when the low bidder won, we simply incorporated the contractor's voluntary program to reach the 20 percent goal into the contract, so that it became enforceable according to our attorneys. So, that is what we had to go through to get all this done.[23]

Two factors contributed to the success of the MBD requirements imposed by Mayor Jackson in the airport construction project. First, the MBD requirements based on the Finley Ordinance had the undisputed backing of the mayor, who enjoyed strong political support from African Americans, who represented a majority of voters in the city. As Adolph Reed observed, Jackson was successful in turning the issue of the airport construction into part of a development policy agenda with the expectation of jobs and economic benefits for blacks in Atlanta.[24] Secondly, even though the *Atlanta Constitution* was initially opposed to the MBD requirements, the editors changed their position and began supporting minority employment and joint venture contracting at the airport. This change in position was the result of quiet negotiations by the Atlanta Action Forum. During 1974 and 1975, the Action Forum discussed the need for united support for the airport project, and there emerged a consensus around the MBD requirements imposed by the Jackson administration.[25]

The MBD policies during Jackson's eight years as mayor did have several positive effects: the percentage of city funds that went to black firms rose from 2 to 33 percent. These purchasing processes were man-

---

[23] Berry, interview, 26 July 2011.

[24] Adolph Reed, Jr., "A Critique of Neo-Progressivism in Theorizing about Local Development Policy: A Case from Atlanta," in *The Politics of Urban Development*, ed. Clarence N. Stone and Heywood T. Sanders (Lawrence: University Press of Kansas, 1987) 202–203.

[25] Michael H. Trotter, *The History of the Atlanta Action Forum* (Atlanta: n.p., 1992) 7.

aged by an Office of Contract Compliance created by the Jackson administration under the Finlay Ordinance. The mayor later claimed that the airport contracting process created at least twenty black millionaires. One of those African-American business leaders in a position to benefit from Mayor Jackson's MBD program was Herman Russell. He learned the construction business from his father and started out working as a plasterer helping build large homes for whites in Buckhead. Russell's construction business grew, and by the late 1960s he was working with architect and developer John Portman on the interior rooms of the Hyatt Regency. When Mayor Jackson required joint ventures for contractors working on the midfield terminal of the airport, Herman Russell had the opportunity for a significant amount of the work. As Russell said, the MBD requirement at the airport "brought some more business to my company because we had the bonding capacity and we had the expertise to form joint ventures, and not to just joint venture in name, but in participation."[26] Russell used the opportunity of the airport MBD program and his entrepreneurial skill to become one of the city's business leaders and the first African American to join the Atlanta Chamber of Commerce.

Another benefit of the Jackson administration's MBD program was the talented human capital that was attracted to Atlanta as a result of the favorable national publicity in African-American publications. Atlanta became a mecca for black professionals who were drawn by the mayor's reputation and the expanding opportunities to work in black-owned businesses. More importantly, Mayor Jackson was fond of telling the media that the midfield airport terminal project was completed on time (it was not delayed by the minority contracting requirement) and under budget. The dedication of the new midfield terminal was held in September 1980.

Mayor Maynard Jackson's legacy with the minority business development program was not limited to the large contracts at the airport.

---

[26] Herman J. Russell (founder and retired CEO, H. J. Russell and Company), interview by authors, 1 May 2012, audio, Special Collections and Archives, University Library, Georgia State University.

According to Commissioner Emma Darnell, other projects involving contracts of less than one million dollars were more significant in providing opportunities for African-American contractors. There were, after all, a larger number of smaller contracts, which provided opportunity for minority contractors and vendors without political connections and with few assets except a record of good performance and the ability to complete a project.[27] While the controversy focused on opportunities for black businesses, Brooke Jackson Edmond recalls that her father had a larger vision:

> It was about minority-owned businesses, female-owned businesses, basically everybody who was not already at the table having the opportunity to be there—not being given a handout because he was emphatic that once you have the opportunity then it is up to you as a business owner to follow through in a way that is as competent or more competent or more outstanding than any other business.[28]

Emma Darnell's position as commissioner of the Department of Administrative Services brought her into conflict not only with whites seeking to do business with the city but also with others within the Jackson administration. In 1977, she lost the support of the mayor, and after much conflict resigned her position. Darnell became a candidate for mayor when Maynard Jackson sought re-election later in 1977. Though she lost that election, Darnell was elected to the Fulton County Board of Commissioners in 1992.

The Finley Ordinance revealed the racial and gender composition of all city contractors, including the banks that held city deposits. Jackson threatened to withdraw city funds from prestigious Atlanta banks if they did not add African Americans to their boards and senior management ranks. Mayor Jackson's daughter Brooke Jackson Edmond, herself a business owner, described her father's approach:

[27] Darnell, interview, 31 January 2012.
[28] Brooke Jackson Edmond (daughter of Maynard Jackson and Executive Vice President, Jackmont Hospitality), interview by authors, 3 February 2012, audio, Special Collections and Archives, University Library, Georgia State University.

He pushed for banks and lending institutions to work with minority-owned businesses because they needed capital to finance their endeavors.... He always started from a big-picture perspective and focused on what were the needs and then kind of methodically said OK, well if this is the need, how do we accomplish that goal. If the minority community needs economic opportunity, economic inclusion, what do we need to do to make that happen, and then he used the tools that were at his disposal to create those opportunities.[29]

After two four-year terms as mayor, the city charter did not permit Maynard Jackson to run again. He left city hall and opened an Atlanta office for a Chicago-based law firm. He was succeeded as mayor in 1982 by former civil rights leader, congressman, and ambassador to the United Nations, Andrew Young. In contrast to the aggressive style of Maynard Jackson, Andrew Young brought his considerable diplomatic skills to the effort to strengthen the partnership between the city's white and black leaders. His administration continued the MBD policies of his predecessor, including city contracts for minority or joint-venture businesses. Young enforced the Finley Ordinance that required all firms receiving city contracts to develop equal employment practices that would move toward the long-term goal of creating a work force that reflects the diverse population of the Atlanta metropolitan area. At the beginning of the Young administration, firms doing business with the city were required to hire at least 20 percent minority workers, and before Young left office, this goal was raised to 25 percent to reflect the increasing minority population of the metro area.[30]

Moving beyond the work of the Jackson administration, Young pressed the city council to enact a new Minority and Female Business Enterprise (MFBE) ordinance, which was adopted in 1982. During each of the subsequent years he was in office, Mayor Young established by administrative order annual goals for minority and female-owned businesses that were participating in any public contracting. In 1985, the city's MFBE goal increased from 25 percent to 35 percent, making At-

---

[29] Ibid.
[30] Horton, *The Young Years*, 117.

lanta's affirmative-action target among the highest in the nation. The city's MFBE program imposed the requirement that firms wishing to qualify as a minority- or female-owned business would need to be certified by the Office of Contract Compliance. The purpose of the certification process was provide a register of certified businesses and to reduce the possibility that companies could make false claims about their ownership. The register of minority and female-owned businesses could be used by majority-owned companies and governmental agencies to identify potential minority and female-owned suppliers, subcontractors, or joint-venture partners. Between 1982 and 1989, more than 1,200 minority and female businesses were certified by the city's Office of Contract Compliance.[31]

As Andrew Young moved to increase Atlanta's MFBE goal, some white business leaders objected to the policy. They argued that their profits would be affected if their businesses were required to share a portion of their revenue from city contracts with minority firms. In contrast to the adversarial relationship between white business leaders and the Jackson administration, Young and his staff negotiated quietly. As Andrew Young recalled in an interview, he would personally ask business leaders if they would rather have 75 percent of something rather than 100 percent of nothing. The diplomatic approach used by Andrew Young and his administration worked more effectively than that of his predecessor. As one business leader said, "Maynard broke a lot of eggs while he was mayor."[32] Mayor Young also enjoyed much more support from business leaders for his policies than his predecessor. This was expressed privately through the deliberations of the Action Forum and publicly in the willingness of business groups not only to hire Young after he finished his term in office but also to dedicate a public plaza

---

[31] Ibid., 118–19.

[32] Sam Williams (initial executive director, Research Atlanta, and retired president and CEO, Metro Atlanta Chamber of Commerce), interview by authors, 8 December 2011, audio, Special Collections and Archives, University Library, Georgia State University.

named in his honor and for a major soft drink maker to endow a policy school that bears his name.

In the perspective of political scientist Clarence Stone, Atlanta has a milieu, a history of biracial cooperation. When challenges to this cooperation arise, the pattern is for black and white leaders to meet, usually in private, to discuss the problem and develop a solution that benefits everyone. The result is a partnership between elected public officials and business leaders to move the city forward. In describing this partnership, Stone quotes Young as saying, "Politics doesn't control the world. Money does. And we ought not to be upset about that. We ought to begin to understand how money works and why money works."[33] The unique "Atlanta Way," as Young described it, was an exchange of power based on electoral control exchanged for a share of the city's economic growth. As Young saw it, his task as mayor was to see that whites got some of the power and blacks got some of the money.

This exchange was at the heart of Atlanta's minority business development program. African Americans made up a majority of both the city's population and its voters, so black elected public officials such as Jackson and Young were in solid control of city hall. Beginning with the MARTA labor contracts (and extending into the program of joint ventures and minority set-asides that followed in the Jackson and Young administrations), this strong political power shaped the MBD policies. As Stone writes, "The black-led city government's policy of promoting minority business enterprises meshed smoothly with the networking efforts of downtown business executives," and these initiatives were part of a new form of biracial cooperation. The alliance was strengthened by the presence of selective incentives that reinforced the attachment of black business executives to the coalition. The black business executives provided campaign funds and various types of civic leadership that are an integral part of black political mobilization in Atlanta. This coalition was self-sustaining through the periods when Jackson and Young occupied

---

[33] Stone, *Regime Politics*, 136.

the mayor's office.[34] The cooperative partnership between black and white leaders in Atlanta unraveled during the tenure of Mayor Bill Campbell, but was re-formed with the administrations of mayors Shirley Franklin and Kasim Reed.

"Regime politics," according to Stone, is the study of how groups work together to get things done. In a later article, Stone elaborated on this point, suggesting a typology of regimes based on the policy agendas of each type. In this framework, the Atlanta regime was described as a "development regime" in which the governing coalition is concerned with changing land uses in order to promote growth. This framework contrasts with "maintenance regimes," which focus on providing routine services and do not attempt to change established social and economic practice. The other options Stone describes are middle-class "progressive regimes" (focused on regulating environmental, historic preservation, affordable housing, linkage programs, and so on) and, finally, regimes devoted to expanding opportunity for lower classes.[35] Few projects had the potential to promote growth like the development of the midfield terminal at the airport by Maynard Jackson. The airport's location on the south side of the city was as an indication of the mayor's skillful ability to define black interests within a pro-growth framework. This enabled the regime to maintain the support of the black community.[36] Other authors writing within the framework of regime theory suggest that Atlanta's black mayors have been adept in providing the selective incentives needed to retain the loyalty of their black constituency, while at the same time pursuing pro-growth policies supported by the city's business leaders. The contracts and other rewards to constituents and contributors provide the basis for "civic cooperation" needed to ensure that regime participants

---

[34] Ibid., 165.

[35] Clarence Stone, "Urban Regimes and the Capacity to Govern: A Political Economy Approach," *Journal of Urban Affairs* 15/1 (March 1993): 1–28.

[36] Adolph Reed, Jr., "The Black Urban Regime: Structural Origins and Constraints," in Michael P. Smith, ed., *Power, Community and the City* (New Brunswick, NJ: Transaction Books, 1988) 83.

"go along to get along."[37] This is confirmed by the high reelection rates of Atlanta's black elected officials.[38] Viewed from this perspective, Atlanta's regime and its leaders worked together to develop the new airport facility. At the same time they produced a minority business development program that increased economic opportunities and employment for many who otherwise would have been denied these opportunities.

The lessons for other cities from Atlanta's MBD programs may have less to do with the policies themselves than with the process of regime decision-making in Atlanta. If a regime is defined as an informal coalition between private interests and public bodies to make and carry out policy decisions, the Atlanta regime faced challenges and considerable stress during the period of the Jackson and Young administrations.[39] Yet, the partnership among leaders in Atlanta carried out several significant policies during this period. The construction of the midfield terminal kept the airport in a preeminent position for air traffic in the region and a major hub for international flights. The Young administration had its share of accomplishments with international investments reshaping the downtown area, the rebuilding of Underground Atlanta, and the beginning of the bidding process for the 1996 Centennial Olympic Games.

All of these accomplishments were a product of cooperation between the city's elected public officials and business leaders—both white and black. The city's minority business development programs were at the center of this system of cooperation based on the selective incentives provided by development opportunities. Andrew Young recalls a conversation in which he was asked to describe the difference between Atlanta and Detroit. Both cities had majority African-American populations and mayors reflecting that political power. In Detroit, Young says, the partnership was formed by the city's black leaders and labor unions. In contrast, in Atlanta the partnership was between a well-educated educated

---

[37] Stone, *Regime Politics*, 192.

[38] Arnie Fleischmann, "Atlanta: Urban Coalitions in a Suburban Sea," in Hank V. Savitch and John C. Thomas, eds., *Big City Politics in Transition* (Newbury Park, CA: Sage, 1991) 98.

[39] Stone, *Regime Politics*, 6.

black leadership and white business leaders, who then were able to bring organized labor along on important development projects. If regimes vary according to local circumstances, it might be fruitful to examine who provides the leadership within various groups and how partnerships are formed in other cities.

What are the lessons from the decisions made by Atlanta's leaders that might be helpful to others? First, it seems obvious that MBD programs invite controversy. The two terms of Mayor Maynard Jackson bore the brunt of the conflict over the 20 percent minority hiring and joint venture program introduced at the airport. Jackson and his commissioner of administrative services, Emma Darnell, were focal point of much of the criticism over the program, which was tested in court and investigated by the newspapers, but withstood the scrutiny. As the mayor said, the goal was efficiency and equity in building the airport terminal.[40] Under the Finley Ordinance, compliance was suggested but not required by the administration. All of the devices such as the pre-qualifying procedure were carefully crafted to avoid court challenges.

Under Mayor Young's leadership, the city awarded contracts totaling nearly $200 million to some 500 different certified minority and female-owned businesses.[41] This increase in minority participation was accomplished with considerably less rancor than took place during the Jackson administration. This suggests that a more diplomatic approach to these types of conflict may be useful in winning support from people involved.

Even diplomacy has limits, and the city's MFBE ordinance was the subject of repeated suits brought by building contractors who were not happy with any minority business goals. The American Subcontractors Association, Georgia Chapter, Inc. filed a legal challenge to the MFBE program in 1983, and the following year the Georgia Supreme Court struck down the initial version of the city's ordinance. The city council amended the MFBE ordinance to suggest that minority and female-

---

[40] Robert A. Holmes, *Maynard Jackson, A Biography* (Miami: Barnhardt & Ashe Publishing, Inc., 2011) 155.

[41] Horton, *The Young Years*, 12.

owned businesses may be used as one of the criteria in determining the most responsible bidder for a specific city contract. The building contractors group filed another suit the following year, but the Fulton County Superior Court upheld the revised MFBE ordinance. While this court decision was being appealed, the United States Supreme Court decided a case against the city of Richmond, Virginia, which had a 30 percent minority business set aside requirement. The litigation continued in the contractors association's suit against the city with the Georgia Supreme Court ruling against the city in early 1989. The mayor hired the economic consulting firm of Brimmer and Marshall to produce a report documenting the present effects of past discrimination in the city's contracting process.

The Brimmer and Marshall report was thorough in its documentation of past discrimination against both minorities and females in contracting and hiring prior to 1973. In two significant findings, the report documented that minority and female contracting by the city dropped from 35 percent in 1988 to 14 percent after the Georgia Supreme Court ruling against the MFBE ordinance. Procurement business by minorities and females also dropped significantly after the court's ruling. The report also showed that minority business with Richmond dropped from 30 percent to 2 percent following the US Supreme Court's ruling in 1989.[42] Reelected in 1989, Maynard Jackson remained committed to the idea of minority business development programs in the city's purchasing, hiring, and contracting. Continuing litigation by contractors had the potential to restrict MBD programs developed by the city and, more importantly, the construction program required for the Olympic preparation by the Atlanta Committee for the Olympic Games (ACOG) between 1990 and 1996. Yet, the city continued its efforts to find ways to meet the requirements of the courts and to use MBD programs to advance the policy goal of providing better access for women and minorities.

---

[42] Andrew F. Brimmer and F. Ray Marshall, *Public Policy and Promotion of Minority Economic Development: City of Atlanta and Fulton County, GA* (Washington, DC: Brimmer and Marshall, 1990) 39.

One conclusion from the decisions made by Atlanta's public leaders is that minority business development is an effective policy tool for re-dressing past discrimination and provides opportunities for minorities and females in purchasing, hiring, and contracting. These opportunities are useful in providing employment for some economically disadvantaged individuals. Such MBD policies are most effective when they have the support of elected public officials such as mayors Jackson and Young. In this sense, local leadership does matter.

There are, however, serious limitations on the effectiveness of local public policy on reducing poverty. During every decade since 1970, the poverty rate for the city of Atlanta has remained above both the percent-ages for the ten-county Atlanta region and for the nation as a whole. Af-ter eight years of the Jackson administration's efforts to promote minori-ty business development, the poverty rate for the city increased from 16 percent in 1970 to 27.5 percent in 1980. The poverty rates within the city remained above 27 percent during the decade of the 1980s, dropped slightly to 24.4 percent in 2000, and climbed to 26.1 percent in the 2010 census.[43]

The causes of poverty are multi-faceted and the subject of much de-bate. The variations in the federal government's methods for measuring poverty make comparisons difficult. The persistence of poverty within the city of Atlanta over many decades reflects two issues that must be considered. First, mayors may have the strongest will to use public policy to improve the lives of their constituents by putting people to work and reducing poverty. However, micro-level policy in a municipality is un-likely to reduce poverty levels in the face of much broader macro-level issues. During the time period when Mayor Jackson was vigorously in-creasing economic opportunities for minorities, the National Bureau of Economic Research reports that there were three separate nation-wide recessions. The recessions of 1973–1975, 1980, and 1981–1982 caused unemployment rates to spike at the time the mayor was attempting to

---

[43] US Bureau of the Census, "Income, Poverty and Health Insurance," http://www.census.gov/hhes/www/poverty/index.html (18 November 2014).

increase minority job opportunities through his MBD program. Most of the national economic problems of the era were caused by the global issue of dramatic increases in oil prices.[44]

A second factor is that the vigorous effort led by mayors Jackson and Young in their MBD programs of purchasing, hiring, and contracting attracted national attention and served as a model for the programs implemented by other cities. Atlanta's African-American public leadership shaped a reputation for the city as the "Black Mecca." While this reputation attracted talented and well-educated blacks, it also drew poor people to Atlanta who had limited job skills and fewer employment opportunities in other places. At the same time, many white residents were leaving the city of Atlanta for suburban locations, resulting in in a higher percentage of blacks (67.1 percent in 1990) and an overall decline in the central city's population from just below a half million in 1970 to fewer than 395,000 residents in 1990.[45]

However, the impact of the MBD programs cannot be seen by looking at the city of Atlanta alone. Atlanta has proven to be an economic engine for a much larger metropolitan region. As they prospered, African Americans joined whites in the surrounding counties, especially Fulton and DeKalb. There are not policies in Atlanta to encourage middle class public employees such as teachers, police officers, and city employees to live inside the city limits. MBD programs were not limited to minority businesses inside the city limits. The median income of African Americans in the Atlanta MSA (metropolitan statistical area) is higher than the median income for other large cities. In 2013, African-American median household income in Metro Atlanta was $41,800

---

[44] "US Business Cycle Expansions and Contractions," Public Information Office, National Bureau of Economic Research, http://www.nber.org/ cycles.html (accessed 18 November 2014).

[45] US Bureau of the Census, Metropolitan and Metropolitan Statistical Areas, Atlanta-Sandy Springs-Roswell, GA" Metro Area," http://www.census. gov/econ/cbp/index.html (18 November 2014).

compared to $34,589 in other large US cities.[46] Relatively high income, higher rates of homeownership, and the continuing influx of African Americans to Atlanta led *Forbes* to rank Atlanta first on its list of best cities for African Americans. The policies established by Jackson and Young continue to produce benefits for the city. The Atlanta MSA has the third-highest total of black households with incomes above $100,000, surpassed only by New York City and Washington, DC.[47] Jackson and Young established policies that changed the opportunity structure for African Americans in Atlanta. The importance of their achievement can be seen in the continued appeal of Atlanta to higher income African Americans and those seeking greater opportunity.

Should the first two African-American mayors of Atlanta have insisted on a policy of minority business development programs? Public policy implementation is related to politics because what a local government chooses to do is based in part on the needs and wishes of voters. In the 1970s and 1980s, both mayors of Atlanta were representing a majority African-American constituency. In an interview, Michael Lomax summarized what was taking place during the Jackson and Young administrations with their policy of minority business development. Lomax said, "African-American mayors did in Atlanta what Boston and New York City mayors did for the Irish."[48] In Atlanta's context, mayors Jack-

---

[46] Joel Kotkin, "The Cities Where African-Americans Are Doing the Best Economically," *Forbes* (15 January 2015): http://www.forbes.com/sites/joelkotkin/2015/01/15/the-cities-where-african-americans-are-doing-the-best-economically/#5ee1a719d1a0 (3 November 2015).

[47] Karen Pooley, "Segregation's New Geography: The Atlanta Metro Region, Race, and the Declining Prospects for Upward Mobility," *Southern Spaces* (15 April 2015): http://southernspaces.org/2015/segregations-new-geography-atlanta-metro-region-race-and-declining-prospects-upward-mobility (3 November 2015).

[48] Michael Lomax (president and CEO, United Negro College Fund), interview by authors, 11 January 2013, audio, Special Collections and Archives, University Library, Georgia State University.

son and Young were following the words of John Wesley Dobbs to follow the *ballot* with the *buck* and the *book.*

The impact of Atlanta's approach to minority business development had a broad and lasting impact. Atlanta's general counsel Marva Brooks described the effect of the "Atlanta Way": "Once it was established that that was going to be way things were done in Atlanta, Atlantans fell in, and I think that whole idea of Atlanta maximizing opportunities for diversity everywhere just began to take off all over town."[49]

---

[49] Brooks interview.

Marvin Arrington, Herman Russell, Robert Holder, and Andrew Young
(Russell Collection)

Maynard Jackson, Andrew Young, Robert Holmes, Jesse Hill,
Herman Russell, and Gerald Durley *(Russell Collection)*

6

Education—The Book

Cities are the creations of the leaders who made them, and one of the remarkable achievements in making modern Atlanta was described by John Wesley Dobbs as "the *book*." Dobbs, insisting that each of his six daughters attend Spelman College, imprinted the importance of education upon them and upon their families, who would come to shape the city. While Spelman College made contributions to the education of women, others came to Atlanta to study and become "Morehouse Men." Spelman and Morehouse are part of a collection of African-American educational institutions known as the Atlanta University Center (AUC) that produced generations of middle-class African Americans.[1] Over the years, graduates contributed to the churches, schools, businesses, and civic organizations that served African Americans within the segregated society of Atlanta. Others got their degrees and realized that a segregated Southern city was not a place where they could realize their full potential, so they joined the out-migration of talented people moving to other places for graduate study and professional lives with fewer restrictions. A few were able to grasp the possibilities of a New South and led the fight to end racial segregation and to expand economic opportunity for mi-

---

[1] Bacote, *The Story of Atlanta University*, 394–98. Initial efforts at cooperation among the institutions now known as the Atlanta University Center (AUC) began in 1929 with Atlanta University, Morehouse, and Spelman forming the Atlanta University System. Clark College, Morris Brown, and Gammon Theological Seminary joined later. These six institutions formed the AUC in 1957 to facilitate cooperation among the schools. Gammon is now part of the Interdenominational Theological Center; Atlanta University and Clark College merged to form Clark-Atlanta University; the Morehouse School of Medicine joined the AUC, and Morris Brown College has withdrawn.

norities. Each of the city's colleges and universities played a unique role in shaping Atlanta.

In the aftermath of the Civil War, thousands of newly freed slaves left the countryside and moved to Atlanta. Of the four million freed slaves in the South, almost all were illiterate because state laws prohibited slaves from learning to read and write.[2] Many of the newly freed slaves were drawn to Atlanta by the protection available from federal troops in the city, as well as the opportunity for jobs in the growing town. Also drawn to Atlanta were three white missionaries from the American Missionary Association (AMA) of the Congregational Church who wanted to open a school to serve the African Americans in the city. The three founded the school that would become Atlanta University. With assistance from the pastor of Friendship Baptist Church, the AMA missionaries began offering classes in an old railroad boxcar.[3] Other missionaries followed from the Freedman's Aid Society of the Methodist Episcopal Church and founded Clark College in 1867. African Americans created some educational institutions for themselves as members of the African Methodist Episcopal Church established Morris Brown College. That same year black Baptists organized the Augusta Theological Institute. It struggled for twelve years before moving to Atlanta where it was renamed Morehouse College. Two white female missionaries organized the Atlanta Baptist Female Seminary in 1881 to train school teachers. John D. Rockefeller provided early financial support for the institution that was renamed Spelman Seminary (later renamed Spelman College) to honor his wife. As the city provided poorly for the education of African Americans, these institutions provided basic education and high school training for many years until they began to offer advanced degrees.

The colleges struggled to raise funds and provide facilities for their students. Spelman Seminary met for several years in the basement of Friendship Baptist Church, which was the city's oldest black Baptist

---

[2] Mays, *Born to Rebel*, 3.
[3] Bacote, *The Story of Atlanta University*, 4.

congregation and whose pastor, the Rev. Frank Quarles, was a strong supporter of education for blacks. Spelman focused initially on the training of teachers who could, in turn, provide instruction to other African Americans.[4] Each institution's founding reflects a story of leaders committed to providing educational opportunity to blacks in the face of adversity. Collectively these institutions produced leaders who would make a significant difference in shaping the future of Atlanta.

Public education for both black and white children suffered from a lack of funding during the nineteenth century. In the immediate aftermath of the Civil War, there were no public schools for children of either race, with only a handful of private tuition academies for more well-to-do white children whose parents could afford the fees. In 1869, the city formed a special committee to design a new school system that would provide free public schools for all of Atlanta's children. In its report the committee called for tuition-free elementary schools and also for secondary schools to educate those whose academic achievement and conduct earned them the right to move up to seek a high school degree. Unfortunately, the committee recommended the provision of educational facilities for white children only, and only last-minute efforts by black citizens resulted in the provision of elementary schools for blacks. In 1872, when the Atlanta school system opened, there were no public high schools for African Americans, while Boys High and Girls High Schools opened for whites. Public high schools for blacks were not available until the opening of Booker T. Washington High School in fall 1924. By denying blacks access to a public high school education, the city's white leaders were using education to buttress the system of racial segregation that required blacks to pay property taxes but denied them the same educational opportunities as whites. This was a deliberate public policy designed to

---

[4] Beverly Guy-Sheftall and Jo Moore Stewart, *Spelman: A Centennial Celebration, 1881–1981* (Charlotte, NC: The Delmar Company, 1981) 5.

keep African Americans "in their place"—a place of subordination and segregation.[5]

Before the opening of Washington High School in 1924, the institutions of the Atlanta University Center offered high school-level degrees for African-American students, who had previously been without access to public secondary education. In 1921, the combined high school enrollment of Clark College, Morehouse College, Atlanta University, and Morris Brown College was 1,139; their college-level enrollment was 527. Blacks were still allowed to vote in local elections in Atlanta but were kept out of state-wide elections by the imposition of a whites-only primary. This permitted black voters to defeat a bond issue that would expand high schools for whites in the city because no provision was made for a high school for black students. Only when authorities agreed to build a high school for African Americans was the next bond issue approved, and the first black public education became available.[6] The opening of Washington High was a source of pride and a springboard for accomplishment for young black students in the city.

White students who finished high school often left town to attend a college or university. The city's white leaders worried about the lack of institutions of higher education, so they sought changes. The Presbyterian church-affiliated Oglethorpe University briefly relocated from Milledgeville, Georgia, to Atlanta in 1870, but a lack of financial support caused the institution to close until reopening in 1913.[7] In the aftermath of the Civil War, Georgia's economy still depended primarily on agriculture. In an effort to encourage diversity, Atlanta's New South spokesman, Henry Grady, sought support from the state government to train mechanical engineers. The state provided $65,000 to establish the Geor-

---

[5] Timothy J. Crimmins, "The Crystal Stair: A Study of the Effects of Caste and Class on Secondary Education in Late Nineteenth-century Atlanta, Georgia," *Urban Education* 8 (January 1974): 404–405.

[6] Mays, *Born to Rebel*, 89.

[7] Paul S. Hudson, "Oglethorpe University," *New Georgia Encyclopedia*, http://www.georgiaencyclopedia.org/articles/education/oglethorpe-university (16 September 2014).

gia School of Technology that opened its doors in 1888.[8] Georgia Tech gradually expanded its academic programs for students and established an Evening School of Commerce that eventually became a separate institution known as Georgia State University. The graduates of Georgia Tech became the architects and engineers who literally built modern Atlanta.

The effort to bring a Methodist-affiliated school for whites was aided by the city's first millionaire, Asa G. Candler, owner of the Coca-Cola Company. After purchasing the formula for Coke from druggist John Pemberton, Asa Candler turned the product into a company producing syrup for soda fountain soft drinks and later for sale to bottlers of Coca-Cola®. As the business prospered, his brother, Warren A. Candler, rose in the ranks of the Methodist Episcopal Church, South, to become a bishop. Bishop Candler was also the president of Emory College, which was founded in 1836 in Oxford, Georgia. When the Methodist Episcopal Church, South, decided in 1914 to establish a university east of the Mississippi River, Asa Candler offered a million dollars for the new school if the church would locate the institution in Atlanta. The offer was accepted, and Bishop Candler became the first chancellor of Emory University.

The generosity of the leaders of the Coca-Cola Company has continued to sustain Emory with gifts to the institution from long-time Coke president Robert Woodruff and the more recent head of the company, Roberto Goizueta, for whom the Emory business school is named.[9] Robert Woodruff had a major influence in making the university a center for medical and health-related research and was instrumental in bringing the Center for Disease Control and Prevention to Atlanta. With the addition of headquarters for organizations that include CARE, the Ameri-

---

[8] Marla Edwards and John D. Toon, "Georgia Institute of Technology (Georgia Tech)," *New Georgia Encyclopedia*, http://www.georgiaencyclopedia. org/articles/education/georgia-institute-technology-georgia-tech (7 April 2015).

[9] Frederick Allen, *Secret Formula: How Brilliant Marketing and Relentless Salesmanship Made Coca-Cola the Best-Known Product in the World* (New York: HarperBusiness, 1994) 375.

can Cancer Society, and Boys & Girls Clubs of America to the city, Robert Woodruff's foundations have contributed in significant ways to shaping Atlanta as a public health and nonprofit center. Emory University has also produced leaders for Atlanta such as Boisfeuillet Jones, who worked behind the scenes to mold the Robert Woodruff Foundation into one of the city's major philanthropic organizations. Jones served as a mentor to Charles H. (Pete) McTier, who became the long-time head of the Woodruff Foundation and provided continuity to the city's major philanthropic organization.[10] The close relationship between leaders of the Coca-Cola Company and Emory University has enabled the institution to evolve from a regional to an international institution.

Another Emory alumnus who was associated with the generosity of the Woodruff Foundation to Emory and to the city is Jimmy B. Williams of the SunTrust Company. For many years, Williams worked directly with Robert Woodruff and continues to serve as a member of the board of the Woodruff Foundation. When asked why Mr. Woodruff was so generous to Emory and to other important causes, Williams said, "Mr. Woodruff wanted everything he was a part of to be successful."[11] This drive for success included not only the Coca-Cola Company, but also the city itself.

The cumulative impact of the colleges and universities in the Atlanta area is difficult to exaggerate as the institutions provide a well-educated workforce. In the city of Atlanta, almost 39.9 percent of the population holds at least a bachelor's degree, while the metropolitan area has a rate of 33.3 percent. Both are higher than the national average of 27 percent. The Atlanta region has the seventh-largest number of students registered in colleges and universities of any city in the nation, and

---

[10] Charles H. (Pete) McTier (retired president, Robert W. Woodruff Foundation, business and civic leader), interview by authors, 19 July 2012, audio, Special Collections and Archives, University Library, Georgia State University.

[11] Jimmy B. Williams (retired head of Trust Company of Georgia), interview by authors, 16 August 2011, audio, Special Collections and Archives, University Library, Georgia State University.

the third-largest concentration of African-American students.[12] The historically black colleges and universities have provided mentoring and educational opportunity for generations of students in the city.

The person most responsible for this leadership in African-American education was Dr. Benjamin Mays. He was born in rural Greenwood County, South Carolina, as the youngest of eight children. During his life on the farm he was unable to attend school more than four months a year, and the possibility that he would earn a college degree and later a doctorate from the University of Chicago seemed remote. Benjamin Mays was determined to get an education and to escape life on a cotton farm.[13]

Mays's determination to pursue his education took him first to Orangeburg, South Carolina, to earn a high school degree from the South Carolina State College, then to Virginia Union for a year of college before transferring to Bates College in Maine, where he finished his college degree in 1921. He attended the University of Chicago for one year before accepting a position as a professor at Morehouse College. After three years in Atlanta, Mays returned to Chicago and completed a master's degree in religion. He returned to the South and served as a pastor for both the Urban League and the YMCA. During his time in Atlanta working for the YMCA, Mays collaborated with fellow minister Joseph W. Nicholson on a national study of African-American churches. In 1933, their findings were published in *The Negro Church*. After a ten-year delay, he returned to Chicago to complete his PhD degree before heading to Washington, DC, to become dean of the Howard University School of Religion. Dean Mays took the weak and struggling school and increased enrollment, established a firmer financial footing, and attained accreditation by the American Association of Theological Schools. Mays

---

[12] Atlanta Regional Council for Higher Education Reports, "The Atlanta Region: National Leader in Higher Education," http://www.atlantahighered. org/default.aspx?tabid=627&Report=5&xmid=557 (21 November 2014).

[13] Mays, *Born to Rebel*, 134–37.

left Howard University in 1940 to accept the presidency of Morehouse College, a position he retained until 1967.[14]

Dr. Benjamin Mays left a unique imprint on Atlanta and especially on the lives of the young men of Morehouse College through his long and distinguished career. He was a mentor to generations of "Morehouse Men," including many who would help to shape the city. Former state senator Leroy Johnson said that, while growing up in Atlanta, he accepted the segregation of blacks and whites unconsciously. When he wished to attend a movie at the Fox Theater, Johnson would enter at the back and climb the stairs to sit in the "colored only" balcony. Then, when Leroy Johnson entered Morehouse as a freshman, the first day of school, President Mays talked to the students about segregation, urging then to refuse to accept it. Johnson said he never again went to a segregated theater, and Dr. Mays made him decide to fight segregation by entering politics. Johnson became the first African American elected to the Georgia General Assembly since Reconstruction.[15]

Benjamin Mays's leadership at Morehouse provided new buildings on the campus, more than $15 million raised in endowment for the institution, and an increase in the academic reputation of the college; Morehouse became the first African-American school to house a chapter of the Phi Beta Kappa academic honor society. Perhaps the most important aspect of his leadership was his mentoring generations of Morehouse students and influencing others far beyond the campus. Mays encouraged Morehouse students in his Tuesday chapel talks to be men, not black men who had to play second fiddle to white men, but rather black men who were not afraid to walk side by side with whites. Mays's most famous disciple was Martin Luther King, Jr., who realized when he entered Morehouse that "nobody there was afraid." The president encour

---

[14] Dereck J. Rovaris Sr., *Mays and Morehouse: How Benjamin E. Mays Developed Morehouse College, 1940–1967* (Silver Spring, MD: Beckham Publications Group, Inc., 2005) 20–32.

[15] Leroy Johnson, interview, 27 July 2011.

aged students to fight fear and racism. "If you are ignorant," Mays told students, "the world is going to cheat you. If you are weak, the world is going to kick you. If you are a coward, the world is going to keep you running."[16] While Dr. King was certainly the most famous of Benjamin Mays's students, others came from throughout the United States to study at Morehouse. One of these young men tells of coming from a farm in rural Alabama to attend Morehouse, where Dr. Mays taught the students lessons of deportment as well as how to dress and speak. Students learned how to conduct themselves, and most Morehouse students graduated with a desire to model their lives on the example set for them by Benjamin Mays. His former student and successor as president of Morehouse, Hugh Gloster, described Mays's leadership by saying, "Dr. Mays was the best and greatest role model that I have ever seen or known."[17]

While he was mayor of Atlanta, Andrew Young said that in every city in the United States, the leading black doctor, the most important black attorney, "most certainly one of the key preachers and probably most of the black elected officials owe where they are to Dr. Mays." In paying tribute to Mays, the widow of Martin Luther King, Jr., Coretta Scott King, said, "Most of the black male leadership in our country during the last forty years has in some way been inspired by you.... Martin Luther King, Jr., called you his spiritual mentor and was greatly influenced by the life and example you set, and you've been a great inspiration to me."[18] Leaders such as Dr. Benjamin Mays not only inspired students, but also served as mentors in nonviolent social protest that helped keep the Atlanta Student Movement of the 1960s relatively peaceful.

Soon after February 5, 1960, when students began the sit-in movement in Greensboro, three Morehouse students met with President Mays to discuss their plans for demonstrations aimed at desegregating

---

[16] David Levering Lewis, *King: A Biography*, 2nd ed. (Urbana: University of Illinois Press, 1978) 21.

[17] Rovaris, *Mays and Morehouse*, 135.

[18] Orville Vernon Burton, "Born to Rebel," in *Walking Integrity: Benjamin Elijah Mays, Mentor to Martin Luther King Jr.*, ed. Lawrence Edward Carter Sr. (Macon, GA: Mercer University Press, 1998) 70.

downtown Atlanta. Led by Lonnie King and Julian Bond, the Morehouse students met with others from the Atlanta University Center schools, and then with the Presidents Council from all of the AUC institutions. The students formed a committee to draw-up a statement making clear why they were demonstrating. The student committee drafted an "Appeal for Human Rights" that was adopted by each of the AUC student bodies and signed by the representatives of each of the student governments before being printed in local newspapers and the *New York Times*. The clarity and eloquence of the appeal showed remarkable leadership for the peaceful, non-violent approach to achieving desegregation that the students advocated. While many such as Mayor Bill Hartsfield praised the "Appeal for Human Rights," the governor of Georgia thought it was so well written that it could not have been done by black students—he thought the document read like a foreign propaganda document.[19]

Even though the students were taking to the streets to demonstrate their impatience with racial segregation, they were still willing to negotiate behind the scenes to avoid conflict. The students met with police chief Herbert Jenkins to discuss their objectives and to seek the protection of police officers during their protests.[20] After the protests at Rich's, the following week more than one hundred students went to jail following sit-ins at eating places located in public or tax-supported buildings such and the rail and bus stations, the Fulton County courthouse and the capitol.

Mayor Bill Hartsfield worried that the demonstrations would harm the city's image, but he was unable to negotiate a quick settlement to end the conflict. When the student leaders met with white businessmen, the demonstrators were told that businesses in downtown Atlanta would not end segregation quickly. Faced with this hostility, the students shifted the focus of their demonstrations to stores that depended on black cus-

[19] Mays, *Born to Rebel*, 290.
[20] Carolyn Long Banks (former student activist and Atlanta City Council member), interview by authors, 1 August 2011, audio, Special Collections and Archives, University Library, Georgia State University.

tomers but did not hire African Americans in any capacity other than menial jobs. Throughout spring and summer 1960, the AUC students continued their demonstrations and calls for a boycott against an A&P supermarket located in an African-American neighborhood. By the end of September, the students succeeded in changing the employment discrimination against blacks in two stores. The following month the students again directed their protests against downtown businesses. This time they invited Dr. Martin Luther King Jr. to join them since he was a Morehouse man and Atlanta was his home. King was not an active participant in earlier demonstrations because he had concentrated his attention on other parts of the South that needed his leadership and organizational skills. By October 20, 1960, King and fifty-seven students were arrested at sit-ins at Rich's and other downtown businesses. The student demonstrators were well led and organized, using two-way radios to coordinate their peaceful sit-ins and picketing.

The demonstrations continued with a change in tactics by the students and Dr. King. Rather than requiring bail to get released following their arrests, the students sought arrest and crowded the jails by refusing to post bond. This led to renewed negotiations conducted by the president of the chamber of commerce (and future mayor) Ivan Allen Jr. By March 6, 1961, business and protest leaders agreed to a compromise that would end the demonstrations in return for a promise to desegregate lunch counters and restrooms in downtown stores no later than mid-October. The young students were impatient with the delay but in a dramatic appeal, Dr. King persuaded them to suspend their demonstrations. In spite of misgivings on both sides, the agreement held and the integration of restaurants and lunch counters in downtown department and variety stores took place without incident on September 27, 1961. Atlanta became the first Southern city to take this voluntary step toward ending segregation. In most other cities in the region where there were lunch counter sit-ins, the businesses responded by closing their eating facilities.[21] Even in the tumultuous 1960s and in the face of student protests and demonstrations, negotiations and settlements, between African-Americans educated in the Atlanta University Center and the Downtown white business leaders continued to be a signature of the Atlanta Way.[22]

In 1954, the US Supreme Court ruled that public schools should end racial segregation "with all deliberate speed." In most cities and states in the south this order was delayed as long as possible. When Little Rock and New Orleans attempted to desegregate their public schools, there was rioting that tarnished the image of both cities. Business leaders of both races and Mayor Bill Hartsfield were determined to avoid this kind of negative publicity for Atlanta.

Mayor Bill Hartsfield was enlisted to continue the negotiations in order to ensure the peaceful desegregation of the city's public schools in fall 1961. While the Action Forum's work remained confidential, Mayor Hartsfield was the public face of the desegregation process. Only 9 African-American students out of approximately 45,000 enrolled in previously all-white schools that fall, but for the more than 200 out-of-town reporters, the peaceful integration of the city's schools was a public relations coup for Atlanta. Compared to other US cities, the process of careful negotiations by white and black leaders resulted in a peaceful outcome. Hartsfield was able to retire as the longest serving mayor in Atlanta's history with a record of relatively progressive race relations.

Over the next decade, integration efforts in the schools lagged. It took further litigation by the NAACP to hasten the process. The federal courts ordered the busing of students to mandate desegregation. Many white residents of the city of Atlanta resisted and moved to the suburbs. This resulted in de facto segregation in the city's public schools.

[21] Harvey K. Newman, *Southern Hospitality: Tourism and the Growth of Atlanta* (Tuscaloosa: University of Alabama Press, 1999) 163–65.
[22] See chapter 2 for a fuller discussion of the Atlanta Student Movement.

Ending segregation in the clubs, restaurants, hotels and other businesses in Atlanta was less difficult than ending conflict over the desegregation of Atlanta's public schools. A newly-formed organization, the Atlanta Action Forum, comprised a white and black business and civic leaders met quietly to discuss how to desegregate the schools peacefully. As participant William Clement recalled, "The Action Forum was a place where there was dialogue behind the scenes between people who had vested interest in moving Atlanta forward. I mean that was the key thing. We wanted to do what is right in order to keep Atlanta moving forward."[23] For many blacks it appeared that the only way to achieve integrated schools was through the massive busing of students from one jurisdiction to another. Many whites were fleeing from the city to suburban racial enclaves where their children would not have to go to schools with black children. Busing children from one place to another would require crossing jurisdictions throughout the metropolitan area in order to achieve racial balance. For many whites, the emphasis on busing to desegregate public schools would lead to more suburban flight and conflict such as some other Southern cities were experiencing. Behind the scenes, black leaders sought control over the city of Atlanta's school system that continued to be led by whites. The solution was to convince black leaders to reduce the demand for massive cross-jurisdiction busing in return for more control over the city's public schools. By this time, former Morehouse student activist Lonnie King was head of the Atlanta branch of the NAACP, the group that was suing the school system to achieve more integration. A deal was reached after lengthy meetings with the Action Forum. Lonnie King said, "I said I want an African-American superintendent of schools. And I want 50 percent of the jobs, and here is a list of the jobs that I want. We have been left out of the school system administration ever since 1960s and now is the time to change it."[24]

---

[23] Clement, interview, 22 July 2011.
[24] Lonnie King, video interview, 9 December 2013.

The national office of the NAACP did not like the proposed solution because for many years the school board had failed to achieve extensive desegregation of the school system and to relieve overcrowding in black schools. In an unusual twist, the national office of the NAACP sued Lonnie King, in an attempt to oust him as chapter president. King won his battle in court against the national office, kept his job, and helped to negotiate the compromise solution. There would be less busing, which neither black nor white parents wanted, and more control of the public school system in Atlanta for African Americans. In return, the Atlanta Board of Education brought in Dr. Alonzo Crim, an African American, to become the superintendent of schools with the authority to hire blacks in half of the system's administrative positions. According to long-time Atlanta public school teacher Carolyn Young, "The school system in the city had a great balance during the 1970s with 140,000 students enrolled in the system when Dr. Crim was the superintendent. And some may say that he did not rock the boat enough, but at the time he was what we needed."[25] The settlement that ended the litigation over the Atlanta public schools was controversial, but both sides got something that they wanted. The dispute was resolved by the biracial coalition that had been a guiding force in Atlanta since the 1940s.

In fall 1969 city elections, the number of blacks on the board of education increased from two to three with the election of retired Morehouse president Dr. Benjamin Mays. After Mays took office in January, his fellow board members elected him president of the school board. For the next twelve years, Dr. Mays guided the Atlanta School Board and worked closely with the new superintendent, Dr. Crim, to focus on excellence in the city's public schools. The compromise between the Atlanta School Board and the local chapter of the NAACP was controversial. Civil rights leaders such as Andrew Young and the Rev. Joseph Lowery, as well as Dr. Mays, supported the agreement to end the litigation. With the flight of large numbers of whites from the city to the suburbs, the

---

[25] Carolyn Young (retired Atlanta school teacher and wife of Andrew Young), video interview, 10 February 2014.

plan could not achieve racial integration within a city school system that was more than 80 percent black by 1973. The unfortunate outcome of earlier school board policies and of white flight resulted in a segregated Atlanta public school system that integrated and then re-segregated. In the process, however, blacks were no longer denied the power to allocate resources and from this point on could provide more equity to all schools in the system.[26]

The integration of the colleges and universities in Atlanta was also a process that required deliberation, careful negotiation, and court orders, but which was eventually accomplished. Most attention focused on efforts that began as early as 1950 to desegregate the flagship institution, the University of Georgia, located in Athens. Under the leadership of segregationist governor Herman Talmadge, the state clung to a defense of the prevailing idea of "separate but equal" as a means of resisting integration of education in the state. There were both provisions in the Georgia constitution and specific legislation passed by the Georgia General Assembly that prohibited integration and required that all state funding be withdrawn from any college or university that enrolled a black student in a white institution. Talmadge's successor, Ernest Vandiver, won election by pledging "No, not one" black would be allowed in the state's white colleges and universities. The efforts by three black women to gain admission to Georgia State in Atlanta began in 1956 and ended unsuccessfully three years later after a variety of legislative and administrative stalling tactics prohibited the students from being admitted. In 1958, two young African-American graduates of Turner High School in Atlanta began the process of applying to the University of Georgia. Both Hamilton Holmes and Charlayne Hunter were initially denied admission. In January 1961, a judge ordered the immediate enrollment of Hunter and Holmes. A group of riotous white students threw bricks at the dormitory in which Charlayne Hunter was staying. However, with the order from the state court supported by a federal court ruling, the two black students continued their education at the University of Georgia.

---

[26] Bayor, *Race and the Shaping of Atlanta*, 247–51.

The court order gave Governor Vandiver the coverage he needed to ignore his "No, not one" pledge, and the university was integrated. Hunter majored in journalism and went on to a distinguished career, and Holmes graduated with a pre-med major and became an orthopedic surgeon.[27] The doors to public higher education in Georgia were finally opened, and soon both Georgia Tech and Georgia State would be integrated. Administrators at Georgia Tech are proud to boast that they admitted three African-American students in fall 1961 without having the courts order the institution to do so.[28]

As a private university, Emory could admit or deny students in any way it chose—except Georgia law required that any nonprofit institution would lose its state tax exemption if it integrated. The university challenged the state law in 1961 and won its case, so that the first black student enrolled the following year. The difference between the desegregation of Emory and most of the state institutions was that Emory sued the state for the right to admit African Americans, rather than being sued by black applicants seeking to enroll.[29] The city's historically black colleges and universities did not have any difficulty over the admission of white students. Most had whites and blacks on their faculties from their founding, so the AUC schools, for the most part, did not object to whites who enrolled. As Benjamin Mays said, "I believe in black colleges.... I do not believe in a black college or university if this means that all students, all faculty and staff members, the student body, and all financial support must be black."[30] Instead, President Mays wanted Morehouse to emphasize academic excellence so that it might attract all well-qualified stu-

---

[27] Thomas G. Dyer, *University of Georgia: A Bicentennial History, 1785–1985* (Athens: University of Georgia Press, 1985) 307–34.

[28] Robert C. McMath, Jr., Ronald H. Bayor, James E. Brittain, Lawrence Foster, Augustus W. Giebelhaus, and Germaine M. Reed, *Engineering the New South: Georgia Tech, 1885–1985* (Athens: University of Georgia Press, 1985) 316–18.

[29] Thomas H. English, *Emory University, 1915–1965: A Semicentennial History* (Atlanta: Higgins-McArthur Company, 1966) 101.

[30] Mays, *Born to Rebel*, 317.

dents of any race. He accomplished his objective, and Morehouse College has provided Atlanta with leaders such as Martin Luther King, Jr., and Maynard Jackson. Morehouse is but one of the network of colleges and universities that have helped produce leaders for the city.

As mayor, Andrew Young recognized the importance of education in the life of the city. He understood that his own family owed their middle-class status to education. He was the son of an educator and the husband of an educator. Jean Childs Young brought her perspective as an educator to her role as Atlanta's first lady. She founded the mayor's task force on education. The task force included an essay contest, a scholarship program, and the Dream Jamboree, a citywide career fair that continued for twenty-five years. In the words of Mrs. Young, the career fair was designed to give students "a life worth dreaming about." The Dream Jamboree was an annual event that brought together all the ninth graders and all the eleventh graders (more than 12,000 students) from the Atlanta public schools to a career and college fair.[31] The first Dream Jamboree was in spring 1983. Mrs. Young began by inviting national and regional institutions offering post-secondary education and training as well as each of the colleges and universities that had featured Mayor Young as a commencement speaker. More than 200 organizations responded to the invitation—including colleges, universities, junior, community and technical colleges, union apprenticeship program, military programs, and corporations. In developing the program, Mrs. Young drew upon her experience as a public school teacher and administrator and a reading teacher at Atlanta Junior College. She insisted on including ninth graders so that these students would have time to adjust their courses to meet admission requirements of programs in which they were interested. College guidebooks were expensive, so students received a book printed by the Georgia Power Company that included information on each exhibitor—application dates, descriptions of the programs, and contact information.

---

[31] Horton, *The Young Years*, 191.

Thousands of students participated each year. As a result, the Dream Jamboree increased the amount of scholarship money awarded to Atlanta Public School students to over $15 million per year.[32] Andrew Young recalled, "One year I can remember that Atlanta had more high school students from public high schools going to MIT on scholarship than any public school outside the state of Massachusetts, and there were seventeen students that got non-athletic scholarships from Notre Dame." For Jean Young, this program was a way to fulfill the promise of Atlanta for each and every child. She said, "The only way we are going to build a better world is by helping those children love themselves; love each other and care for one another.[33] Jean Young was lost to cancer in 1994. In recognition of her service to Atlanta, Southwest Middle School was renamed Jean Childs Young Middle School.

Andrew Young continued to leave an imprint on education in the city. In recognition of his leadership as a member of Congress and as mayor, the Coca-Cola Company endowed the Andrew Young Center for Global Leadership at Morehouse College and the Andrew Young School of Policy Studies at Georgia State University. Both programs are committed to carrying on the legacy of his life and work in Atlanta and beyond.

As John Wesley Dobbs often said, "*the book*" was an important stepping stone for the uplift of the race. His words have been prophetic; there are currently 47,548 African-American students out of a total of 176,171 enrolled in higher education institutions in the Atlanta area. The days are long past when these students had to go elsewhere to pursue their education. Once they finish, these students no longer need to go elsewhere for employment opportunities. This concentration of talent

---

[32] Ibid., 192.

[33] Jean Young interview, WXIA archives, in "Andrew Young's Making of Modern Atlanta," video, Special Collections and Archives, University Library, Georgia State University.

makes Atlanta a leader in higher education among American cities and enriches the economy.[34]

---

[34] Atlanta Regional Council for Higher Education Reports, "The Atlanta Region: National Leader in Higher Education."

Andrew and Jean Young at Dream Jamboree, above *(Young Family Collection)*
Clarence Bacote leading Graduation Procession, below
(Bacote Collection, Woodruff Library AU)

Benjamin Mays and Andrew Young
(Young Family Collection)

7

Hospitality—Atlanta Style

Throughout much of the city's history, the leaders of Atlanta sought to do things in a way that set the city apart from other places in the region. Using the network of intersecting railroad lines that gave birth to Atlanta, the city played host to a series of three expositions during the nineteenth century that helped establish its reputation as a center of the New South. Promoters like Henry W. Grady, the managing editor of the *Atlanta Constitution*, made speeches urging sectional reconciliation and Northern investment to bring industrialization to Atlanta. Early in the twentieth century, a new generation of leaders promoted the city in the Forward Atlanta campaign to continue investment in industry and commerce. In the post-World War II period, the city's longest-serving mayor, William B. Hartsfield, built an interracial voting bloc between blacks and whites that not only contributed to relatively peaceful desegregation, but also gave some truth to his opt-repeated slogan that Atlanta was the "city too busy to hate." Compared to other places in the region, Atlanta's citizens achieved a level of racial cooperation that contributed to the city's economic development. The business of tourism was an important component of Atlanta's growth. Building on its transportation connections, initially, with the railroad, and, later, with highways and an airport, Atlanta's leaders sought to attract development through expositions, conventions, and other forms of tourism. Keeping visitors coming to the city required racial tranquility, as well as, facilities constructed with public and private cooperation. The need for constant negotiation across racial lines and between business and political leaders gave rise to a distinct way of using tourism to promote the growth of the city. City leaders used Southern hospitality to create support for tourism as an economic development policy and to attract tourists to come, visit, and do business. Their efforts helped to build Atlanta as a regional, national, and increasingly international tourism destination.

While other cities attracted tourists with scenic lakefronts, beaches, riversides, or other natural attractions, Atlanta had to depend upon business travelers to fill hotel rooms, restaurants, convention and meeting facilities, amusements, and other tourism-related businesses. These tourism businesses extended hospitality to visitors to promote Atlanta as a place to visit and to do business. The initial settlement of the town took place after the state of Georgia decided to build a railroad line in 1838. When the first locomotive arrived a few years later, the city's leaders realized they needed to build a hotel for arriving passengers. This business travel-related tourism set a pattern that has continued for more than 170 years through changes in transportation technology, hotel architecture, and other aspects of the tourism industry. For example, in 1881, Atlanta's leaders hosted the "International Cotton Exposition," the first of three such events during the late nineteenth century designed to promote the city as a site for investment in textile manufacturing. With a population of only 37,000 in 1880, Atlanta's leaders built hotels, the exposition grounds, and buildings. The 1881 exposition resulted in more than $2 million in manufacturing investment during the months following the event.[1] The best known of the three expositions was the 1895 Cotton States and International Exposition that featured a speech on opening day by Booker T. Washington. This exposition also included a pavilion showcasing the progress of Atlanta's black citizens.[2] The series of three nineteenth-century expositions positioned the city at the center of the New South movement. The theme of all these events was to promote the idea that the region had entered a new era and was open for investment with a population eager to assume jobs in factories instead of traditional agricultural work. City leaders promoted this vision of New South growth and prosperity based on industry, commerce, and tourism.

---

[1] Jack Blicksilver, "The International Cotton Exposition of 1881 and Its Impact Upon the Economic Development of Georgia," *Cotton History Review* 1 (1960): 182.

[2] Walter G. Cooper, *The Cotton States and International Exposition and South, Illustrated* (Atlanta: Illustrator Company, 1896) 344.

In 1885, four years after the initial cotton exposition, Atlanta's leaders hosted the city's first national convention of chamber of commerce officials. This led to increased attention to the city as a place for investment and economic growth, contributing to a population increase of 75 percent during the decade ending in 1890. Early in the twentieth century, Atlanta's political and business leaders worked together to attract other conventions and established a Visitors Bureau to promote meetings in the city. Their vision was to make Atlanta a city of national importance. In spite of a variety of strategies to market the city, including the "Forward Atlanta" campaign of the 1920s, Atlanta remained a rather small, provincial Southern town whose growth was retarded by the poverty of the region and the Great Depression.[3]

This situation was about to change as a result of decisions made by Atlanta's leaders in the period following World War II. Influential leaders as far back as Henry Grady and Booker T. Washington promoted Atlanta as moderate on race to facilitate the city's economic growth. Mayor William Hartsfield continued that tradition, with sophisticated pressure from Atlanta's African-American leaders. In exchange for gradual improvements in the city's approach to separation of the races, African-American leaders supported Hartsfield's reelections in a governing coalition that promoted a vision of economic growth and expansion for the city.[4] Hartsfield, in turn, went so far as to proclaim Atlanta "A City Too Busy to Hate" when welcoming conventions to the city and in the national magazine *Newsweek*.[5] As cities like Little Rock and Birmingham struggled with violence over racial integration in the 1950s and '60s, At-

---

[3] Harvey K. Newman, *Southern Hospitality: Tourism and the Growth of Atlanta* (Tuscaloosa: University of Alabama Press, 1999) 90–122.

[4] Clarence N. Stone, *Regime Politics: Governing Atlantat, 1946–1988* (Lawrence: University Press of Kansas, 1989) 28.

[5] Mayor Hartsfield made his famous statement in an interview with William Emerson that appeared in *Newsweek*, 10 October 1959 (Harold H. Martin, *William B. Hartsfield, Mayor of Atlanta* [Athens: University of Georgia Press, 1978] 142).

lanta's leaders managed the transition away from segregation without violence.

Investment capital began to flow into Atlanta from other parts of the US during the decade of the 1960s, making a reality of the earlier leaders' vision of the city as a place of national importance. As symbols of Atlanta's "major league" status, professional sports teams arrived with the Braves, Falcons, Hawks, and a short-lived hockey franchise known as the Flames. Mayoral leadership by Ivan Allen, Jr., (1962–1970) continued the close working relationship between city hall and the city's blacks and whites. At considerable political risk, Allen testified in 1963 in support of the proposed Civil Rights Act that would guarantee the desegregation of hotels, restaurants, and other places serving the public not only in Atlanta, but in cities throughout the nation. The following year after passage of this landmark legislation, the test cases for the desegregation of hotels and restaurants came from Atlanta. As the *Atlanta Daily World* reported, both local restaurants and hotels were ordered to serve African-American customers, and the law was enforced by federal marshals.[6]

In addition to Allen's success in continuing the pattern of relatively peaceful desegregation in the city, he made several decisions that aided tourism and promoted economic development in Atlanta. In 1961, the city opened a jet-age airport that by 1964 ranked fourth nationally in passenger enplanements and fifth in commercial operations. The city also built a major league stadium for baseball and football and a new civic center to host convention groups. Atlanta also passed a referendum permitting the sale of liquor by the drink, which put the tourism businesses in the city on par with those in other places and gave local businesses a competitive advantage over surrounding jurisdictions that remained dry. Mayor Allen also prompted the state to create a Metropolitan Atlanta Rapid Transit Authority (MARTA) in order to study the feasibility of a rail transit system for the area.

---

[6] Harmon G. Perry, "Lester Maddox, Leb Restaurants Make Protests of Laws," *Atlanta Daily World*, 4 July 1964, 1, 6; "Maddox Hearing Monday," *Atlanta Daily World*, 19 July 1964, 1; and "Heart of Atlanta Head Asks for Liberty to Segregate," *Atlanta Daily World*, 6 October 1964, 1, 6.

Private sector investment in tourism quickly followed the initiatives led by the city's mayor. By 1965, Mayor Allen announced that the number of hotel rooms in the city had more than doubled since 1945.[7] One of the major contributors to this process was John Portman. Although born while his mother was visiting relatives in South Carolina, Portman grew up in Atlanta. He recalls that Atlanta at the time was viewed as a "big country town." Portman graduated from the architecture program at Georgia Tech and began work in a design firm during the 1950s. Short of capital, but full of imagination, Portman redesigned an abandoned garage building for use as a wholesale merchandise mart to serve the needs of clothing retailers from the region. Soon the merchandise mart was bringing an estimated 200,000 people per year to Atlanta, but the older hotels in downtown could not handle the crowds. This success led Portman to design and build a much larger merchandise mart on Peachtree Street in downtown Atlanta that opened in 1961. He was able to borrow money for the financing, so that he became both the architect and the developer of the Merchandise Mart.[8] The new mart attracted more visitors to downtown, leading Portman to expand by constructing a new hotel, the Hyatt Regency, which opened in 1967. Part of his plan to construct a high density area, Peachtree Center would reshape a major section of the downtown. Portman's strategy was to use the merchandise mart as a center for a collection of buildings that would be within easy walking distance of one another. At a time when many other developers were moving their investments to the suburbs, Portman, as both architect and developer of Peachtree Center, exercised his preference to remain in the central portion of the city. Portman remembered the decisions of that era, "the 60s were the beginning of the white flight and cities all over the country were really beginning to feel that and the disintegration of cities.

---

[7] Newman, *Southern Hospitality*, 172.

[8] Mickey Steinberg (retired executive vice-president of the Portman Companies), interview by authors, 23 September 2011, audio, Special Collections and Archives, University Library, Georgia State University.

So we decided to anchor. We wanted to anchor and we wanted to do everything possible to be a force growing in the other direction."[9]

With the innovative hotel architecture of the Hyatt Regency and its location across the street from the Merchandise Mart, the occupancy rate of the hotel was 95 percent within a few months of opening. One of the first national meetings held in the new hotel was the annual convention of the Southern Christian Leadership Conference. It would be Dr. Martin Luther King's last convention, but it led to a lasting bond between the hotel and Andrew Young. Today, there is an Andrew Young suite in the aptly named International Tower. At the request of the Hyatt Corporation, Portman added 200 more rooms to the hotel, bringing the total to 1,000. The openness of the hotel's atrium lobby was so spectacular that Hyatt used the design in other hotels across the country, enhancing Portman's reputation as both an architect and developer. In 1968, Portman doubled the size of the merchandise mart building and added the first office tower to the Peachtree Center complex. Eventually, he would add two larger hotels to Peachtree Center, the Westin Peachtree Plaza in 1976 and the Marriott Marquis in 1985. The number of buildings in Peachtree Center would expand to occupy all or part of seventeen city blocks, making it one of the largest private developments in any city. In a recent interview, Portman indicated his only frustration with Peachtree Center was his inability to include housing in its development. Portman's boyhood home was only a few blocks from Peachtree Center, and he anticipated that people would eventually want to live and work near downtown once again. As Peachtree Center expanded, Portman was unable to attract financing for apartment or condominium development. Portman's prediction about the return of downtown housing would come true, but it would take other leaders to make that dream a reality.[10]

The business of tourism was growing in the downtown area of the city. Public and private sector financing greatly expanded the tourism

---

[9] John Portman (founder and chairman, John Portman & Associates), interview by authors, 15 September 2011, audio, Special Collections and Archives, University Library, Georgia State University.
[10] Ibid.

infrastructure in Atlanta during the 1960s. In addition to the visitors attracted to Atlanta's Peachtree Center, Mayor Allen spearheaded the drive for the financing and construction of the Civic Center, which gave the city the ability to host more and larger meetings. Allen also led the process of building the Atlanta-Fulton County Stadium, which attracted professional baseball and football teams to the city. According to his son, Inman Allen, the addition of the stadium and professional sports teams were part of Mayor Allen's vision for the city.[11] These also served as attractions for the city's tourism business. During the decade, the city also committed to financing a new coliseum to house basketball and hockey teams.[12] In 1960, the Convention and Visitors Bureau reported that 251 conventions (attracting 120,000 visitors) were held in Atlanta. A decade later, the city attracted 525 conventions attended by 420,000 tourists. This made Atlanta more competitive with its major regional rivals such as Miami and Dallas, as well as with national leaders in the convention business such as Chicago; New York; Washington, DC; Atlantic City; and Los Angeles.[13]

The increased numbers of conventions meeting in the city along with the business travelers coming to Portman's growing Peachtree Center gave public and business leaders renewed hope for the future of downtown Atlanta. At the same time, there was concern about the lack of attractions for the amusement of residents and visitors alike. In 1966, the city's recently established historic preservation advisory board, the Urban Design Commission, issued a report calling attention to an area of old storefronts and warehouses from nineteenth-century Atlanta, left behind as the city built viaducts to span the railroad lines that converged

---

[11] Inman Allen (civic leader and son of Mayor Ivan Allen, Jr.), interview by authors, 13 April 2012, audio, Special Collections and Archives, University Library, Georgia State University.

[12] Heywood T. Sanders, *Convention Center Follies: Politics, Power and Public Investment in American Cities* (Philadelphia: University of Pennsylvania Press, 2014) 299.

[13] Atlanta Convention and Visitors Bureau, "Annual Report: Atlanta Convention and Visitors Bureau" (Atlanta: ACVB, 1970).

in downtown. Other cities had restored older portions of their down-
towns such as French Quarter in New Orleans and Gaslight Square in
St. Louis. Two young college graduates seized the report and set out to
obtain rights and leases to the area that came to be called Underground
Atlanta. The venue opened for business in 1969 with a mixture of restaurants, clubs, museums, and shops. A year later the area was bustling with
sixty-five establishments that appealed to a variety of tastes. Success came
almost too easily for the original Underground Atlanta. The development expanded rapidly but exercised little control over the mix of tenants. Public safety concerns arose as teenagers from throughout the metropolitan area were able to buy drinks at eighteen; the resulting unruly
behavior scared away older adults. The gradual decline in patrons led
business closings, and the last restaurant in the old Underground Atlanta
shut its doors in 1982.[14] There was an immediate call from convention
hotels, elected public officials, and others for a revival of the city's best-
known tourist attraction.

Atlanta's reliance upon the automobile was a source of concern for
political and business leaders. Soon after the failure of the city's transit
referendum in 1968, Mayor Allen decided against seeking a third term,
leaving an open position to be filled in the 1969 election. For the first
time in decades, the candidate supported by the city's business leadership
lost to one who was supported by a coalition of black and liberal white
voters. The election brought into office Atlanta's first Jewish mayor, Sam
Massell, and a young African-American attorney, Maynard Jackson, who
became vice-mayor. Together they renewed efforts to hold another transit referendum, which passed in 1971 with strong support from both
whites and blacks. The Metropolitan Atlanta Rapid Transit Authority
(MARTA) immediately took over the operations of the city's aging bus
service, lowered fares, and began planning for two lines of rapid rail
transit.[15] The success of the MARTA referendum was hailed as one of
the most significant accomplishments of Mayor Massell's term in office.

[14] William E. Kent, "Underground Atlanta: The Untimely Passing of a
Major Tourist Attraction," *Journal of Travel Research* 22 (Spring 1984): 2–7.
[15] Massell, interview, 28 July 2011.

This investment in transit would prove critical to Atlanta's ability to attract national events and the visitors that followed.

The US Census report for 1970 showed significant changes in the city of Atlanta's population, which for the first time in the city's history, was majority African-American. Testing the new-found political strength of this majority was former executive director of the Southern Christian Leadership Conference, Andrew Young, who ran for the US Congress in 1970 against a white incumbent. Although Young lost the election, the coalition of voters he put together enabled him to win the congressional seat two years later, and pave the way for a successful challenge by Vice Mayor Jackson who defeated incumbent Mayor Massell the following year. Young became the first African American representative elected to Congress from the South since the Reconstruction era following the Civil War. As a member of Congress, Young asked to serve on the Banking and Urban Affairs Committee so that he could assist the city in getting funding for the construction of its rapid transit system and other transportation improvements.

Equally important with the construction of the rapid rail system for the city's hospitality businesses was the expansion of the airport. As Mayor Massell led the successful referendum for the transit system, the building of the new terminal and runways at the airport was the achievement of Mayor Maynard Jackson.[16] Elected to office in 1973, Mayor Jackson and his staff proposed that anyone seeking a contract with the city of Atlanta must have 20 percent minority employees or develop a joint venture partnership with a minority firm in order to work on the new airport. The order extended to all contractors including law firms, architects, engineering and construction firms, and others. With $305 million in bonds required to finance the new terminal and runways, the airport was the most expensive project ever undertaken in Georgia. White business leaders were adamant in their objections to the minority business requirements for the airport, but Mayor Jackson was equally firm. Refusing to change his program, the mayor stated that he would let

---

[16] For a full discussion of the airport, see Chapter 4.

weeds grow on the proposed construction site before he would sign any contracts that did not include the 20 percent minority business provisions. After significant delay, both sides agreed to the minority business development requirements and construction began. One problem was the need to expand the number of runways at the airport, but this was restricted by the location of the city's beltway, Interstate 285 that was already too close to the airport. With assistance from Congressman Young who enlisted support from other representatives from Georgia, federal funding enabled the city to move the interstate so that the field could be expanded. With the leadership provided by Mayor Maynard Jackson, Congressman Andrew Young, and others, the vital link in the city's transportation, the new airport runway and terminal opened in 1980, on time and under budget.[17]

Mayor Jackson had a public disagreement with many white business leaders during his early years in office. This split in the long-standing partnership between city hall and businessmen was reflected in newspaper stories depicting the city's downtown convention area as crime ridden and frightening. The mayor responded by holding "pound-cake summits" to meet informally for breakfast in his office with business leaders to promote unity. Jackson and the head of the chamber of commerce also toured major US cities to promote the relocation of businesses to Atlanta and to show harmony within the city.[18]

In spite of the show of unity by Jackson and the chamber of commerce, the public criticism of Atlanta's African-American mayor by the newspaper had consequences for the tourism business in the city. In August 1975, a large national convention of Elks Club members cancelled its convention scheduled for Atlanta the following year. Mayor Jackson blamed the newspaper for the economic loss to the city, and cited the ongoing criticism of his administration and its handling of the crime problem. The downtown business organization Central Atlanta Progress responded by funding a study by the Metropolitan Crime Commission

---

[17] Berry, interview, 26 July 2011.
[18] Newman, "Hospitality and Violence," 550.

on the safety of downtown. The study authors found that downtown was "one of the city's most crime-free areas." The editor of the *Constitution* added that "perhaps these statistics will put a stop to some of the loose talk about how dangerous downtown is." As if to make amends, the newspaper published a seven-part series on the varied nightlife offered to visitors in downtown Atlanta. The series reminded readers that in 1974 convention visitors spent an estimated $40 million on entertainment, and those attending sports events contributed an additional $25 million in spending. The articles featured movies, restaurants, lounges, and night-clubs that were available for entertainment.[19]

The expanded airport connected visitors with downtown hotels, but there were other components of the tourism industry that were also significant. In 1974, business leaders and a pro-business governor of Georgia convinced the state to approve funding for a new convention building known as the Georgia World Congress Center. Proponents of the new facility argued that the Civic Center was too small and poorly located to keep the city competitive in the race to attract large conventions and trade shows. Influential consultant Philip Hammer pointed out in a report to business leaders that the city lacked the financial capacity to build the new, larger facility and that other states had recently supported investment in convention facilities in Philadelphia, Indianapolis, and Birmingham. This report helped convince state government leaders to create an entity known as the Georgia World Congress Center Authority to finance, build, and operate the convention hall.[20] When the $35 million facility opened two years later, its 640,000 square feet of exhibition space made it the world's largest indoor hall. The facility enabled Atlanta to increase both the number of conventions and attendance between 1975

---

[19]Jim Merriner, "Jackson Blames Paper's Series," *Atlanta Constitution*, 6 August 1975, 9A; Jim Gray, "Study Finds Crime Low in Downtown," *Atlanta Constitution*, 29 October 1975, 10A; Frederick Allen, Paul Jones, Art Harris, and Bill Mahan, "Night Life's Not Dull in Atlanta," 16 November 1975, 1, 14A; Allen, et al., "Money, Honey, Is What Entertainment's All About," *Atlanta Constitution*, 17 November 1975, 1, 8A.

[20] Sanders, *Convention Center Follies*, 303–308.

and 1980. In 1975, the city hosted 710 conventions attended by 545,000 people. Five years later, with the World Congress Center in operation, 1,090 conventions were attended by 1,002,900 people.[21] The construction of the convention facility also stimulated new hotel construction in the downtown area. Closest to the World Congress Center was the Omni complex, developed by Tom Cousins. The complex contained the Omni International Hotel and was adjacent to the Omni sports arena. In addition to the hotel, restaurants, shops, and an ice skating rink, the complex housed a $17 million indoor amusement park called the World of Sid and Marty Krofft. After opening in the spring of 1976, the amusement park closed by November.[22] The hotel and entire complex struggled financially for several years until 1985 when Ted Turner bought it and converted the Omni into CNN Center. The Omni International Hotel continued to operate within the CNN Center.

Competition between developers such as Tom Cousins and John Portman led to the construction of new additions to the city's tourism businesses at opposite ends of downtown. The Omni International Hotel developed by Cousins opened in 1976 while Portman opened the Westin Peachtree Hotel later that year as part of the expansion of his Peachtree Center complex. At the time it opened, the Westin was the tallest hotel in the world. The seventy-three-story black glass cylinder contained 1,100 rooms and a dazzling lobby featuring a half-acre lake and a five-level sky-lit atrium.[23] The building of these hotels and others such as the

---

[21] Atlanta Convention and Visitors Bureau, "Annual Report: Atlanta Convention and Visitors Bureau," (Atlanta:
ACVB, 1975, 1980).

[22] DeWill Rogers, "$20 Million Fantasy: The World of Sid and Marty Krofft Aims 'to Make You Feel Good,'" *Atlanta Constitution*, 17 May 1976, 1, 16A; Rex Granum, "$31.4 Million Building Contract on WCC OK'd," *Atlanta Constitution*, 16 July 1974, 14A; DeWitt Rogers, "Kroffts' World Folds Up," *Atlanta Constitution*, 10 November 1974,1, 6A; Frederick Allen, "End in Sight: Bickering Nearly Over, WCC Nearly Done," *Atlanta Constitution*, 9 April 1976, 1, 18A; George Rodrique, "Atlanta Facility Dedicated," 17 August 1976, 8A.

[23] Paolo Riani, *John Portman* (Washington, DC: American Institute of Architects Press, 1990) 155.

downtown Hilton indicates not only the competition between developers but also the close relationship between the public and private sectors in the city's tourism development. Public sector investment in the Georgia World Congress Center spurred the investment by the private sector in new hotel facilities. The city also aided the process with the investment in the expanded capacity of the new midfield terminal at the airport. The Georgia Dome (an indoor sports facility built for the Atlanta Falcons), the Westin, and most downtown hotels were accessible by MARTA, Atlanta's rapid rail system that also connected downtown to the airport.

Business leaders found that Mayor Andrew Young was someone who listened to them and was willing to move forward with them in partnership. One of the ideas they suggested to Mayor Young was the revival of Underground Atlanta as an important element in the city's tourism industry. Underground Atlanta was the city's best-known attraction prior to the closing of its last business. Young reached out to the Rouse Company, the successful developer of similar projects in Baltimore and Boston, and asked them to produce a feasibility study on the reopening of Underground Atlanta. Again, the city's business leaders formed a partnership with elected public officials to rebuild the tourist attraction. The Atlanta Action Forum commissioned a study by Research Atlanta that helped bring cooperation to raise private and public sector dollars for the project. The total cost for Underground's redevelopment was $144 million. The city used its power of eminent domain to acquire most of the land for the project. The original Underground Atlanta was a collection of small parcels with multiple owners, which limited overall control over the complex. For the new development the city bought the land from the owners and then conveyed it to the Downtown Development Authority, which issued $85 million in revenue bonds to finance much of the construction. Other public sector contributions came from an $18.5 million urban development block grant and a community development block grant from the federal government.[24]

---

[24] Underground Festival Development Corporation, "Briefing Paper on the Underground Atlanta Project," 22 December 1986, 1–2.

Atlanta's public and private sector investments in Underground Atlanta's revitalization were designed to provide convention visitors with an entertainment facility of shops, clubs, and restaurants. These would, in turn, provide employment for residents, as well as sales and property tax receipts. There was also a new parking deck that would provide spaces for visitors to the offices of Fulton County government during the day and Underground Atlanta in the evenings. Mayor Young's administration raised the minority business requirement to 35 percent in all phases of the Underground Atlanta project. This provided more opportunities not only for African Americans but also for women-owned businesses to participate in the contracting for the project. The revitalized Underground Atlanta opened in June 1989 with much celebration. During its initial year of operation, an estimated 13 million people visited the attraction.[25]

While serving as mayor, Andrew Young observed,

> It dawned on me that every plane that came into Atlanta, everyone that came in first-class probably spent $1000 a day and everyone that came in coach spent a couple hundred, and that includes students. I began to realize that that was the best way to bring money into the city. It was quick, it was affordable, and we had the hotel capacity. This was why one of the first things I tried to do was to rebuild Underground Atlanta as a downtown entertainment district.

Young also noted that,

> Every hotel creates one job per room. Now people think of those as not good paying jobs. They think of it as menial jobs. I followed the Hyatt very closely because we had one of the first conventions in there in 1967, so when I go back to meet with the Hyatt when they have their annual employee award dinners and the like, I meet people that have been there thirty to forty years. And they have found a way to make good lives for themselves and for their children. The other thing is, hotels require a lot of part-time labor, so in a student center like Atlanta,

---

[25] William E. Kent and J. Thomas Chesnutt, "Underground Atlanta: Resurrected and Revisited," *Journal of Travel Research* 29 (Spring 1991): 37–38.

being a banquet waiter is a good part-time job on the weekend for a student.

In describing the city's hotel business, Mayor Young said,

> I used to always try to tip the doorman at the Downtown Hyatt, but he wouldn't take my tip. He said, "Look Mr. Mayor, I know what you make." My salary was $50K as a mayor. He said, "I make more than that in tips, so keep your money." So before homeland security, the guy shining shoes at the airport was making better than $100K a year. Tourism starts at the airport. It's not just the passengers coming in, it's the fact that 25 percent of that airport was owned originally and operated by minority- and female-owned employees and managers. And they developed that, so that by the time I left the mayor's office in 1989, the airport was employing 60,000 people directly and was making $31.5 billion a year. Now the 2010 figures expanded from the airport proper to include the hotels and convention space. Their figures from 2010 were that there were 435,000 jobs and $52.8 billion directly from that airport.

As mayor, Andrew Young also developed a close friendship with architect and developer John Portman. Young said,

> John Portman has two big conventions a year, and each one of them is almost equivalent to the Super Bowl because people come in for the Super Bowl for a couple of days. But people come in for the Portman America's Mart for five or six days. And they do all their ordering of their goods and services from the Apparel Mart and the Merchandise Mart, and they do that in January and in July. And in between, they have specialty shows so that we keep our hotels full.

Young added,

> The other thing was that for a long time we started out when I was mayor, we had something like 5,000 hotel rooms downtown, and it was 67 percent occupancy. And we could never get that occupancy up, and so at one point they wanted to stop building hotels. But we kept on and then we got up to 50,000 hotel rooms, and by that time, I realized that they were neglecting black conventions. So simply by adding black conventions and getting churches, family reunions, [and] college visits…we increased our hotel occupancy rate. The main conventions were from Monday to Friday. But the black conventions and church conventions quite often come in on Friday and stay 'til Monday, and the family re-

unions come during the summer time. So by my understanding that the market is not just a big business market, and by promoting things like church conferences, fraternity/sorority meetings, and going after that market, we got our hotel occupancy up to almost 89 percent, and that was before the Olympics.

Recognizing the importance of Atlanta's tourism and convention businesses, Andrew Young remarked,

Business investments follow the visitors. Well, what happens is nobody invests in a place they don't know. And we made it a special effort to start training our taxi drivers, the maids in the hotels, the waitresses/waiters for the most part as much as we could since they were more temporary. But the permanent employees all went through some kind of training to make them ambassadors for tourism and they knew what the city was all about. They had to take a course to get a taxi license, for instance. In London, taxi drivers have to go to school for over a year just to get a taxi license. They had to know everything there is to know about the city of London. We didn't go quite that far, but you have to believe everybody in your supply chain is a recruiter for business. People have a way of thinking that taxi drivers will tell you the truth and newspapers might lie. If you have a bunch of angry taxi drivers who talk about how crooked the city is and how bad the mayor is and how the police are mean, they kill your investment. You take some time to make them feel important. We actually had a situation where a taxi driver was waiting in front of Peachtree Plaza, and these two Japanese guys got in the cab and the driver had been waiting there for several hours in the sun, waiting for a fare to the airport, and when they wanted to go right to the Omni which was two blocks away, he started fussing about having to wait there all day long. And they finally said, "That's all right. Take us to the airport." Later on, we found out that they were there planning to make an offer of $150 million to the Omni, which the taxi driver killed by his attitude. So if you're going to go into tourism, you have to start from top to bottom and from bottom to top. And we convince people that if you're nice and you can talk to people about the city. And instead of a $2 tip, you get a $5 tip. You have to help them to sell themselves in order to sell the city.

Private sector investments in hotels increased during the time that Andrew Young served as mayor. Between 1982 and 1987, more than 16,000 new hotel rooms were added throughout the metropolitan area.

This increased hotel capacity contributed to a decline in the occupancy rate which had been at 65 percent for the 30,000 rooms in the metropolitan area. The occupancy rate for the entire area declined to 63 percent during the period of rapid new hotel development. At the same time in 1985, Atlanta hosted a record number of conventions, with 1,400 meetings in the city attended by 1.5 million people.[26] City leaders, especially Mayor Young, were anxious to increase both the number of conventions and visitors to Atlanta. One way of showcasing the city on television from coast to coast was the hosting of a national political convention. Young and former President Carter used their influence to convince the Democratic Party to hold its July 1988 nominating convention in the city. Like a household in the South getting ready for company, the city government spent more than $22.5 million in preparation for the Democratic National Convention. A hotel tax on rooms was dedicated to improving sidewalks, parks, and streetscapes to welcome the convention. The pedestrian corridor between the Georgia World Congress Center and the major convention hotels received new sidewalks and trees planted along the route. The seating capacity of the Omni sports arena was enlarged, and skyboxes were installed for the use of television crews covering the convention. Newspapers in the city spread the message that Atlanta was a "Southern city with a heritage of racial tolerance and a reputation for good business sense." The *Constitution* went on to describe the preparations for the Democratic National Convention as a "Super Bowl of civic pride, a high-wire prance between hospitality and hype put on for the benefit of more than 5,300 delegates and alternates, 13,500 journalists and 10,000 members of the political and corporate elite." Mayor Young officially welcomed the convention in its opening session, saying, "We hope you enjoy our Southern hospitality." He added that he hoped the delegates would have all the greens, ribs, and grits they wanted to eat before they went home.[27] From an economic-development per-

---

[26] Atlanta Convention and Visitors Bureau, "Atlanta Convention and Visitors Bureau: Fact Sheet" (Atlanta: ACVB, 1987).

[27] Tom Walker, "Hotel Occupancy Rates Drop Here, 13,000 Rooms Added Over Past Five Years," *Atlanta Journal-Constitution*, 24 April 1987, 1C; Ma-

spective, the Democratic National Convention was a success in publicizing the hospitality of the city and in its ability to host large events with
convention facilities, hotels, and other components of the tourist business.

With a tourism industry centered in a downtown convention business, Atlanta experienced the benefits of hosting large groups such as the
National Democratic Party—and the drawbacks when those groups left,
resulting in occupancy rates as low as 15 percent. This put pressure on
the Atlanta Convention and Visitors Bureau to increase their efforts to
bring more conventions and tourists to the city. The city's leaders knew
that for Atlanta's remaining a viable tourist destination required a combination of hard work, new attractions, and promotion. Mayor Young's
efforts to attract more African-American groups to Atlanta began to pay
off. While many of these were small events held by churches and families, the meetings were usually held on the weekends when hotel and
conference space was not in high demand. Other black groups included
the NAACP, the Alpha Phi Alpha fraternity, and the National Baptist
Convention. For example, the meeting of the National Baptist Convention in 1992 brought more than 40,000 delegates to the Georgia Dome,
the indoor sports facility that served as the home of the Atlanta Falcons.
Two years later, the Atlanta Convention and Visitors Bureau announced
that a recent poll had named Atlanta as the most preferred city in which
to hold African-American meetings and conventions.[28]

---

ria Saporta, "'Mythbusters' Setting the Record Straight for Convention Crowd,"
AJC, 11 June 1988, 1, 8A11; Hal Straus, "Decision 88: Convention to Be Rich,
Varied Stage," *AJC*, 17 July 1988, 1, 22C; Andrew Young, "Decision 88: Atlanta
Welcome, 'Need to Elect Another Democratic President,'" (text of speech deliv-
ered by Mayor Andrew Young) 19 July 1988, 16C; Scott Shepard, "Democratic
Convention Price: $22.5 Million and Bills Still Coming," *AJC*, 29 September
1988, 1, 8A; Sheila Poole, "Occupancy at Metro Hotels Trails behind National
Rates," *AJC*, 7 November 1989, 1B.

[28] Gayle White, "Black Baptists Fear Convention Politics," *Atlanta Journal-
Constitution*, 5 September 1992, 6E; Susannah Vesey, "Courting Black Conventions," *AJC*, 24 February 1994, 1D.

Another way to fill hotel rooms is to host an event that has become among the largest on the planet. In 1987, a young Atlanta attorney named Billy Payne noticed that Nashville planned to invite the International Olympic Committee (IOC) to hold the 1996 summer games in their city. He reasoned that if Nashville's leaders thought it was reasonable to make a bid for the Olympics, then Atlanta's could also enter the bidding process. Payne asked Mayor Young for an appointment to discuss the idea. Andrew Young says that at first he thought the young attorney was crazy, but he soon realized Payne was both persistent and persuasive. Together with a handful of business leaders, Billy Payne and Mayor Young formed a partnership to move forward with Atlanta's bid to host the Olympics. They formed the Atlanta Organizing Committee (AOC) to prepare the official invitation.

An intangible, but significant nonetheless, result of the 1996 Olympics was the increased perception of Atlanta as an international city. While what constitutes an "international city" may be vague, the city's leaders had declared this goal in the early 1970s. The publicity of hosting the Olympics and the global television coverage of the opening ceremony, the competitions, and the closing literally put the city on the international map. In an international survey conducted before the Olympics, many respondents said that they liked Atlanta, especially the city's casinos—indicating that in many parts of the world Atlanta and Atlantic City were confused. After the 1996 Olympic Games, few people in the world did not know about Atlanta, and many held a favorable image.

With the continued expansion of the Hartsfield-Jackson International Airport, including the opening of the new international concourse, Atlanta became an aviation hub with the largest number of arriving planes and passengers of any airport in the world. Atlanta's leaders continue to project Atlanta's image as a gateway to the world for transportation, visitors, and commerce. Atlanta can also offer lessons to other places on how it has grown from a small country town to a place of international importance. A significant element in this process was the ability to move beyond a history of segregation as elected officials worked with business leaders of all races.

Atlanta's tourism business is the product of a complex partnership between political and business leaders. Black and white leaders often meet behind closed doors in informal settings to discuss major issues. Their consensus leads to action that involves government and business in the solution. Even the most controversial proposals, such as the 25 percent minority business requirement set up by Mayor Jackson for the airport project, eventually were accepted by this informal group and the city's business moved forward. As Andrew Young said in expanding the minority business development requirement to 35 percent during his administration and to 40 percent during the Olympic preparations, white business leaders can do the math that an expanding pie worth an estimated $5 billion is valuable to everyone. In a growing city, increased economic opportunity for women and minorities benefits everyone.

As mayor, Andrew Young encouraged Atlantans to view hospitality as the city's core industry. The city's tradition of hosting visitors has proven to be an effective strategy for promoting economic development and capturing dollars from the many people who use the interstate transportation network—the planes, trains, and automobiles that come through Atlanta. The steady growth of the Merchandise Mart and its tens of thousands of business visitors give the hotel and convention industry in Atlanta a baseline of patrons. The ease and frequency of transportation into Atlanta through the airport and the access to downtown hotels on MARTA create a synergy that feeds the expansion of business and convention travel. To continue to expand the convention business that is the heart of the industry in the city has required not only cooperation between white and black business and political leaders but also hard work, constant promotional efforts, and new attractions. These same ingredients keep people coming to a county fair and also to the next convention held in a major city like Atlanta. As Andrew Young said, "Business investments follow visitors," and Atlanta has long used tourism as an economic development strategy in the expectation that tourists will come, visit, and want to do business in the city.

8

Public-Purpose Capitalism

As he assumed office as mayor in 1982, Andrew Young's inaugural address called for a new sense of cooperation in Atlanta. During the 1960s, the civil rights movement allowed residents of the city to advance socially. In the decade of the 1980s, Young hoped Atlanta would advance economically. Young's background brought qualifications that allowed him to be a catalyst for cooperation. Atlanta's leaders were not unique in using public investment and tax-exempt bond financing to develop public assets. The city has been particularly successful, however, in using these tools to leverage significant public benefits in its public-private partnerships. Over the years Atlanta's taxpayers have shown their willingness to absorb the risk and underwrite major development projects ranging from the Omni Arena to MARTA to the airport. As a result, these public-private partnerships are an economic engine for the region. When he became mayor, Andrew Young continued the pact between Atlanta's business community and Atlanta's African-American community. He supported projects to expand the economy, with the proviso that Atlanta's African-American citizens were able to participate as business partners, as well as, employees.

Speaking to the National Conference of Black Mayors in 2012, Young described his strategy:

> I call what we do "public-purpose capitalism." Now if you define your public purpose...you have to do that. Our public purpose was the airport, our public purpose was the sewer system, our public purpose was Underground Atlanta, our public purpose was the Olympics, and once we define the public purpose then we go to the capitalists who got the money and we work out a deal where they fund what we want. But now we let them not only fund it, but we let private contractors build it and manage it—but we set it up. The private contractors can't make any money until all the debt is paid. You can do almost anything.

On the surface, Andrew Young was an unlikely candidate for strengthening the relationship between business leaders and government. A self-styled "New Testament socialist," he had been adept at securing federal resources for Atlanta's needs as Atlanta's congressional representative from the 5th Congressional District of Georgia. He ran for Congress on a promise of serving as "Atlanta's errand boy in Washington." Direct federal aid to cities was supported by a US House of Representatives controlled by Democrats still inspired by the goals of President Franklin Roosevelt's New Deal and President Lyndon Johnson's Great Society. Young's association with Dr. Martin Luther King, Jr., and his engaging manner with people from all walks of life made his endorsement of liberal white members of Congress especially useful. He was sought after by members of Congress seeking to mobilize African-American voters in their campaigns. Andrew Young used the political capital that he earned campaigning for the powerful, liberal chairmen of congressional committees to maintain a steady stream of federal funds flowing to Atlanta, connecting federal funds to Atlanta's public purpose.

Prior to Young's election to Congress, Mayor Ivan Allen gained the favor of Washington when he testified in favor of the civil rights legislation introduced by President John Kennedy and enacted with the leadership of President Lyndon Johnson. Federal funds enabled Atlanta to develop important elements of Mayor Ivan Allen's framework for economic growth through the expanding expenditures of the federal government. George Berry, who became Atlanta's commissioner of aviation, was given responsibility of oversight for federal grants under Mayor Allen. Soon after Lyndon Johnson became president, he recalled,

> We would get calls saying "We've got a three-million-dollar grant up here for you. Have an application in by next Friday"—and we would. We would work all night and on weekends to write up this application for some worthy cause that we thought the city needed and get it up to Washington and in a few days we would have a check. Fairly soon this young, thirty-year-old accountant in the finance department was running a budget about the size of the Atlanta General Fund.

Berry attributed Atlanta's good fortune to Allen's courage in testifying in support of the Civil Rights Act of 1964. He said, "I've always assumed, without any direct evidence, that President Johnson said to his cabinet, 'I want you to have a grant ready for the city of Atlanta when they ask for it.'"[1] He could find no other explanation for the flood of federal funds that poured into Atlanta.

Ivan Allen described the environment for cities during the Johnson administration:

"We knew that we couldn't rely on state aid and that the only answer was Washington. I asked for, and got, the creation of the position of director of governmental liaison, which in essence called for a man to run back and forth between Atlanta and Washington carrying a bag to hold federal funds." Mayor Allen was a vocal supporter of President Johnson's Great Society programs—"Head Start, Jobs Corp, Urban Renewal, Model Cities, all of them."[2]

Urban Renewal funds cleared the land for the Atlanta Stadium and the first professional sports team in Atlanta.[3] Urban Renewal Funds also made way for the Atlanta Civic Center, supporting the city's growing business travel and hospitality industry. These projects improved the city's public amenities but displaced hundreds of families from areas that were close to employment opportunities and city services. The federal dollars were used in a way that had a disproportionate impact on Atlanta's African-American citizens and business owners. Urban Renewal for the stadium, hotels, and civic center dislocated more than two hundred black-owned businesses and nearly two thousand families. Only the stadium clearance displaced a small number of white families, as well as large numbers of blacks.[4] Very little relocation assistance was provided to businesses or families in the urban renewal program.

Mayor Sam Massell used tax-exempt municipal bond financing to continue Atlanta's expansion as a "big league" city. Massell had a background and family connections in real estate. He was careful to limit the taxpayers' exposure on the bond deal to build the Omni Coliseum, home

---

[1] Berry, interview, 26 July 2011.
[2] Allen and Hemphill, *Mayor*, 135–36, 151.
[3] Ibid, 155.
[4] Newman, *Southern Hospitality*, 137–38.

for Atlanta's new professional basketball team, the Atlanta Hawks. Developer Tom Cousins proposed an arena for the team adjacent to parking decks that he owned on the west side of downtown Atlanta. Massell recalled,

> When I did the Omni Coliseum, I had been in real estate for twenty-two years…. And I was able to structure that one as where if you never sold a single ticket, the public wouldn't have to pay anything, because he [Cousins] pledged his income from those parking lots that were already built, they were already making money and we sold…the revenue bonds, so he had a real low interest rate. It was a win-win arrangement.

Espousing what was a central tenet of Atlanta's approach to bonds, Massell added, "you work hard enough to get that pencil sharp enough to where everybody comes out well, you never have to regret it."[5] Massell was liberal about city amenities, such as MARTA, and conservative about taxpayer funds. Getting that "pencil sharp" was the role of Atlanta's civil servants, people such as George Berry and Richard Stogner, who sharpened pencils and scrubbed numbers to protect Atlanta taxpayers from overly optimistic projections. These dedicated city employees are often not famous, but they contribute to making the city a well-run and efficient place.

The election of Richard Nixon as president in 1968 did not end Atlanta's access to federal grant dollars. Federal funds were secured in 1971 for MARTA, following the referendum to approve a penny sales tax to pay for Atlanta's percentage of the construction cost. Federal money accounted for 90 percent of the construction costs for the MARTA system, and the city put up the remaining 10 percent.

In addition to securing funds to move I-85 to make space for the expanded airport, Young was also able to preserve part of the Chattahoochee River, north of Atlanta in a federally supported Chattahoochee Recreation Area. The inflows of federal assistance to cities continued as the Congress enacted housing assistance for cities. Atlanta's leaders used federal programs—such as the Housing and Community Development

---

[5] Massell, video interview, 5 August 2013.

Act, the Neighborhood Housing Services Project, and Low and Moderate Rental Housing Project—to improve housing for thousands of residents. Through a $10 million federal grant under the Comprehensive Employment and Training Act (CETA), Mayor Jackson was able to expand employment opportunities for low-income African Americans and even support some of his initiatives in the arts. By Jackson's final year in office, the city had received $90 million in CETA funds.[6]

Andrew Young's election as mayor coincided with the "Reagan Revolution," which abruptly halted the federal government's direct aid to cities. Ronald Reagan, the actor and former governor of California, defeated Georgia's Jimmy Carter in 1980. President Reagan moved quickly to send block grants to states rather than direct aid to cities. For Atlanta, the effects on the city's budget were catastrophic. Atlanta received little support from the state. The days of phone calls from Washington inviting Atlanta to request funds had come to an end. Young knew that the city would not be able to count on generous direct grants of federal funds from Washington. He had been President Carter's ambassador to the United Nations and served on the House of Representatives Committee on Banking and Urban Development. If the city was going to continue to meet the needs of the citizens for jobs and growth, he was going to have to find money elsewhere—leveraging private investment for public purposes.

Young used his knowledge from years of public service for the benefit of Atlanta. He explained,

> I learned, while I was on the banking committee, that there were places in the world where they were generating billions of dollars and didn't know what to do with it; in fact the Arabs were paying the Swiss banks interest to keep their money. They weren't making anything on it; they were charging them to keep it, see, and I said the Japanese are generating so much wealth they don't know what to do with it. They can't spend it all in Japan.... We started these trade missions to places like

---

[6] Alton Hornsby, Jr., *Black Power in Dixie: A Political History of African Americans in Atlanta* (Gainesville: University Press of Florida, 2009) 153, 159, 178.

Germany, like Japan, like Saudi Arabia. We didn't get any Saudi money that was labeled as Saudi money, but we got money from Luxemburg, money from Holland, you know, and the billions of dollars that was probably money that was being managed by those companies for the Arabs who had surplus capital. And I said everywhere there was money available, we went and invited them to bring it into Atlanta.

As President Carter's United Nations ambassador, Young had generated tremendous goodwill around the world. The Carter administration had made peace and human rights core tenets of diplomacy.[7] However, Young's tenure as U.N. Ambassador ended abruptly with his resignation following a conversation with Representatives of the Palestine Liberation Organization (PLO), a move that was in conflict with U.S. policy at the time. In his last act as ambassador, Young led a business delegation to Africa that resulted in more than a billion dollars of contracts and investment in African countries. The trip was put together to allow Young to leave Carter's administration on a high note.

President Carter's chief of staff, Atlanta attorney Jack Watson, authorized the delegation and a plane for the Africa trip. Julius Hollis, a former Young staff person, was with the Export-Import Bank of the US. An Atlanta native who attended Morehouse College, Hollis had worked in Young's congressional office and was well-versed in the "Atlanta Way." He reached out to Atlanta powerbroker, Jesse Hill, to ensure the trip had maximum impact. He had been trying to push through trade deals in Africa on behalf of US companies and was unable to finalize the terms with the governments of several African countries, including Nigeria. Hollis recalled, "So, I called Jesse Hill…and with his help, suddenly I'm sitting here with $1.3 billion in commitment for Westinghouse…M. W. Kellogg, Archer Daniels Midland on projects in Nigeria, Kenya, and

---

[7] Carole Cadwalladr, "The Observer: Jimmy Carter," *The Guardian*, http://www.theguardian.com/world/2011/sep/11/president-jimmy-carter-interview (accessed 11 February 2016).

Tanzania.... Andy came back with a billion dollars of contracts, signed."[8] Working behind the scenes, Hollis and Watson organized the delegation to include John Moore, Jr., the chairman of the Export-Import Bank; Bruce Llewellyn, president of Overseas Private Investment Corporation; and senior executives from several major U.S. corporations, such as Westinghouse, General Electric, Archer Daniels Midland, Consolidated Petroleum Industries, and International Harvester. According to Hollis, these deals had been languishing, but because of Andrew Young's stature with the key governments, the deals were signed. Accompanying the delegation was a reporter from *Ebony* magazine, who wrote, "...the leaders of business and governments were interested enough to do $1.75 billion worth of business with the trade members."[9] The *Washington Post* quoted Theodore A. Adams, president of Unified Industries, Inc., an electronics company based in Alexandria, Virginia, summarizing the impact of Young's leadership: "It is because they like Andy Young that we are able to get to the right people. I accomplished in two days in Liberia what would normally have taken one year."[10]

When he was elected mayor, Young had a record of leading an effective trade mission and establishing tremendous good will from the legacy of his work with both Martin Luther King, Jr., and President Carter. This savvy and goodwill translated into tremendous international access for Atlanta business leaders. Architect and developer John Portman recounted the increase in access that resulted from traveling with former ambassador Andrew Young. Portman described an Atlanta business trip to France:

> I went there with a delegation with Andy, and we called on Mitterrand and Chirac, and Andy got us in everywhere and everybody treated

---

[8] Julius Hollis (founder and chair, Alliance for Digital Equality), interview by authors, 30 January 2012, audio, Special Collections and Archives, University Library, Georgia State University.

[9] Robert E. Johnson, "Ambassador Young's Last Official Visit to Africa," *Ebony* (December 1979): 31–42.

[10] Leon Dash, "African Respect for Young Aids Trade Mission," *Washington Post*, 11 September 1979, 1.

Andy like he was, you know, visiting royalty. It was amazing. I was standing in the window of the Élysée Palace where Mitterrand was, looking out on the yard, and there was the gate with the gold tips and all that, and the people out there were looking in. And I was standing there in the window with Charlie Loudermilk, and we were waiting to go in to see Mitterrand with Andy. And I said, "You know something, Charlie?" I said, "I've been coming over here for so many years and I was always one of those guys out there looking through, but it took Andy Young to get me inside. I'm going to see the president."[11]

During his years as mayor, Young led annual international trade missions with the Metro Atlanta Chamber of Commerce. Young and Atlanta Chamber delegations visited Jamaica and Trinidad in 1983; Scandinavia in 1984; the United Kingdom and France in 1985; Japan, the People's Republic of China, and Hong Kong in 1986; Italy and Switzerland in 1987; Japan and Taiwan in 1988; and the Soviet Union in 1989.[12] He made other trips with the Atlanta Visitors and Convention Bureau, the Atlanta Business League, the Atlanta Organizing Committee for the Olympic Games, and others. Young described his approach to the international trips:

I would go to Japan and one of the big businesses, Marubeni, would host me, and they would set me up in their offices and all their group. They'd have their automobile people coming in in the morning; they'd have the plastics people coming in at 10:00; they'd have the textile people coming in at 12:00 or usually at 12:00 they had the bankers, you know, the big money people for lunch.... And then I'd have I could meet with more than a hundred companies in one day. My pitch was that Atlanta is really the center not only of the US market, we're the center of the world. I said you can get anywhere...you can get to 80 percent of the United States within two hours and most of them you can get back the same day to Atlanta. So in terms of your executive travel time, you have much more access and must less time flying in and out of Atlanta.

---

[11] Portman, interview, 15 September 2011.
[12] Horton, *The Young Years*, 111–12.

To spur investment, Young created a "one-stop shop" and gave each investor a city employee to manage the permitting process: "We didn't offer them any tax breaks, we just said we will guarantee you honest and efficient service. You won't have to pay anybody under the table, and if we agree to a certain date, we will make sure you get open by that date. And I said the one thing we pride ourselves in is doing everything on time and within budget, if not under budget."

In some cases the city did use tax breaks to promote housing downtown and an industrial park to steer employers to provide jobs near low-income communities. When John Portman built Peachtree Center, he envisioned the type of urban environment he had seen in Europe—people living, working, shopping, and experiencing entertainment in a walkable area. This approach was the reverse of the move to the suburbs and the commute by car that had become Atlanta's way of life. Portman used the concept of a "coordinate unit" to plan a multi-faceted walkable central city. Portman described what he called a "coordinate unit":

> If you walk from where we are eight to ten minutes and you do a circle, that's a tremendous area. Now if you take that area and you put all your jobs, your offices, your entertainment, all this stuff, and you fringe it with housing, what I was trying to do with the coordinate unit is to get people out of the car and on their feet and have a pedestrian environment that you could walk to the corner drugstore, you know, get a newspaper or you could go to the grocery store…. We were premature, and the concentration on building the coordinate unit was to build a job base first.[13]

Portman's vision of a livable, walkable city depended upon having commercial buildings providing jobs before it would be possible to have residents downtown. Other policies would be needed to bring people back to the central city. Mayor Young shared that vision of people living downtown. East of the downtown business district, the city created a "residential enterprise zone," which made building in the city more affordable. Young used tax incentives that gradually increased over time:

---

[13] Portman, interview, 15 September 2016.

You don't pay full property tax until you've been in the house ten years. That has given us a way to balance out the high cost of land in the city with the low cost of land in the suburbs, and we made it more convenient and more economical to live in downtown. My goal when we set aside those residential enterprise zones was that we could have fifteen to twenty thousand units of housing downtown.

Longtime Young supporter, Herman J. Russell recalled, "Mayor Young wanted to have more people living in the downtown area, making downtown more accessible."[14] Russell Construction was the first company to take advantage of the Residential Enterprise Zone. Along with McGill Place and McGill Park, Sienna at Renaissance Park Condominiums and other developments brought the total new residential units to nearly 1000 before Young left office.[15] In a city known for sprawl and single family homes on large, wooded lots, these developments demonstrated that middle class citizens would seek out higher-density housing options near downtown. The real impact of the policy would take hold in the years after the Olympic Games. The policy did achieve the goal of encouraging developers to build housing near downtown and making these units affordable because of the tax breaks offered during the first ten years.

Jobs were a major concern for Atlanta's African-American community. The compact with Atlanta's business community was based on improving conditions for the African-American community in exchange for supporting projects to promote economic growth. Access to quality jobs was an important part of that compact. Andrew Young's passion for job creation was rooted in his experience with the civil rights movement. (While Martin Luther King, Jr.'s, "I Have a Dream" speech at the March on Washington is remembered for its stirring cadence and eloquence, few recall that the call for the march was "Jobs and Freedom.")

[14] Herman J. Russell (founder and retired CEO, H. J. Russell and Company), interview by authors, 1 May 2012, audio, Special Collections and Archives, University Library, Georgia State University.
[15] Horton, *The Young Years*, 323–25.

The Young administration used tax incentives and federal funds to create an industrial park near a public housing project known as Bank-head Courts. There were also several of Atlanta's working class African-American communities in the area. The Atlanta Industrial Park became home to dozens of distribution and light manufacturing companies providing more than 2,000 jobs.[16] Young's commitment to attracting employers to Atlanta was intense, and so was his determination to prevent corruption. He gave executives interested in locating in Atlanta his phone number. He recalled a meeting with a Japanese investor:

> I said, well, we have an industrial park right out here in Bankhead area, and I said I'm pretty sure we can build a building to your specification.... So we sat there, and we found a developer who said he had a building that met those specifications, and that we could get him located in three or four months. So, the guy was amazed so I did to him what I did with everybody—I gave him my phone number at home and at the office, and I put him in touch with somebody to get him going.

Later, when the investor ran into a roadblock, he called Mayor Young from Japan.

> He said, "They won't turn on the lights, they won't turn on the electricity." ...I said it's 3:00 in the morning here...I'm sure we can work this problem out. I woke up the guy who was in charge of building permits. He said, "It's simple, Mr. Mayor. We just need his insurance company and the number of his policy." So I called him back...he gave me the name of the company and the number of the policy, and I said, "When you call tomorrow, the lights will be on."

With a series of phone calls, Mayor Young produced jobs for city residents and enhanced Atlanta's reputation for fairness among global companies.

The redevelopment and renewal of Underground Atlanta was the touchstone of Mayor Young's approach to leverage private resources for public purposes. During the campaign, Young pledged to revitalize Underground Atlanta. In addition, there was a need to anchor Atlanta's historic downtown business district—the site of the original railroad cross-

---

[16] Ibid., 327–28.

ing and Coca-Cola's first soda fountain. Underground Atlanta had been born in 1969 as an entertainment complex at the ground level of Atlanta's first train crossings, underneath the viaducts that spanned the railroad tracks and grew to hold held the city's modern bank towers and office buildings. One attraction of the original Underground was the availability of liquor by the drink since the counties surrounding Atlanta were dry. Underground offered supper clubs and bars and became Atlanta's answer to New Orleans's French Quarter. Honky-tonks and blues clubs co-existed with a restaurant named Dante's Down the Hatch that featured the Paul Mitchell Trio playing sophisticated jazz. At its peak, Underground attracted 3.5 million visitors.[17]

Several factors contributed to the decline of the old Underground Atlanta. The construction of the MARTA rapid rail line eliminated a third of the Underground area. This was followed by a fire and, finally, a broken water pipe that flooded the remaining businesses. No sooner had the last business closed in Underground before business leaders began asking city hall to reopen the tourist attraction. In several US cities, festival marketplaces were opening as part of a new downtown redevelopment strategy. The initial and most successful of these festival marketplaces were the work of the Rouse Company that had transformed Boston's Faneuil Hall and Baltimore's Harbor Place. Mayor Young hired the Rouse Company to conduct a feasibility study that recommended the revitalization of Underground Atlanta. While there were drawbacks, the mayor moved the project from the planning stages toward construction. The largest hurdles involved the financing of the revitalization effort.

The city had a number of tools to use to finance public-private partnerships such as Underground Atlanta. The state of Georgia had authorized cities and counties to establish development authorities to enable public bond financing of important projects. In March 1992, the city council approved the Atlanta Downtown Development Authority (ADDA).[18] The ADDA could issue industrial revenue bonds to finance pro-

---

[17] Scott Henry, "From boom to bust and back again: A timeline of Underground's many twists and turns," *Creative Loafing* (24 January 2007): 1.

[18] Horton, *The Young Years*, 80.

jects, thus using the funds of private investors rather than direct funding from city taxpayers. Nevertheless, these projects were guaranteed by city taxpayers, and it was incumbent upon Atlanta's civil servants to ensure that city taxpayers were not left holding the bag for these projects.

Richard Stogner, the city's financial manager, was tasked with making the Underground Atlanta project come together. Stogner was a native of Atlanta and a graduate of Georgia Tech with an MBA from Georgia State. He started with the city as a junior accountant under Charlie Davis, the legendary curmudgeon who served as chief financial officer of Atlanta. Davis had the confidence of the bankers and business leaders to keep Atlanta's bond rating high. Another former CFO, Pat Glisson, also trained under Davis. Glisson recalled that one of the keys to the city's success in municipal bond financing for a variety of projects, including Underground Atlanta, was to be strict about using the bond proceeds only within the covenants of the bond issue and not for other purposes.[19] Richard Stogner served under Atlanta's first African-American mayor, Maynard Jackson; Fulton County's first African-American chairman, Michael Lomax; and DeKalb County's first African-American chairman, Vernon Jones.[20] Stogner described Underground's financing as a "puzzle." One portion of the financing involved federal Urban Development Action Grants (UDAG) for which cities across the country had to compete. Atlanta's Underground proposal was returned to the city by HUD four times. At the last minute, the project needed an infusion of private sector cash. Dan Sweat, then president of Central Atlanta Progress, took on the challenge of filling the financing gap. Harvey Newman recalls Sweat, a proud graduate of the school, bounding into a class at Georgia State where he was scheduled to deliver

---

[19] Pat Glisson (former chief financial officer, City of Atlanta and the Atlanta Committee for the Olympic Games), interview by authors, 19 July 2012, audio, Special Collections and Archives, University Library, Georgia State University.

[20] Richard Stogner (retired chief financial officer, City of Atlanta, Fulton County, and DeKalb County), interview by authors, 27 September 2012, audio, Special Collections and Archives, University Library, Georgia State University.

a guest lecture: "He said, 'I just raised twelve million dollars over breakfast.'" This was the way of public-private partnerships in Atlanta. Dan Sweat, former chief administrative officer to mayors Ivan Allen and Sam Massell and long-time head of Central Atlanta Progress, closed the financing gap for Underground Atlanta in one breakfast meeting. This was power, the "Atlanta Way," and was an example of Atlanta's regime politics that allowed Atlanta to overcome hurdles to economic development projects.

After its reopening in 1989 for more than a decade, Underground served as the city's town square, its civic gathering space. Atlanta residents celebrated at Underground Atlanta when the city won the bid for the Centennial Olympic Games. The city hosted a Peach Drop at Underground on New Year's Eve, its answer to New York's Times Square.

There have been problems associated with Underground Atlanta since its redevelopment. In 1991, Atlanta did not escape the riots that occurred around the nation in the wake of the acquittal of Los Angeles police officers charged with the brutal beating of Rodney King, a beating that was video recorded and shown around the world. Protestors spilled into Underground Atlanta, damaging stores in the area and causing fear among middle-class Atlanta citizens.

Another blow came when the Atlanta Olympic Committee centered many Olympic ceremonies in a new amenity, Centennial Park, rather than at the plaza at Underground Atlanta. Nevertheless, Underground Atlanta anchored the revitalization of Atlanta's downtown historic district and bridged the corridor of state, city, and county government buildings and the commercial district. As of 2016, the city is in the process of rejuvenating the area by selling Underground Atlanta to a developer who promises to add housing and other amenities to the area.

In 1984, the Atlanta Zoo was named the worst zoo in the nation by *Parade*, a syndicated publication that appeared in the Sunday edition of newspapers across the nation. The poor conditions at the zoo caused a major image crisis for Atlanta. Mayor Young faced a decision whether to close the zoo or improve it. One of Young's skills was to find innovative solutions to complicated problems. Marva Brooks, city attorney under mayors Jackson and Young, recalled of Young, "He was willing to think outside the box about solving problems. He never accepted from me [...] options A, B, and C that there really wasn't a little bit of B that could be added to A that could be added to C that made a new way forward—the 'Atlanta Way,' if you will."[21] The decision was made to keep the zoo open with a new vision and a public-private partnership. A new nonprofit corporation was created, the Atlanta-Fulton County Zoo, Inc., a private entity with a public purpose. Young convinced Terry Maple, a research scientist at the Georgia Institute of Technology, to serve as director for the new entity.[22] The corporate community rallied behind the zoo, and the facility was transformed. Animals were seen outdoors in appropriate habitats, such as a rainforest or savannah, rather than in tile-lined cages. Willie B., the charismatic gorilla named for former Mayor Hartsfield, was given a grassy hillside to survey his kingdom. In 1985 the zoo was renamed Zoo Atlanta, and its international reputation for science, research, and education was secured in 1999 with the loan of pandas from China.

South of downtown Atlanta was a city-owned parcel of land that had been the home of the Southeastern Fairgrounds. The Music Corporation of America and Pace Entertainment Group were interested in building an outdoor amphitheater in Atlanta. Mayor Young persuaded them to consider this section of the city that was economically depressed as a result of the closure of a nearby General Motors assembly plant. Young saw an opportunity to create small businesses for the residents in the community. Involving local residents in businesses related to the new venue would have the added benefit of reducing crime that might otherwise occur to the patrons attending events at the entertainment venue, a major concern of the developers. Shirley Franklin who was chief administrative officer under Mayor Young said, "He wanted to be sure that

---

[21] Marva Brooks (former city attorney), interview by authors, 7 March 2012, audio, Special Collections and Archives, University Library, Georgia State University.

[22] Francis Desiderio, "Zoo Atlanta," *New Georgia Encyclopedia*, http://www.georgiaencyclopedia.org/articles/geography-environment/zoo-atlanta (1 October 2014).

young entrepreneurs, business people in that area, that we were not plop-
ping a development in their community but that they were part of it."²³

This was public-purpose capitalism at its best, creating business
owners, rather than simply employees. Young said,

> I put the responsibility for putting the deal together on the shoulders of
> Eugene Duffy, a Morehouse man who had come into politics with
> Maynard Jackson. The first thing we did [was to form] a security com-
> pany of people who were in the neighborhood who had some military
> training, had been in ROTC, had been Boy Scouts—anybody who had
> any kind of discipline training—we pulled them together to create a se-
> curity company. And they became a joint venture, they owned 51 per-
> cent, but they became a joint venture with a national company, which
> provided them with uniforms and training. I asked local developer
> Herman Russell to head construction of the amphitheater, but with one
> stipulation…hire everybody he could in the neighborhood that he could
> hire and take them with him on his next job. He said "If I train them I
> don't want someone else to take them.

Russell remembered, "You know, it was just always a part of me. Whatever I could do to improve the quality of life for people regardless of the
race I just believe in that."²⁴

Young then turned to the issue of women in the community, saying,

> Well most of the women [...] were single mothers. We said we will give
> you the [amphitheater] concessions. You can own the cotton candy, the
> hot dogs, you know, the fried chicken, whatever, ice cream…. It's your
> store, but we joint-ventured them with [a company] that supplied them
> with what they needed, but [the women owned] 51 percent of every
> store.

The older men were organized to manage the parking lots, and
younger men sold T-shirts. The involvement of the community in the
private development has resulted in a safe and popular entertainment

---

²³ Shirley Clarke Franklin (former mayor, City of Atlanta), video interview,
1 May 2015.
²⁴ Russell, interview, 1 May 2012.

venue seating 18,000 known as the Lakewood Amphitheatre that opened in 1989 and continues in operation without major incidents.[25]

Mayor Young had a number of tools to implement his vision of public-purpose capitalism, and he used all of them, sometimes in combination. At every juncture, he was supported by some members of the business community, creating effective public-private partnerships. In his quest to expand Atlanta's economy as well as the job and business opportunities for African Americans, he sought international business investment, promoted development in under-resourced communities, and invested in downtown Atlanta. Minority business participation and job creation for African Americans were essential factors in allowing Young to support economic development while retaining political support in the African-American community.[26] To redevelop Underground Atlanta in the heart of downtown, he used private support from Atlanta business leaders, federal dollars, and the city's development authority to issue bonds. To preserve a zoo in the city of Atlanta, he supported the creation of a nonprofit entity that would solicit private support, rather than rely on tax dollars, and turned over city-owned property to that new entity. This strategy was used to preserve a number of community attractions while reducing the burden on the city for funds. Piedmont Park, the city's largest park, the Atlanta Botanical Garden, and other public amenities that could garner private funding sources were turned over to nonprofit organizations. He used tax incentives to encourage private companies to build middle-class housing near the city's downtown business district. This strategy reflected Young's belief that the private sector was best at creating sustainable jobs. He was open to turning over public sector resources to public-private partnerships if it resulted in better services at a lower cost to tax payers. This type of leadership helped create the city of Atlanta. "Public-purpose capitalism" was a creative approach that protected the interests of the pro-growth governing regime by bringing more people into roles as business owners, improving city

---

[25] Horton, *The Young Years*, 333.
[26] Stone, *Regime Politics*, 148.

amenities, and including diverse stakeholders in the decision-making process. This innovation allowed for more "win-win-win" solutions to the challenges facing Atlanta.

9

Big-League Town

In the years after World War II, sports would play an important role in the desegregation of Atlanta, but for most of the city's history strict segregation of the races was the rule in school yards and stadiums. Minor league baseball was popular in Atlanta beginning early in the twentieth century with the formation of the all-white team known as the Atlanta Crackers. For African Americans there was a separate team known as the Atlanta Black Crackers. The Black Crackers played with uniforms and equipment often handed down from the white team. For many years, the two teams often shared the same field known as the Ponce de Leon Ballpark. The Black Crackers would play on the field when the white team had away games and at other times would use the fields of Atlanta University or Clark College. The Black Crackers played other teams in the Negro Southern League, which was generally considered a group of farm teams associated with the black leagues that operated nationally. Negro Southern League franchises were never financially stable. Visiting and home teams furnished two balls per game, and often games had to be stopped to retrieve the balls. Because the teams carried only about twelve players, the athletes played more than one position, and membership on the teams changed constantly. Relief pitchers were nonexistent, and pitchers moved to the outfield to finish games after pitching a few innings.[1]

The Ponce de Leon Ballpark was among the finest minor league baseball facilities when it was built in 1907. The old wooden grandstand burned in 1923 and was replaced by a concrete and steel facility the next

---

[1] Tim Darnell, "Atlanta Black Crackers," *New Georgia Encyclopedia*, http://www.georgiaencyclopedia.org/articles/sports-outdoor-recreation/atlanta-black-crackers (24 April 2013).

season. The Ponce Ballpark's seating was consistent with the pattern of segregation at the time with a grandstand for 10,000 whites, bleachers in one outfield for 2,500 whites, and an equal number of bleacher seats in left field for blacks. The ballpark was unique in having a magnolia tree located in the outfield, and according to the ground rules of the field, any ball that hit the tree was considered a home run. The white Atlanta Crackers were among the best in the Southern Baseball League, winning the championship seventeen times between 1901 and 1965. The desegregation of major league baseball by Jackie Robinson and the Brooklyn Dodgers in 1947 had a significant impact on both Atlanta professional minor league teams. The white Crackers and the ballpark were segregated, but in 1949 the Crackers made history when they played against Jackie Robinson and the Brooklyn Dodgers in a three-game exhibition series. The final game of the series on April 10, 1949, drew an all-time Ponce de Leon crowd of 25,221, including 13,885 black fans. The Crackers won one of the three games, and the series marked the first time in Atlanta history that blacks and whites competed against each other in a professional sports event.[2] In the years that followed, the integration of other major league teams drained the talent of the Atlanta Black Crackers, leading to the demise of the all-black team and its league. In 1965, the Atlanta Crackers played their final season in the recently constructed Atlanta-Fulton County Stadium and disbanded the following year when the Milwaukee Braves relocated to the city.[3]

Since the 1870s, sports in Atlanta were limited to minor league baseball, amateur athletics, high school sports, and college teams. For many years, these sports followed the pattern of racial segregation. Until 1948, when the second high school for African Americans, David T. Howard High School, opened, teams from the older Booker T. Washington High had played their games against all-black teams from places

---

[2] Tim Darnell, *The Crackers: Early Days of Atlanta Baseball* (Athens: Hill Street Press, 2003) 46, 88–89.

[3] Tim Darnell, "Atlanta Crackers," *New Georgia Encyclopedia*, http://www.georgiaencyclopedia.org/articles/sports-outdoor-recreation/atlanta-crackers (29 August 2013).

as far away as Birmingham, Alabama, and Asheville, North Carolina, as well as Macon, Savannah, Augusta, and Columbus in Georgia. With a second black high school, Washington High School began a rivalry with Howard High. Home football games were typically played in Herndon Stadium at Morris Brown College. Black high school baseball games were sometimes played at the Ponce Ballpark. Rivalry between Howard and Washington High Schools was so intense that extra security was usually needed to keep peace between the teams, coaches, and fans.

The integration of high school sports followed many of the patterns of the "Atlanta Way" with strong leadership forging relationships between whites and blacks that resulted in a relatively peaceful desegregation. The carefully negotiated integration of public schools began on a small scale in 1961. Two years later there were still only fifty-four black students attending desegregated schools in the city. Nevertheless, the peaceful process and tone of moderation convinced Sid Scarborough, a white man and longtime athletic director of the Atlanta Public Schools, that integration was inevitable. He also realized that sports could play a significant role in the desegregation process within the schools and the city as a whole. Although the state, like others in the South, had separate high school sports organizations for blacks and whites, Scarborough began holding interracial meetings between coaches and athletic directors within the Atlanta Public Schools. A few of the white coaches were not pleased with these meetings, but they attended anyway and began to get to know their black coaching counterparts. Scarborough led the group to plan for the desegregation of high school sports in the city by having black high schools begin playing traditionally all-white schools. Games between black and white high schools in non-contact sports such as track and field, baseball, and basketball would be played before football.[4]

One of the first of these desegregated contests was a basketball game between all-white Therrell High and the all-black Price High that was coached by Frank Glover. At halftime, Glover's team was ahead, so

---

[4] Raymond Williams (former coach and athletic director, Turner High School), interview by author, 7 August 2015.

he told his players in the locker room that during the second half they would be opposed by seven men—five from Therrell and the two white referees. Sure enough, as the second half began, the game became rough with no fouls called against the white team. At that point, Glover stopped play, walked to mid-court, and called to the white coach of Therrell High, Bennie Farmer, to meet him there. The two coaches knew one another from the meetings with Sid Scarborough. Together they called the two referees into the conference and told them to call the game fairly before someone was hurt, or be reported to the Georgia High School Association. Glover knew that he should have been kicked out of the game for walking out on to the court and stopping play, but after the conference at mid-court, the referees did not disqualify him or even call a technical foul. The game continued with more balanced officiating, and Coach Glover's Price High team won. Sid Scarborough's leadership in bringing black and white coaches together before integration paved the way for the smooth integration of high school basketball in Atlanta.[5]

On September 2, 1966, the first high school football game in Atlanta between a black and white high school team took place. The all-black Archer High team played the all-white Dykes High team at Grady Stadium.[6] The Archer High coach of this game, Raymond Williams, recalled that the Atlanta Police Department brought out extra security for the stadium with police dogs and officers on horseback to patrol the field. Williams said, "My players were quicker than the whites who played for Dykes High, so we were able to score on deep passes down the field." The Archer Eagles defeated the Dykes Colts by a score of 28 to 0 and were named by the newspaper as the "team of the week" in prep football circles. One of the city's white school coaches called Raymond Williams following the game and asked, "How do you coach quickness?" Williams explained that it was innate, prompting the white coach to reply, "The only way we can beat you in the future is to have some black

---

[5] Frank Glover (former coach and National Football League referee) interview by author, 6 August 25, 2015.

[6] Allen Hauck, "George, Northside Meet in Top High School Game," *Atlanta Constitution*, 2 September 1966, 52.

players." As a black football coach, Raymond Williams summed up the process: "We had to prove ourselves on the field to earn their respect."[7] That is exactly what happened. High school sports played an important role in the peaceful desegregation of the city thanks to the leadership of Sid Scarborough, who became head of the Atlanta Stadium Authority, where he helped build the field that would make Atlanta a big-league town.[8]

College sports in Atlanta were somewhat slower than the high schools to desegregate their athletic teams. In fall 1969, Georgia Tech enrolled an African-American quarterback to play football for the Yellow Jackets.[9] The time of racial change put enormous pressure on black athletes. While the basketball team of the University of Georgia integrated in 1970, the football team did not integrate until 1972. The flagship institution in the state was one of the last three football teams in the Southeastern Conference to integrate.[10] Vince Dooley, who served as football coach and athletic director at the University of Georgia for forty years, described the process of desegregation in football: "When it came to integration, college football didn't lead the way—it couldn't. The pipeline had to be created, and that was the job of Georgia's high schools."[11] Colleges in the state were much better prepared for integration after African-American athletes began to perform successfully on the field in places like the city of Atlanta.

---

[7] *Atlanta Constitution*, "Archer Cited for Big Win," 5 September 1966; Williams interview.

[8] Darrell Simmons, "Unforgettable Man: On Eve of Retirement, Sid Scarborough Looks Back," *Atlanta Constitution*, 1 July 1979, 31.

[9] Robert C. McMath, Jr., Ronald H. Bayor, James E. Brittain, Lawrence Foster, Augustus W. Giebelhaus, and Germaine M. Reed, *Engineering the New South: Georgia Tech, 1885–1985* (Athens: University of Georgia Press, 1985) 318.

[10] Charles H. Martin, *Benching Jim Crow: The Rise and Fall of the Color Line in Southern College Sports, 1890–1980* (Urbana: University of Illinois Press, 2010) 220, 288.

[11] Jim Galloway, "Vince Dooley and a search for the glue that holds the South together," *Atlanta Journal-Constitution*, 22 July 2015, 1.

Some local leaders, such as long-time Mayor Bill Hartsfield, wanted to keep the city's professional teams playing minor league ball. Mayor Hartsfield regarded professional sports as an invitation to gambling, and he kept the city government from encouraging the relocation of a major league team to Atlanta. With the election of former chamber of commerce president Ivan Allen, Jr., as mayor in 1961, attitudes toward major league sports began to change. Mayor Allen felt that having the city's name in the sports pages of newspapers across the country on a daily basis was publicity the city needed. It announced that Atlanta was a big league city and a place of national importance.

Soon after his election, Mayor Allen invited the owner of the Kansas City Athletics, Charles Finley, to the city in hopes that Allen could coax the Finley to move his American League baseball team to Atlanta. During the visit, Finley pointed out the advantages of locating a new stadium near the intersection of the three interstate highways close to downtown. Although Finley could not get permission from the American League to move his franchise to Atlanta, his recommendation for the stadium's location inspired Allen to move forward with the project. The mayor's connections to fellow business leaders made the financing of the new stadium possible. The president of the Citizens and Southern Bank (now Bank of America), Mills B. Lane, Jr., was a close friend of Mayor Allen, and with the support of the bank, the stadium was "built for a team we did not have, with money we did not have, on land we did not own."[12] The stadium's location was on property that was part of what was called the Rawson-Washington urban renewal area in the neighborhood of Summerhill. An entity known as the Atlanta-Fulton County Recreation Authority was responsible for issuing the $18 million in revenue bonds used to finance the stadium.[13]

---

[12] Robert (Bob) Hope (retired public relations director, Atlanta Braves), interview by authors, 8 September 2011, audio, Special Collections and Archives, University Library, Georgia State University.

[13] Kenneth R. Fenster, "Atlanta-Fulton County Stadium," *New Georgia Encyclopedia,* http://www.georgiaencyclopedia.org/articles/sports-outdoor-recreation/atlanta–fulton-county-stadium (11 August 2015).

The quest for a major league baseball franchise eventually led to an agreement for the Milwaukee Braves to relocate to Atlanta. The Braves had a contract with the City of Milwaukee that did not expire until 1966, so even though the new stadium was constructed on a fast track in order to be ready for occupancy in 1965, the team was not able to move. The Atlanta Crackers played their final season in the city in the new major league stadium. Finally, on the evening of April 12, 1966, the Braves opened their season in Atlanta in a game against the Pittsburgh Pirates with Mayor Allen throwing out the ceremonial first pitch. Even though the Braves lost the extra-inning game, all the seats in the new stadium were sold, and the next morning newspapers across the country carried the news that professional sports had arrived in Atlanta.

Major league professional sports were new to the South, and the city attracted fans who drove from surrounding states on the developing network of interstate highways that came together near the site where Mayor Allen and Charles Finley had decided the new stadium should be built. The mayor described the new stadium as the "real symbol of the new Atlanta—the single structure that signified our arrival as a national city.... Its baby-blue seats and gleaming light towers glistening in the sun, the stadium was visible and literal proof that Atlanta was a big-league city."[14] Local leaders were not the only ones who recognized the significance of major league professional sports to Atlanta's growth. The former president of the Birmingham Chamber of Commerce, Frank Young, said in a recent interview, "I remember when the Braves franchise moved to Atlanta really, realizing then for the first time that Atlanta was moving into a world all its own and was leaving places like Birmingham and Charlotte and Chattanooga and other places behind."[15] Major league professional sports teams in football and baseball would be reluctant to locate in a city with a toxic racial climate, and the relatively peaceful process of desegregation in Atlanta helped get the edge on other Southern cities.

---

[14] Allen and Hemphill, *Mayor*, 152–53.
[15] Frank Young (former president, Birmingham Chamber of Commerce), video interview, 14 October 2013.

The circular stadium was designed by a local architectural firm known as FABRAP and constructed by Heery and Heery, another local firm. This joint venture's success in building the stadium within one year and under budget enhanced their reputations so that the firms won contracts to design and build other major league stadium projects in Cincinnati and Pittsburgh.[16] According to Cecil Alexander, his partner Bill Finch was responsible for the modern design of the stadiums, and Alexander's role was to secure the contracts.[17] After the success in landing the Braves, the city's leaders convinced the National Football League to award an expansion franchise to Atlanta. The team, the Atlanta Falcons, played their initial regular season game in the stadium in 1966. The multi-purpose stadium also became the home of a professional soccer league team called the Atlanta Chiefs the following year. Among the three sports teams calling Atlanta Stadium home during the 1960s, the soccer franchise won their league championship in 1968.

The name of Atlanta Stadium was changed in 1975 to recognize the role of Fulton County in the Recreation Authority that jointly maintained oversight of the facility. The Atlanta Falcons were dissatisfied with the stadium, and after the 1991 season moved to the new Georgia Dome. The Braves continued to use the old stadium until 1997 when they moved to Turner Field. The old Atlanta-Fulton County Stadium hosted the baseball competition for the 1996 Olympic Games and was demolished the following year.[18]

During the first three seasons in Atlanta, there was little for fans to cheer about at Braves games. In 1969, the team improved and won the Western Division of the National League, losing to the "miracle Mets" in four straight games. If the teams did not provide many winning moments during their early years in Atlanta, there were individual players

---

[16] Robert M. Craig, "FABRAP: Finch, Alexander, Barnes, Rothschild, and Pascal," *New Georgia Encyclopedia*, http://www.georgiaencyclopedia.org/articles/arts-culture/fabrap-finch-alexander-barnes-rothschild-and-pascal (21 August 2013).

[17] Alexander, interview, 30 June 2011.

[18] Fenster, "Atlanta-Fulton County Stadium."

who captured the attention of fans. The most important of these was the home-run hitting outfielder for the Braves, Hank Aaron. He was a black athlete from Mobile, Alabama, who had been a star for the team in Milwaukee, but was concerned about playing major league baseball in a Southern city. In an interview, Aaron remembers the pressure he was under to deliver for his new city: "I knew I had to have a good year in order to sell the fans on my ability because they had never seen me before."[19] Hank Aaron won many fans by hitting so many home runs that the new stadium quickly earned the nickname "the launching pad." By fall 1973, Aaron began closing in on the all-time home run record of 714 held by Babe Ruth. Crowds of fans and members of the media gathered for each home game, hoping to see the hit that would break Ruth's record. The season ended with Aaron's home run total just one behind Ruth—and Aaron received hate mail and death threats from those who resented the success of an African-American athlete.

The 1974 baseball season began with three road games for the Braves. During these games, Hank Aaron hit one home run to tie Ruth's record. When the team returned to Atlanta Stadium on April 8, the game was sold out as people crowded in to watch history being made. His record-breaking home run ended the quest for Aaron to become the all-time home run leader. At the time fans did not realize how difficult this period had been for Aaron. For security against the threats, Aaron had lived at the stadium and even had to endure the stress of a kidnap plot against his daughter, who attended college in Nashville. Instead of joy over the prospect of breaking the record, Aaron felt the time was "probably one of the hardest things that happened to me in my baseball career."[20] Bob Hope, who served as the public relations director for the Braves at the time, said "Aaron was just marvelous. I mean he was such a gentleman in every way and that reflected so well on our city, but also reflected well on the entire race because people watching and saying, how is this man going to react under pressure, and he was a guy that did his

---

[19] Henry (Hank) Aaron (retired outfielder and homerun hitter for the Atlanta Braves), video interview, 21 August 2013.
[20] Ibid.

very best at what he did in his trade. He could not have been classier all the way through that process."[21]

The Braves as a team continued to lose games, and by 1975 there were discussions of moving the franchise to Toronto. Instead, Ted Turner, the owner of a billboard company who had bought a small local cable television station, agreed to buy the team for $11 million. He proved to be a remarkable team owner, marketing genius, and television pioneer. Turner had been televising 100 of the Braves games per year on his cable station, but he needed additional programming to fill air time. The purchase of the Atlanta Braves enabled him to broadcast all of the games. Most other television station owners at the time worried about other stations around the country stealing television signals, especially from sports programming. According to Bob Hope, the thought was if you are televising your baseball game in Atlanta and suddenly somebody steals your signal, they can put it up on a satellite, and show it for free in Phoenix or anywhere in the country. Other station owners felt they would be losing revenue from this, but Turner felt that it was okay for people to steal his signal. If enough people steal his signal, then he would have a network. It took advertisers a while to understand the idea that there were viewers watching Braves' games in places across the nation. Turner used the idea to gain more revenue because the station's signal was reaching a larger audience. Bob Hope said, "People thought Turner was crazy. When we were starting out we were hardly super, but we called it the superstation."[22]

Ted Turner recalled that he bought the Braves like buying a house with a mortgage—no money down and regular monthly payments. What he needed after buying the Braves was people to attend the games. Turner called Bob Hope, his marketing director, and said, "Hope, you and I have the magic touch," adding that they would increase attendance

---

[21] Hope, interview, 8 September 2011.
[22] Ibid.

with promotional activities.[23] As a result, they planned a colorful promotion for every game. Turner remembers pushing a baseball with his nose from third base to home plate in a race against someone pushing a ball from first base toward home plate. The event left Turner's face bleeding, but he was excited to win the competition. The Braves served a spaghetti dinner for fans on the field after one game. At another, radio announcer Skip Caray asked listeners to call in if they would be interested in getting married at home plate after a game. Seventeen couples responded, so the Braves invited all of them to get married together. The superstation had a wrestling match scheduled before the game, so Hope and Turner came up with the promotion for "Wedlock and Headlock Day." Sports writers from across the country loved the Braves' promotional events, and the Braves succeeded in selling tickets during seasons when the team was not playing well on the field.

The new owner of the Braves made one other significant change in the team. He hired Bill Lucas to become the first African-American general manager in baseball history. As Hank Aaron recalled, "It would take somebody like a Ted Turner in order to help put baseball where it should be. He wanted Bill Lucas to be the general manager, so he gave him the job. And it was not just a camouflage job. It was his job to run the organization, and that is what he did. He did a very good job." Aaron added, "I was proud. I was very proud."[24] Lucas had formally been in charge of the well-regarded Braves farm club system and player development within the organization. Lucas remained general manager until his sudden death in 1979 at the age of forty-three. Bill Lucas's role within the organization and Hank Aaron's position as a star of the team sent a message to the city's black community that the Braves accepted African-American leadership and were willing to help change the face of major league baseball.

---

[23] Ted Turner (former owner of the Atlanta Braves and CNN), interview by authors, 9 February 2012, audio, Special Collections and Archives, University Library, Georgia State University.

[24] Aaron interview.

Ted Turner's competitive nature enabled him to win the America's Cup yacht race and to turn the Atlanta Braves into a profitable franchise. Even though the Braves lost more games during their first twenty-five years in Atlanta than any other team in baseball, the purchase proved profitable due to Turner's constant promotion and his innovations in the broadcast industry. Turner Broadcasting System sold the Braves in 2007, but the team is still supported by the airline and the soft drink company. Following the Centennial Olympics in 1996, the stadium built for the Olympics was reconfigured for baseball and renamed Turner Field in honor of the Braves owner, whose competitive nature turned the franchise into the most successful one in baseball during the 1990s.

In the same way that the Braves suffered defeats during their early years playing in the city, the Atlanta Falcons began operations in 1966 and rarely posted winning seasons. The popularity of football in the state and region enabled the team to continue to sell out their games in spite of their poor record. The football franchise was owned by Rankin Smith of the Life Insurance Company of Georgia and his family. During its first dozen years in the city, the franchise posted only two winning seasons, but it remained attractive to fans. In 1991, the Falcons left Atlanta-Fulton County Stadium and moved to a new enclosed stadium known as the Georgia Dome with a seating capacity of 71,000. After years of frustration, the Falcons reached the NFL championship Super Bowl in January 1999, only to lose to the Denver Broncos. The co-founder of the Home Depot, Arthur Blank, purchased the Falcons from the Smith family in 2002, pledging to change the long-time losing team into winners. The Falcons enjoyed some success under the leadership of the coaches hired by Blank and, beginning in 2017, will play in a new stadium with a retractable roof.

Arthur Blank and his co-founder of Home Depot, Bernie Marcus, became wealthy in the process of transforming the building supply retail business. Both men have become leading philanthropists within the city. Marcus has donated funds for a variety of religious causes, children's health initiatives, and the Georgia Aquarium, which has become a major attraction for visitors and residents. Blank has also established a foundation that has provided support for a variety of children's developmental and environmental activities. Although neither Blank nor Marcus is still involved in the management of the company they created, both have become pillars of the Atlanta philanthropic community.

The biracial coalition among business leaders in Atlanta also changed the way in which sports franchises were owned. In 1968, a small group of business leaders (that included developer Tom Cousins, former Georgia governor Carl Sanders, Anne Cox Chambers, and Charlie Loudermilk) bought the St. Louis Hawks franchise of the National Basketball Association and relocated the team to Atlanta. Once the team arrived, the owners invited black businessman Herman Russell to invest in the Hawks franchise. When he joined the ownership group, Russell became the first African American in the nation to share in the ownership of a major league sports team. The Hawks played their games in the Omni Coliseum that had been developed by Tom Cousins. The team enjoyed only modest success on the court in spite of the presence of St. Louis veteran Lou Hudson and drafting an exciting college player, the shooting guard "Pistol Pete" Maravich.

Team sports were not the only professional athletic contests that drew attention to Atlanta. In 1967, the Olympic heavy-weight and undefeated professional champion Cassius Clay was disenchanted with the involvement of the United States government in the Vietnam war. When he was called to report to his draft board for induction into the army, Clay refused, citing the teachings of his new religion of Islam. Clay changed his name to Muhammad Ali, but he was refused status as a conscientious objector to the war, arrested, and stripped of his heavy-weight boxing title. While the appeal of his legal situation wound through the court system, Ali could not fight in most US cities. No boxing commission would issue a license to him; however, Georgia had no state law governing boxing commissions. In 1970, State senator Leroy Johnson was contacted to see if he could arrange for Ali to fight in Georgia. As the man who desegregated the state's general assembly, Johnson had become a powerful and influential member of the state senate. Senator Johnson quickly secured the approval of the mayor, Sam Massell, and the Atlanta City Council. The next step was approval by the staunch segregationist Governor Lester Maddox.

In his meeting with the governor, Leroy Johnson told Maddox that he had an opportunity to put Ali into the ring. He said, "I want to have the fight in Atlanta, and I came to you because you are the governor. I wanted to make sure that you had no opposition to my doing so." Maddox did not start throwing things or anything like that, so Johnson added, "Governor, Ali does not want to go on welfare, and I know how you feel about welfare. He doesn't want to go on welfare, and the only thing he knows how to do is fight. He is a boxer, and that is what he wants to do, and I think he deserves a second chance."[25] Governor Maddox did not object, so Ali was given a license to fight in Atlanta.

The fight between Muhammad Ali and Jerry Quarry took place at the city's Municipal Auditorium in downtown Atlanta. The auditorium held only around 5,000 people, but it marked Ali's successful return to boxing. The political clout of Senator Leroy Johnson was backed by the powerful black business influence of Atlanta Life Insurance executive Jesse Hill and developer Herman Russell. Cities across the US had denied a license for Ali to fight, but Senator Johnson was able to secure it from the city and state governments in Georgia. Ali knocked out Quarry in the third round of the fight in less than nine minutes. Ali would also win his court fight a year later and have his professional heavy-weight title restored. Even though the crowd who saw the fight was small, the context attracted attention throughout the nation. Ali won the title three times, and was named *Sports Illustrated*'s "Athlete of the Century." Near the end of the twentieth century, Muhammad Ali would return to Atlanta as part of the city's greatest athletic moment.

In 1972, Herman Russell and his business partners also acquired a National Hockey League franchise, the expansion team known as the Atlanta Flames. The Flames shared the Omni Complex with the Hawks. In 1977, the majority ownership of both the Hawks and Flames was sold by Tom Cousins to media entrepreneur Ted Turner. The hockey team usually managed to make the playoffs—only to lose in the first round. Attendance suffered in part because Atlanta residents were unfamiliar

---

[25] Johnson, interview, 27 July 2011.

with the sport of hockey. In 1980, Turner sold the team, and the franchise relocated to the cooler climate of Calgary.

The arrival of professional sports in Atlanta validated the claim that the city had attained national prominence and, at the same time, provided a source of civic pride for local residents. Local leaders also regarded the sports teams as important tools for economic development since visiting fans spent money in the city and media outlets provided the intangible benefits of increased national coverage. In many ways, the acquisition of professional sports teams and the building of facilities for the games was a continuation of the traditional "Atlanta Way." Key business leaders required the cooperation of public officials to move their plans forward. Not only did the sports franchises provide an example of black and white athletes representing the city's teams but the ownership also showed the biracial cooperation that was a hallmark of the way things were done in Atlanta. However, decisions made by public and business leaders, beginning with the construction of Atlanta-Fulton County Stadium in the 1960, often neglected the needs of low-income city residents.

The location of the stadium for the Braves and Falcons in the Rawson-Washington Urban Renewal area meant that the city had already declared the area a slum, making the land eligible for acquisition by the city through eminent domain for the use of a public facility that would largely benefit private franchise owners. Under the policy of urban renewal, the owners of properties taken by eminent domain were repaid with federal dollars; however, many of the residents of the areas needed for the stadium and parking lots were renters. Most of these neighborhood residents were simply ordered to move with no relocation assistance provided.

Because it was racially mixed, the Rawson-Washington area was unique among urban renewal areas in the city. Part of the neighborhood consisted of "bottom land" with creek beds whose adjacent banks suffered from poor drainage and unsanitary conditions. Also included in the Rawson-Washington urban renewal district, along Georgia Avenue, were many small businesses that served the community. The stadium construction required that 75 of these small businesses and 948 families (of whom 32 percent were white) relocate. The moves from the urban renewal areas were difficult for both individuals and businesses, which lost their customer base in the process of relocating.[26] This urban renewal policy created a persistent legacy of distrust, not only among families and businesses displaced by the program, but suspicion of other projects planned by city government and business leaders.

There were two major differences between the urban renewal programs and later projects planned by Atlanta's business and public leaders. First, recent projects provided more adequate relocation assistance for churches, businesses, and families displaced for newer sports facilities. Secondly, since 1974, the public officials who negotiated with business leaders were African-American and needed to represent the political interests of their majority black constituents. Since these African-American constituents were often the ones affected by development projects such as new sports facilities, this was a delicate situation for Atlanta's black mayors.

Some scholars describe Atlanta's black mayors, including Maynard Jackson and Andrew Young, as continuing the pattern set by their white predecessors by promoting development in the city even at the expense of the interests of low-income black constituents.[27] One of the strongest of these critics is Adolph L. Reed, Jr., who dismisses the idea that the election of an African-American mayor in cities like Atlanta results in changes in the alliance between the local black public officials and the white business elite. He cites the example of Maynard Jackson's use of

---

[26] Eric Hill Associates, *City of Atlanta, Georgia, Report on the Relocation of Individuals, Families, and Businesses* (Atlanta: Community Improvement Program, 1966) 142. The white families relocated from the Rawson-Washington area were among the few whites in Atlanta moved from urban renewal land. Ninety-one percent of the families moved in the city's urban renewal program were African American, giving some validity to the program's nickname "Negro removal."

[27] For example, see Clarence N. Stone, *Regime Politics: Governing Atlanta, 1946–1988* (Lawrence: University Press of Kansas, 1989) and Clarence Stone, "Urban Regimes and the Capacity to Govern: A Political Economy Approach," *Journal of Urban Affairs* 15/1 (March 1993): 1–28.

the airport location on the south side of the city as an indication of the mayor's skillful ability to define black interests within a pro-growth framework. The regime was able to maintain the support of the black community.[28] Manley Elliott Banks says that each of the black mayors who came after Maynard Jackson was pro-growth and increasingly "more politically conservative than his predecessor."[29] The construction of the Georgia Dome sports facility for the use of the Atlanta Falcons is frequently cited as an example of this conservative pattern of favoring the interests of business leaders over the needs of low-income city residents. However, this controversy over the construction of the indoor stadium illustrates that the balancing act between the desires of downtown business leaders and the needs of the city's low-income residents was more complicated than the term "neo-conservative black political regime" might suggest.

In 1987, Rankin Smith, the owner of the Falcons, announced that he was unhappy with the Atlanta-Fulton County Stadium his team shared with the Braves baseball team. Smith hinted that he would move the team to Jacksonville, Florida, if other arrangements could not be made in Atlanta. This resulted in a flurry of activity with plans by the state of Georgia to join the city and county to build a new indoor stadium called the Georgia Dome. The new facility would be located near the World Congress Center and operated by the same state agency that ran the convention facility. The chosen location for the Georgia Dome presented a problem. The neighborhood around the World Congress Center was a low-income black area known as Lightning and part of a larger community called Vine City. Over the years the downtown business community supported a variety of redevelopment projects proposed for the Vine City area. One plan involved the state's Department of Labor's

---

[28] Adolph Reed, Jr., "The Black Urban Regime: Structural Origins and Constraints," in Michael P. Smith, ed., *Power, Community and the City* (New Brunswick, NJ: Transaction Books, 1988) 86–87.

[29] Manley Elliott Banks, "A Changing Electorate in a Majority Black City: The Emergence of a Neo-Conservative Black Urban Regime in Contemporary Atlanta," in *Journal of Urban Affairs* 22 (Fall 2000): 273–74.

erecting an office building in the neighborhood. Strong community opposition defeated this proposal, suggesting that state government and
business interests do not always prevail in Atlanta politics.

The Georgia Dome proposal was different in several respects. First,
it would virtually eliminate the Lightning neighborhood for the construction of the stadium and nearby parking lots. Next, the proposal not
only was supported by the business community but also enjoyed the support of Mayor Andrew Young, the majority African-American Fulton
County Commission, and the state of Georgia. Finally, there were five
black churches in the immediate area of Vine City that would be harmed
by the proposed stadium. Among the churches was Friendship Baptist,
the city's oldest black Baptist church, which had been relocated previously. This set the stage for a confrontation between Mayor Young and other black elected officials on the one hand and two groups of constituents
who had been among the mayor's strongest supporters: low-income black
neighborhood residents in Vine City and a well-organized coalition of
black ministers. The organization known as Concerned Black Clergy of
Atlanta (CBC) was a large and politically influential group that decided
to use its power to win support for relocation assistance for neighborhood
residents, businesses, and the five churches in the area of the proposed
stadium.

Responding to pressure from constituents, Mayor Young and Fulton County Commission chair, Michael Lomax, promised support for
the relocation assistance. Both leaders said they supported the proposal
to build the Georgia Dome, but they also recognized the need for funds
to relocate residents, businesses, and the churches. The majority black
Atlanta City Council and Fulton County Commission also supported
the two issues of construction of the sports facility and relocation assistance; however, the state was unwilling to accept the financial burden of
the relocation payments. The conflict raged through summer and fall
1988 before the state government agreed to pay $25 million in relocation
assistance. During the following year, detailed agreements were worked
out with the two largest churches in the area. Friendship Baptist Church
would receive money for construction of a buffer to mitigate the worst
impact of the stadium, and Mount Vernon Baptist Church would relo-

cate if the members voted to do so. The three smaller Vine City churches claimed that the initial buyout offers were short of what would be needed to relocate their congregations. The CBC again took up the cause of the three smaller churches, and eventually the state agreed to the demand for added relocation assistance.[30]

The case of the Georgia Dome controversy illustrates the delicate balance that Mayor Young and other African-American public officials needed to strike between pro-development business interests in retaining the professional football team in the city and the interests of neighborhoods affected by the proposed stadium. In contrast to the 1960s when the Braves' stadium was built, the black elected officials needed to respond to both business and neighborhood interests. No mayor wanted to suffer the loss of the city's professional football team to another city. This means couching the construction of the new stadium in terms of the pro-development interests of business leaders and many residents of Atlanta. At the same time, elected public officials needed to minimize the impact of the new facility on neighborhood residents, businesses, and churches. The final agreement on the Georgia Dome managed to keep this balance among competing interest groups. If local residents were not pleased with the decision by their elected officials, they might have punished the mayor and others at the ballot box. The high reelection rate among black leaders suggests that a majority of residents were not dissatisfied with the outcome of conflicts such as the construction of the Georgia Dome.[31] These same conflicts are taking place as the city prepares to tear down the Dome and build a new stadium with a retractable roof for the Falcons in the area of Vine City. Again, neighborhood residents, small businesses, and churches will receive relocation assistance and economic development funds for those who remain in the area. The city's oldest

[30] Harvey K. Newman, "Black Clergy and Urban Regimes: The Role of Atlanta's Concerned Black Clergy," in *Journal of Urban Affairs* 16 (March 1994): 27–29.

[31] Arnold Fleischmann, "Atlanta: Urban Coalitions in a Suburban Sea," in H. V. Savitch and John Clayton Thomas, eds., *Big City Politics in Transition* (Newbury Park, CA: Sage, 1991) 106–108.

black Baptist congregation, Friendship Baptist Church, has agreed to move to a new location as part of the agreement.

If stadium construction has caused tensions within the city's biracial political coalition, sports teams have also united local residents on those special occasions when the teams have achieved success. In 1990, the Atlanta Braves finished in last place within their division of the National League. The following year, they went from worst to first, playing in the World Series against the Minnesota Twins of the American League. The club's owner, Ted Turner, had finally made good on his commitment to improve the performance of the team that drew huge crowds during the regular season and the playoffs. The turnaround of the Braves began in 1985 when Turner hired Bobby Cox as the team's general manager. Cox followed the course set previously by Bill Lucas and rebuilt the team through the Braves' farm system. After five years as general manager, Cox fired the field manager of the Braves and moved to the position himself. Ted Turner hired John Schuerholz to be the new general manager. As manager, Bobby Cox took the team to eight consecutive division championships and five World Series. In 1995, the Braves defeated the Cleveland Indians to become World Champions. More than 500,000 people lined the downtown streets of Atlanta to watch the team and celebrate the victory. During this series of winning seasons, black and white, rich and poor residents of Atlanta could find common ground talking about the Braves. Strong fan support and sellout crowds at the stadium became regular events during the decade of the 1990s.

The city's leadership has long recognized the potential of sports not only to promote the image of the city but also to bring in revenue from fans. One of those events was a college football a post-season game, the Peach Bowl. The event was begun as a fundraiser by the Lions Club in 1968 and took place for three years at Georgia Tech's Grant Field. In 1971, the game moved to Atlanta-Fulton County Stadium, but the outdoor venue suffered from cold and rainy weather. The lack of fan support was something of an embarrassment to the city, so in 1985 the Metro Chamber of Commerce formed a special organization known as the Atlanta Sports Council to take over the management of the Peach Bowl. With more resources, the game sold more tickets and moved from the outdoor stadium to the new Georgia Dome in 1992. Under the management of the Atlanta Sports Council, the game grew in prestige and attracted corporate sponsorship from Chick-fil-a. In 2013, the Peach Bowl became one of the rotating college football playoff sites.[32]

The Atlanta Sports Council broadened its focus to include hosting other collegiate and professional sporting events. When the Georgia Dome became available, the council partnered with city, county, and state governments to invite the National Football League to play the Super Bowl in Atlanta. The league decided in 1990 to award the 1994 game to the city. The city's hospitality businesses were delighted with the decision, which would provide an estimated $150 million boost to the local economy. While the costs to the participating government organizations reduced this impact, Atlanta's leaders looked forward to the media attention attracted by the Super Bowl. The Sports Council considered the event a net benefit to the city and worked with the mayor in a successful bid to host the Super Bowl XXXIV in 2000. There is no doubt that the promotional resources of the Atlanta Chamber of Commerce and the Atlanta Sports Council have contributed to the city's economic development. Among other important sporting events promoted by the council include the Centennial Olympic Games, two NCAA Women's Final Four basketball games, four NCAA Men's Final Four basketball games, three ACC Men's basketball championships, WrestleMania XXVII, two PGA championships, and the MLB, NBA, and NHL All-Star games.[33] The Atlanta Sports Council promoted the Southeast Conference championship football game that moved to Atlanta in 1994 and that is also played in the Georgia Dome.

Another local organization, the Atlanta Track Club, has also worked closely with the Sports Council to promote amateur athletics in the city. Started in 1964 by a small group of track enthusiasts, the track

[32] Chick-fil-a Peach Bowl, "The Bowl: Peach Bowl History," http://www.peachbowl.com/the-bowl/bowl-history/ (accessed 3 July 2015).

[33] Metro Atlanta Chamber of Commerce, "Atlanta Sports Council," http://www.metroatlantachamber.com/docs/default-source/sports-council-files/asc-toolkit_12-31-14.pdf?sfvrsn=2 (accessed 18 March 2016).

club's signature event is the annual July 4th Peachtree Road Race. The 10-kilometer race down Peachtree Street began with 110 runners in 1970, but within a few years formed a partnership with the *Atlanta Journal-Constitution* to expand the race to become the largest race of this distance in the world with 55,000 runners. The Peachtree Road Race also includes a wheelchair event and a variety of related activities, such the Peachtree Jr. for children. The Peachtree Road Race, which attracts top professional athletes as well as recreational runners of all fitness levels, provides an annual opportunity for runners to parade down the city's most famous street from the Buckhead area to the finish in Piedmont Park. The race reflects the mission of the Atlanta Track Club to create an active and healthy Atlanta through world-class events, training programs, and community outreach activities. With more than 21,000 members, Atlanta Track Club is the second largest running organization in the United States.[34]

Atlanta's leaders have made sports an important aspect of the city's life. The biracial partnership between business and political leaders is reflected in the decision-making on stadium and sports facility construction from the initial building of the Atlanta-Fulton County stadium to the present. African-American business leaders such as Herman Russell were able to join the partnership that owned local sports franchises in the city and in so doing set an example that helped the leagues desegregate their ownership structure. At the time of striving for recognition as a city of national importance, Atlanta's leaders recognized that professional sports would contribute to the image they sought for the city as a place of national importance. While these professional teams have not always achieved consistent success on the field, fans are often able to find common ground to support the local franchises. This has been especially true of professional football, since this sport is the most popular with fans in the city and state. Professional hockey has been the least favorite sport with two franchises—first the Atlanta Flames and more recently the At-

---

[34] Atlanta Track Club, "Mission," http://www.atlantatrackclub.org/mission (accessed 3 July 2015).

lanta Thrashers—that have failed to draw large crowds on a regular basis. Both relocated to more hockey-friendly cities in Canada. The North American Soccer League's Atlanta Chiefs achieved success on the field but did not draw large crowds during its brief time in the city. With a larger and more diverse metropolitan population, Arthur Blank, the owner of the Falcons, plans to bring a new Major League Soccer team to Atlanta in 2017 and the opening of the new stadium.

College and other amateur sports continue to play an important part in the city with a fan base supporting local teams and large numbers of participants in individual sports. The Atlanta Sports Council, with the support of the Metro Chamber of Commerce, provides leadership that makes many athletic events in the city possible and helps draw national attention to Atlanta through the sponsorship of events like the Peach Bowl and NCAA championship games. The council also worked with other local leaders to garner international attention as host to the 1996 Centennial Olympic Games.

The vision of Atlanta leaders regarding the role sports could play in the promotion of the city was realized. Mayor Ivan Allen's gamble to bring a professional baseball team to Atlanta was the start of a winning development formula for the city, setting a standard for each amryo that followed.

Herman Russell with Atlanta Hawks player Lenny Wilkins
(Russell Collection)

Ted Turner and Bill Lucas
(Courtesy of Rubye Lucas)

10

Creative Class—Arts, Culture, and Media

Atlanta is a city born through the application of creativity and imagination. The city's leaders invented the ideal of "A brave and beautiful city," and Atlanta has grown through audacity, imagination, and innovation. Without harbors, rivers, or other natural resources, its primary tools for growth were creativity and human capital. The pattern of creativity and imagination is applied in a variety of contexts: in the promotion of the city itself, the evolution of social and political arrangements, and the approach to business. Coca-Cola, the world's most famous soft drink, created a beverage category, invented the independent bottler system as a mechanism for production and distribution, and perhaps created the market itself through advertising. Creativity and imagination are seen in Alonzo Herndon's development of the Atlanta Life Insurance Company, the partnership between William Hartsfield and Atlanta's black community on matters of economic growth, Dr. King's vision of American's potential, John Portman's design of the Hyatt Regency, Ted Turner's conceptualization of CNN, the evolution of Southern hip-hop, and Andrew Young and Billy Payne reaching for the Centennial Olympics.

In 1960, metropolitan Atlanta had a population of one million. In the era of racial segregation, even a listing of the top 25 metro areas of the United States would not include Atlanta, Georgia. By the 2000 Census, the Atlanta metropolitan area was among the top ten most populous regions in the United States.[1] As the work of modern cities moved away from industrial production and physical labor toward knowledge and creative work, Atlanta's creative approach to race relations paid unexpected dividends. It was a bold move for a segregated Southern city to proclaim

---

[1] U.S. Census Bureau, "Population Distribution and Change: 2000–2010," March 2011, Table 3, 6.

itself "too busy to hate." Atlanta became an island of tolerance in the South, a haven for innovative, non-traditional thinkers and their diverse personal characteristics of race, religion, sexuality, and national origin.

Scholar Richard Florida argues that creativity is the driver of the modern economy. The workers who define the "Creative Class" are "people in science and engineering, architecture and design, education, arts, music and entertainment, whose economic function is to create new ideas, new technology, and new creative content. Around the core, the creative class also includes a broader group of *creative professionals*." Atlanta was rich in a diverse constellation of educational institutions in the early 1960s. Economic growth depended on whether those young people stayed in Atlanta for their careers. In *The Rise of the Creative Class*, Florida describes the "3T's of economic development: talent, technology and tolerance. Each is a necessary but by itself insufficient condition: To attract creative people, generate innovation and stimulate economic growth, a place must have all three." Florida created a "Creativity Index" designed to measure the presence of talent, technology, and tolerance in a given metro area. The Atlanta Metro area was tied with Denver for number 13 on this index of 268 regions with more than one million in population. Houston and Dallas, in the heart of oil country, were the only major Southern cities ranked higher. One oversight in Florida's listing of creative class occupations is that he does not include the chefs, event planners, and hoteliers who make up the hospitality industry, a core industry in Atlanta. Nevertheless, it is a useful theory that helps to explain Atlanta's extraordinary transformation. Florida's creative capital theory states "regional economic growth is powered by creative people, who prefer places that are diverse, tolerant and open to new ideas."[2]

From the time of the post-Civil War Reconstruction Era, Atlanta leaders embraced moderation on race relations for economic reasons, from impressing Northern industrialists after the Civil War to attracting

---

[2] Richard L. Florida, *The Rise of the Creative Class: And How It's Transforming Work, Leisure, Community and Everyday Life* (New York: Basic Books, 2002) 8, 247–49.

investment after World War II. It was a wise choice that included encouraging the flourishing of higher education institutions serving African Americans as well as whites, both women and men laying the foundation for a modern, knowledge-based economy and a welcoming environment for diverse members of the creative class. There are many examples of tolerance, technology and talent that are among the essential components in the making of modern Atlanta.

Tolerance

People with new ideas and creativity are attracted to place with an atmosphere of tolerance. Two couples, Martin Luther and Coretta Scott King and Andrew and Jean Childs Young, were members of DuBois's "Talented Tenth," African Americans who were expected to use their educational opportunities to lift their own community.[3] Each had the opportunity to earn graduate degrees from educational institutions in the North and leave the South—and Jim Crow segregation—permanently. Committed to service, they attempted to serve in other Southern cities. They found that their talents and families could thrive in Atlanta. The city's relatively tolerant racial climate, the presence of Dr. King's family, the network of African-American institutions, and the transportation network made it an ideal base of operations for Dr. King's new organization, the Southern Christian Leadership Conference, founded after the success of the Montgomery Bus Boycott. As a result of his choice to return to Atlanta, the city became the intellectual center of the civil rights movement with the offices of SCLC and SNCC, the Student Nonviolent Coordinating Committee, led by Atlanta Student Movement leader Julian Bond and Nashville sit-in veteran John Lewis. Veterans of

---

[3] *The Negro Problem: A Series of Problems by Representative American Negroes of Today,* W.E.B. DuBois, "The Talented Tenth", ed. Booker T. Washington (New York: James Pott and Company, New York, 1903) 31. W. E. B. DuBois objected to the emphasis that Booker T. Washington placed on industrial education. He argued that African-American leaders needed a classical liberal arts education. The Youngs and the Kings earned liberal arts degrees.

the movements in Montgomery, Alabama; Nashville, Tennessee; Charleston, South Carolina; St. Petersburg, Virginia; and the Freedom Rides converged on Atlanta. Dr. King's ideas of non-violence and civil rights emanated from Atlanta. It was that vision that attracted Andrew Young and many others to Atlanta. Young had initially planned to go to a training program in Tennessee, but an intolerant state government closed the site known as the Highlander Folk School, calling it a communist training center. Young recalled, "I had a grant to train local leaders, we said we were trying to train the people who were natural leaders in the community. We defined it as the people who had PhD minds but who never had a chance to get an education...like Fannie Lou Hamer."[4]

Young found a place with Dr. King's organization in Atlanta. From offices on Auburn Avenue, Young planned to travel to recruit local leaders across the South and bring them to workshops at Dorchester Center, an old American Missionary Association school in South Georgia. Atlanta would be a base and that would "give me an opportunity to be in the movement but not in the mix of it," Young said. Atlanta served as a safe haven from the perils of the movement, especially for Dr. King, because "everywhere he went his life was at stake, and he didn't want to throw it away. He had been bombed, his home had been bombed, he had been jailed a number of times, he'd been sued by the state of Alabama, the bus company, and everybody else. He had been stabbed in Harlem."

---

[4]Fannie Lou Hamer was born into a family of sharecroppers in rural Mississippi and never had a chance to receive formal education. When she attempted to register to vote in 1962, Hamer was pushed off the cotton plantation where she had lived and worked. She became a civil rights activist, worked for the Student Nonviolent Coordinating Committee, and became a founder of the Mississippi Freedom Democratic Party that brought national attention to the struggles of African Americans in her home state. When Hamer died in 1977, Andrew Young gave her eulogy, saying, "None of us would be where we are today had she not been here then." Young said that the progress of the civil rights movement had been made through "the sweat and blood" of activists like Hamer. On her tombstone is written one of her most famous statements: "I am sick and tired of being sick and tired."

Auburn Avenue pulsated with the creative energy of the civil rights movement and the business activity that gave the street its nickname, "Sweet Auburn." One of the people who was witness to this scene was a young woman named Rita Samuels who had moved to the city from the small Georgia town of Forsyth. After coming to Atlanta, Samuels took a job working as a secretary for the SCLC. She recalls that Auburn Avenue was filled with such hustle and bustle that "It took Dr. King forty minutes to walk three blacks down the street" as people wanted to stop him and talk.

As the movement expanded to Selma, Birmingham, and Mississippi, Atlanta remained the staging area, the intellectual center. Civil rights workers poured into Atlanta from around the United States. Jean Young "was an active supporter of her husband's work, and they opened their home to civil rights workers needing food and/or shelter."[5] The Quakers and other groups hosted group homes for the activists, who would come into Atlanta before being deployed to Albany, Georgia; Selma, Alabama; Chicago, Illinois; and Cleveland, Ohio. Atlanta was teeming with people who were social justice strategists, planners, organizers, writers—people dedicated to designing a new society based on equality, a society without racism, and fighting in the war on poverty. Working together they applied creative non-violence to challenge the policies and practices of centuries of injustice toward African-Americans.

Following the successful passage of the Civil Rights Act of 1964 and the Voting Rights Act of 1965, King, Young and others focused on the crisis of poverty. The poverty of African-Americans, especially in the rural South brought Dr. King to tears. In his last Sunday sermon he told of his visits to America's poor, "I would remind you that in our own nation there are about forty million people who are poverty stricken.... I have just been in the process of touring many areas of our country and I must confess that in some situations I have found myself literally cry-

---

[5] Andrea Young, *Life Lessons My Mother Taught Me* (New York: Tarcher/Putnam, 2000) 87.

ing."[6] It was during the mobilization for the Poor People's Campaign March on Washington, the Dr. King took a detour to the garbage worker's strike in Memphis. Young remembered that when King was killed, "I just got mad…for him leaving us, I said you drag us into this and you going up to heaven with your reward and leave us with all this hell, you know I did not know where we would go or what we would do. But I realize he had done all that he could but, I didn't understand then that even though his body was gone his spirit will remain with us."

Immediately after Dr. King's assassination, his widow, Coretta Scott King sought to preserve his legacy and the message of non-violent social change, establishing the Martin Luther King, Jr., Center for Non-Violent Social Change with the support of Andrew Young, then executive vice president of SCLC. "Coretta had her own sense of mission," Young remembered. She had her own gift for leadership and truly came into her own making speeches for Martin against the Vietnam War. She wanted to train people in non-violence. Young continued, "Coretta tenaciously set about establishing the Martin Luther King Center for Non-Violent Social Change to preserve and share Martin's legacy into the twenty-first century."[7]

Long before Mrs. King succeeded in establishing Dr. King's birthday as a national holiday, she convened world leaders in Atlanta to observe King Week with workshops on non-violence and an international interfaith service on Dr. King's birthday. Atlanta developer Blaine Kelley, a white Presbyterian, was pleased to be asked by Jesse Hill, the Center's board chair, to join the advisory board. Kelley said, "I was asked to…be the moderator over the Monday Morning Ecumenical Service and…every year there would be some prominent guest of honor, Jimmy Carter, George Bush, Sr., I remember, and Bill Clinton…. It was a big deal, and I was impressed that the little King Center was quite an epi-

---

[6] Martin Luther King, Jr., *A Testament of Hope: The Essential Writings of Martin Luther King, Jr.*, ed. J. M. Washington (San Francisco: Harper and Row, 1986) 272.

[7] Andrew Young, *An Easy Burden: Civil Rights and the Transformation of America* (New York: Harper Collins, 1996) 479.

center of something good."[8] The presidents were joined by civil rights leaders, international peace activists, labor leaders, and major figures in human rights struggles around the globe.

Mrs. King also established the Historic District Development Corporation to preserve and improve the neighborhood around the King birth home. She and Jesse Hill went to see Henry Ford II, the CEO of the Ford Motor Company, for the lead gift to build a center to preserve Dr. King's legacy. Her special assistant, Benetta Ivey, came to Atlanta to work with Julian Bond and spent more than a decade traveling with Mrs. King as she supported the causes of peace, non-violence, freedom in South Africa, women's rights, and human rights. She remembers that Mrs. King was determined to "institutionalize the teachings of Dr. King. She very carefully built the infrastructure to do that—she reissued his books, she developed the archives, she build a building to house the work, she brought in Dr. Clayborne Carson, an African-American professor at Stanford to build the collection of Dr. King's papers, every speech, every letter painstakingly documented in multiple volumes."[9] As part of the King Center, Mrs. King built a plaza and reflecting pool as a resting place for the marble crypt that holds Dr. King's earthy remains on Auburn Avenue. Next door is the Ebenezer Baptist Church where Dr. Martin Luther King, Jr., his father, Martin Luther King, Sr., and grandfather, A. D. Williams, had all served as pastor. The area was designated the King Historic District and included the King birthplace. Mrs. King ensured that the vision of Dr. King for a world where, "justice rolled down like water and righteousness like a mighty stream," would never be forgotten, and the King Center ensured that vision would forever be linked to Atlanta.

---

[8] Blaine Kelley (former developer and CEO, Landmarks Group), interview by authors, 20 January 2012, audio, Special Collections and Archives, University Library, Georgia State University.

[9] Benetta Ivey (former special assistant to Coretta Scott King), interview by authors, 24 November 2015.

Atlanta was firmly established as a city that could host a center that continued the work of an international figure when Jimmy Carter's presidency ended. The Carter Center and Presidential Library were developed in partnership with Emory University and the National Archives. Initially conceived as a place for mediation, the Carter Center programs expanded to promoting peace and good health around the globe. As with the King Center, Andrew Young was an adviser and founding board member. The fundraising campaign for a building to house the library and the Carter Center, where President and Mrs. Carter would continue their international humanitarian work, was led by Ivan Allen III, the son of Mayor Allen. The largest pavilion at the Carter Center was named in honor of the mayor's son.

From this base near downtown Atlanta, President and Mrs. Carter toured the globe observing elections, advocating democracy, eliminating diseases, and promoting a core philosophy around the things that make for peace and hope. Former president Carter described his work in a press conference:

> We deal with individual people in the smallest and most obscure and suffering villages—in the deserts and in the jungles of Africa. We've had programs in 80 different countries for the poorest and most destitute people in the world. And that has been, I'd say, far more gratifying personally, because we actually interact with families and with people who are going blind...or who have Guinea worm and so forth. Going into the villages and learning about the people and what the actual needs are, then meeting those needs with a superb Carter Center medical staff, I think, has been one of the best things that ever happened to me.[10]

President Carter is the first to acknowledge that his rise to prominence was enabled by the civil rights movement. He took Rita Samuels from SCLC into the governor's office, the first African-American woman to serve in the office of the governor, and to the White House. It is well known that he selected Andrew Young as his ambassador to the

---

[10] President James Earl (Jimmy) Carter, Jr., transcript of press conference, Atlanta, The Carter Center, 20 August 2015.

United Nations largely because of Young's relationship with King. The Freedom Park surrounding the Carter Center includes two of Atlanta's most iconic works of public art, *Homage to King*, a sculpture that portrays Martin Luther King, Jr., in the act of waving to crowd at the March on Washington by Xavier Medina-Campeny and *The Bridge* by self-taught Alabama artist Thornton Dial that commemorates civil rights leader John Lewis and the struggle for the right to vote in Selma, Alabama.

The Carter Center and the King legacy are both a result of and a have made immeasurable contributions to Atlanta's culture. These institutions are the result of Atlanta's journey from legally mandated segregation and social separation of the races, through periods of accommodation and tolerance, to an era of striving for inclusion and the celebration of diversity. They are repositories of the history of that struggle, as well as the wisdom born of that struggle. As internationally significant entities that broadcast a message of civil and human rights and respect and concern for the well-being of each human being around the world, they also burnish the city's reputation for tolerance.

Technology

New technology typically evolves as the solution to a fresh set of problems. Atlanta was behind Los Angeles and New York in developing the technology for the telecommunications industry. Thanks to the vision, creativity, and tenacity of Ted Turner, Atlanta was first to develop the technology and expertise to send and receive news, continuously around the world, twenty-four hours a day. Turner came to Atlanta as a very young man, having inherited a billboard company following his father's tragic suicide. Turner became a larger-than-life presence, demonstrating boundless energy and determination in his pursuits, whether the America's Cup of sailing or the favor of one of America's most fascinating women, Jane Fonda. As Hartsfield foresaw that the future of transportation was moving from rail to air, Turner anticipated the movement of advertising from billboards to television.

Turner began by acquiring a small television station with a signal so weak that Turner could not get it at his own home. He conceived the notion of a "superstation" using the new satellite technology at a time when Atlanta lacked an uplink to the new system. Undaunted, Turner enlisted Glen Robinson of Scientific Atlanta, whose company developed the cable-to-satellite connections that enabled Turner to connect his station across the nation. Since he owned the Braves, Turner had access to quality programming at no additional cost, so the baseball games of the Atlanta Braves were seen around the country. The fledging cable industry was in search of programming and television stations that would allow it to compete with free, broadcast signals. The success of the "superstation" confirmed that there was a role for specialized niche stations.

Turner went into the cable news business in part because at the time cable television was not regulated by the Federal Communications Commission (FCC). Turner said, "If we go straight onto the cable and we have a news channel, the FCC has no say at all over what we put on the air."[11] Another issue was the larger, well-established broadcast networks, whose stations televised news only at six o'clock in the evening. Turner thought people might want to get their news around the clock, so he started the Cable News Network (CNN).[12] Bob Hope began working with Turner as a public relations assistant with the Atlanta Braves baseball team. "He [Ted] wanted to be the first person on earth to be able to communicate with everyone," recalled Hope, "and show everyone what it's like to be in the other guy's shoes. One man's terrorist is the other man's freedom fighter. He wanted to show both sides of the story in a war so people would understand each other and come together and bond."[13]

Ted Turner wanted his station headquartered in Atlanta rather than New York, Los Angeles, or Chicago. He felt that the business climate in his hometown was better suited to his start-up media empire. While

---

[11] Robert (Bob) Hope (retired public relations director, Atlanta Braves), interview by authors, 8 September 2011, audio, Special Collections and Archives, University Library, Georgia State University.

[12] Wyatt Thomas (Tom) Johnson (retired president of CNN), interview by authors, 17 November 2011, audio, Special Collections and Archives, University Library, Georgia State University.

[13] Hope interview.

some business leaders thought Turner was crazy to try to build a television empire around the Braves and cable news, there were some who were willing to support his efforts. Among these were Tom Cousins, a real estate developer who built the Omni Center and eventually sold it to Turner who renamed it the CNN Center. Other supporters included Glen Robinson of Scientific Atlanta, whose company developed the cable-to-satellite connections that enabled Turner to connect his stations across the U.S. and eventually around the world. Two of Atlanta's largest corporations, Delta and Coca-Cola, also purchased advertisements on the superstation that helped assure the profitability of Turner's networks. "No one in this city had anymore devotion to the city of Atlanta than he did," said Hope. Turner lived on top of CNN Center in a tiny apartment and was known to pick up trash around the building.[14]

As he had with Bill Lucas and the Atlanta Braves, Turner continued to seek out the best talent, regardless of race. Bernard Shaw made history at CNN as the first African-American anchor of a network prime-time broadcast. Ted Turner remembered, "He knew something about journalism. I didn't...when we started off, all the other guys had white males as their lead anchors. And our lead anchor was a team of a woman (Mary Ann Williamson) and a black man. So I thought it was real good."[15] Shaw continued in the anchor chair for twenty years, covering the first Gulf War live from Bagdad.

CNN was for Atlanta in the late twentieth century what Ralph McGill's column had been in the middle of the century. Anne Cox Chambers, former chair of Cox Communications, remembered her father's intentionality in promoting a message of tolerance: "My dad put Ralph McGill's columns on the front page because he was against segre-

---

[14] Ibid.
[15] Ted Turner, Special Event, "A Farewell Tribute to Bernard Shaw," Aired 2 March 2001, 5:30 p.m. ET, CNN.com Transcripts, http://transcripts.cnn.com/TRANSCRIPTS/0103/02/se.07.html.

gation and wanted to promote a New South."[16] Cox Newspapers and McGill used the communications media of their era to spread the value of tolerance and promote an end to segregation in Atlanta and around the Southeast. Turner's CNN spread the awareness of Atlanta around the world. Tom Johnson was a Georgia native who had worked in President Johnson's White House. He came to head CNN from a post as publisher of the Los Angeles Times. He said,

> When Ted asked me to become the president of CNN in 1990, I said, "Ted, what is it that you want of your next president of CNN?" And he said, and I quote him precisely, he said, "I want it to be the best news network on the planet, pal. I want it to be the best network on the planet, pal." And I said, "What else?" He said "That's it, that's it.... Your job is to make it the best news network on the planet."

He remembered that he put Turner to the test for the coverage of the first Gulf War. He requested funds for independent satellite access and communication from the hotel in Baghdad that housed anchor Bernard Shaw, foreign correspondent Peter Arnett, and others:

> So, sure enough, I think it was January 16, 1991, Allies attacked, all the communications go down, all the signals for NBC, CBS, ABC, the BBC, and everybody else totally lost, and there we are. At that time, you know, CNN was called the "chicken noodle network" by some of our competitors. Well, we showed that through the technology and the resources.... And you know, and then Bernie he started, when it first came out, he said "The skies over Baghdad are illuminated." I'll never forget those words.[17]

CNN was able to broadcast the allied invasion of Iraq live from the Al Rasheed Hotel in Baghdad. CNN joined Coca-Cola as an Atlanta-born company, known and valued around the world.

Turner Broadcasting includes CNN and an ever-expanding group of cable networks and programming adjacent to the campus of the Geor-

---

[16] Anne Cox Chambers (owner of Cox Communications), interview by authors, 19 April 2013, audio, Special Collections and Archives, University Library, Georgia State University.

[17] Tom Johnson interview.

gia Institute of Technology. Turner's creative vision generated countless problems for engineers and other members of the creative class to solve. As problems were solved, new jobs were created and business opportunities expanded. Atlanta was not merely a consumer of entertainment programming, but a producer with all of the technical expertise to create, produce, and distribute information and entertainment around the world. Ted Turner realized his dream of creating a platform that could be used to promote mutual understanding around the world, through the simple means of sharing information. He later continued that commitment with a $1 billion donation to the United Nations. Although CNN was careful in its neutrality, Andrew Young remembered a dinner with Ted Turner, Jane Fonda, Tom Johnson, former first lady Rosalynn Carter, and former president Jimmy Carter. Young looked around the table and commented, "Atlanta has developed its own capacity to influence international affairs."

Talent

Andrew Young says, "Atlanta was always an international city, we just didn't know it." That global interaction may explain the aspiration to imagine a more important city and embrace art and culture. Many of Atlanta's civic, business, and political leaders had international experience and exposure. Robert Woodruff, as president of Coca-Cola, ran a global business. The presidents of the Atlanta University Center schools were well traveled. Dr. Benjamin E. Mays, president of Morehouse College, served on the board of the World Council of the YMCA and had attended the induction of India's first elected prime minister, as well as international conferences in Geneva and London. Anne Cox Chambers, who became publisher of the family-owned *Atlanta Journal and Constitution* newspaper, was educated at the exclusive Miss Porter's School for Girls in New York and had a love affair with French culture that began as a student in Paris.[18] Later in her life, Anne Cox Chambers was ap-

---

[18] Amanda Heckert, "Anne Cox Chambers: A conversation with the famously private billionaire," *Atlanta Magazine*, 20 July 2011,

pointed by President Carter as the US ambassador to Belgium where she made important contributions to European diplomacy. The mother of Maynard Jackson, Atlanta's first black mayor, earned a doctorate in French at the University of Toulouse.[19] While they did not have scholarship or research to anchor their positions, these leaders knew from their international experience that in order for Atlanta to become an important city it must have arts and culture. The arts are the very heart of the creative class. The arts nurture and enhance the creativity of other disciplines and help attract the most talented of the engineers, designers, educators, and creative professionals to a community.

Two tragedies galvanized the city to mobilize resources to support art and culture. One was the funeral of Martin Luther King, Jr., an event of international significance that focused the attention of the world on Atlanta. The other event was a plane crash outside Paris. On June 3, 1962, more than one hundred Atlanta civic leaders and patrons of the arts died in a crash as their plane was departing Orly Field.[20] Mayor Allen flew immediately to Paris to take charge of the crisis. The victims of the crash were members of the Atlanta Arts Alliance and leading figures in Atlanta's small arts community. Laura Jones Hardman, civic leader and daughter of Boisfeuillet Jones, the former president of the Woodruff Foundation, remembers the Orly tragedy as a "devastating event that wiped out the city's art patrons." Atlanta paid tribute to those who died, and almost immediately efforts began to build an arts center to honor their memory. The Woodruff Foundation made a gift of $4 million. Laura Jones Hardman observed,

---

http://www.atlantamagazine.com/great-reads/anne-cox-chambers1/#sthash.NuUaA5Q3.dpuf (accessed 17 November 2015).

[19] Gary M. Pomerantz, *Where Peachtree Meets Sweet Auburn* (New York: Penguin Books, 1996) 231.

[20] Donald R. Rooney, "Orly Air Crash of 1962," *New Georgia Encyclopedia*, http://www.georgiaencyclopedia.org/articles/history-archaeology/orly-air-crash-1962 (30 August 2013).

The Woodruff Arts center is an example of support for the city. Mr. Woodruff himself was not a particular connoisseur of the arts, but he really understood the value of the arts in the community, and so he invested in the art center which is now named for him. It wasn't named for him until much, much later because you know he did many other things anonymously. Simply, after the tragic Orly incident I think [that] Atlanta coming together to build an arts center had a big impact in this city and has been supported by Coca-Cola, by Mr. Woodruff, and many, many others in Atlanta.[21]

Anne Cox Chambers described how she "learned philanthropy from her parents," and was among the city's leaders who responded. She and twelve other women founded the Forward Arts Foundation in 1965.[22] The following year, construction began on the arts center that would house the Atlanta College of Art, the Alliance Theater, the Atlanta Symphony, and the High Museum of Art. Anne Cox Chambers's philanthropy in Atlanta continues with a gift of $6.1 million for a new wing of the High Museum that is named in her honor.

Fifty years after the tragedy, Pearl Cleage was artist-in-residence at the Alliance Theater and wrote a poem that captures the vision of the dedicated Atlanta arts patrons who perished in the Orly crash:

It began with a dream; a big dream,
And a big idea about what it took to be a world class city,
To be a place fully engaged in the international flow of art and ideas. It be-
    gan with you.
Your actions were intentional.
You already knew that the city you loved could not prosper without the
    presence of artists to show ourselves to ourselves,

---

[21] Laura Jones Hardman (civic leader and trustee of Emory University), interview by authors, 7 May 2012, audio, Special Collections and Archives, University Library, Georgia State University.
[22] Chambers, interview, 19 April 2013.

And then to the wider world you already knew was waiting to welcome us.[23]

Talent in Atlanta often developed along disparate paths, and the arts and culture were no different. At Atlanta University, there was another avenue to promoting the arts in the city. The painter and educator Hale Woodruff, with the support of President Rufus Clement, organized an "Exhibition of Paintings by Negro Artists" in 1942. This was the first national juried exhibition of artworks by African-American artists in the United States. The national jury included artist Aaron Douglass, from Fisk University, another institution founded by the American Missionary Association. Continuing the tradition of biracial collaboration that was part of the legacy of Atlanta University, Louis Skidmore, director of the High Museum, was also a member of the jury. This became an annual event that developed a generation of collectors and artists. According to art historian Dr. Amalia Amaki, "It became a principal gathering place for people in the arts and a source of collecting and gaining information about art and artists for patrons, collectors, would-be collectors, and arts enthusiasts."[24] Following their arrival in the 1961, Andrew Young's wife, Jean, and Lillian Miles (who later married civil rights leader John Lewis) were among the art enthusiasts who attended the exhibition each year. The exhibition series known as the Atlanta University Annuals continued until 1970 and resulted in Atlanta University acquiring more than 350 works of the leading African-American artists of that period. Margaret Borroughs, African-American artist, reflected on her participation in the Annuals in a volume commemorating the seventieth anniversary of the annual art competition:

---

[23] Pearl Cleage, "Wish You Were Here (In Memoriam)," https://www.woodruffcenter.org/~/media/Sites/www,-d-,woodruff,-d-,org/About-Us/wish-you-were-here-by-pearl-cleage.ashx?la=en (accessed 1 December 2015).

[24] Amalia Amaki and Andrea Barnwell Brownlee, *Hale Woodruff, Nancy Elizabeth Prophet and the Academy* (Seattle and London: Spelman College Museum of Fine Art in association with University of Washington Press, 2007) 36.

For most of us, the Atlanta Show provided the first memory, the first mention and the first knowledge of the black arts presence...through this great cultural vehicle, founded by Hale [Woodruff] and nurtured by this great University, through this Annual, Atlanta because an oasis in the Southern desert, not only for the black artists of the South, but for those also in the East and West as well.[25]

The Atlanta University Annuals established Atlanta as a premier venue for the best in African-American creative expression. In 1973, Atlanta University came together with the High Museum of Art to organize a touring exhibition titled "Highlights from the Atlanta University Collection of Afro-American Art" with the opening event held at the High Museum featuring Hale Woodruff.

In November 1973, at Maynard Jackson's inauguration, an internationally acclaimed opera singer, who had performed for Queen Elizabeth and who was accompanied by the Atlanta Symphony, sang for the new mayor. The singer was Mattiwilda Dobbs, the aunt of the new mayor and one of the six daughters of John Wesley Dobbs. Michael Lomax, president of the United Negro College Fund, was an English professor at Spelman College at that time. He observed, "It was an olive branch to Atlanta's white arts community and a huge signal of the cultural sophistication in the black community."[26]

Jackson's commitment to the arts may have flowed in part from his own family history. Valerie Jackson recalled that Maynard Jackson came "from a family that has a strong, creative sense—the music. His aunt, Mattiwilda Dobbs, the great opera singer, the first black to sing at LaScala...all of those girls, those Dobbs sisters, all had to take piano while they were in school for ten years, so there was a lot of singing and piano playing and so forth and that legacy was even carried over into our

---

[25] *In the Eye of the Muses: Selections from the Clark Atlanta University Art Collection*, eds. Tina Maria Dunkley and Jerry Cullum (Atlanta: Clark Atlanta University, 2012) 25.
[26] Michael Lomax (president and CEO, United Negro College Fund), interview by authors, 11 January 2013, audio, Special Collections and Archives, University Library, Georgia State University.

family." Another aunt, Millicent Jordan, encouraged Jackson to establish an ad hoc committee on the arts that was chaired by Shirley Franklin, who later was the first woman to be elected mayor of Atlanta. Eventually, Maynard Jackson's commitment to the arts led to the creation of the Bureau of Cultural Affairs with Michael Lomax as the first commissioner. Valerie Jackson recalled the mayor's values with respect to the arts:

> He set up the special bureau, the Bureau of Cultural Affairs, because he really believed that art, that public art is a very influential force on developing a sense of community because if there is a piece of art out on display and it belongs to the city, that means it belongs to everybody. The people can feel a sense of ownership if nothing else but in that piece of artwork, and they can also see an opportunity for creativity and imagination, and both of those things were very important. Maynard and I strongly believed in the power of the imagination. So, art triggered something in the soul and I think when your soul is touched you have a tendency to be a better human being.[27]

Lomax remembered that while the white community had the symphony and the High Museum, the African-American community had talent with "no place to showcase it, no way to make a living."[28] The important Atlanta University art collection was housed in the basement of Trevor Arnett Library. Morehouse was producing students such as actor Samuel L. Jackson and director Spike Lee with no theater in which to practice their craft. Through the Bureau of Cultural Affairs, Lomax was able to hire artists and to make grants. A neighborhood arts center was established on Atlanta's south side. Federal funds from the Comprehensive Employment and Training Administration (CETA) program were used to staff the center. Maynard Jackson's own family offered proof that careers in the arts need not be limited to wealthy people with trust funds. He acted to expand opportunities for careers in the arts with long-term results for the role of the arts in Atlanta.

In 1980, Atlanta Life Insurance Company under the leadership of Jesse Hill sponsored a national art competition in the spirit of the Atlan-

---

[27] Jackson, interview, 18 November 2011.
[28] Lomax interview.

ta University Annuals. According to Henrietta Antonin, the choice to host an art competition emerged from the need to choose art for a new headquarters building. Antonin selected professor of art and culture Richard Long and artist and art historian Samella Lewis as judges for the competition. Opening night was a black tie affair in the atrium of the new building with an overflow crowd. One VIP guest of Ms. Antonin was Michael Lomax, the commissioner of the bureau of cultural affairs, soon to be chair of the Fulton County Commission. One evening, Lomax shared with Antonin, "Henrietta, this is just so wonderful.... I wish we could do something like this, not just with the visual arts, but with theater and music and everything.... I'm going to have a national black arts festival."[29]

In 1988, Fulton County, the city of Atlanta, the National Endowment for the Arts, the Georgia Humanities Council, forty-seven corporations, and fifty-eight independent arts organizations came together to present the first-ever National Black Arts Festival. The ten-day festival featured eight artistic disciplines, including the visual arts, dance, theater, and music. More than 500,000 people attended the festival that included more than 2,000 artists participating in 124 events involving 344 presentations. An additional 1200 people took advantage of educational workshops and master classes offered through the festival.

The arts continued to expand under Andrew Young as mayor of Atlanta. The Atlanta Jazz Series offered free concerts in the city's Piedmont Park and Grant Park with funding from the city of Atlanta, the National Endowment for the Arts, and local companies. Famous jazz musicians including Miles Davis, Sarah Vaughn, and Wynton Marsalis (like Young, a native of New Orleans) performed as part of the Jazz Series.[30] Mayor Young's tenure featured a continuation of the special relationship between Atlanta's art community and France with an International Arts and Cultural Exchange—two years of exchanges between Atlanta and the French Ministry of Culture. Young extended the one percent for the

---

[29] Antonin, interview, 15 July 2011.
[30] Horton, *The Young Years*, 288–90.

arts program, a legacy program begun by Maynard Jackson in 1977 to ensure the presence of public art in all new capital projects that included public financing. The new city hall building commissioned during Young's administration included $300,000 for new works of art to grace the new building. The architect, Paul Muldawer, created an atrium inspired by the Toulouse City Hall that could be a gathering place for Atlanta citizens. Lev Mills won the commission to design a floor for the atrium, and internationally-known sculptor Elizabeth Catlett created a figurative relief. Other public art pieces around the city included a sculpture commissioned for Margaret Mitchell Square, in honor of the author of *Gone with the Wind*.[31]

One legacy of the National Black Arts Festival can also be found in the emergence of Atlanta as a production center for music and film, especially entertainment reflecting the experience of African Americans in the South. In 1989, Antonio "L.A." Reid and Kenneth "Babyface" Edmonds relocated to Atlanta from Los Angeles and established LaFace Records. Shanti Das, an Atlanta native, began working for the duo following her graduation from Syracuse University. She recalled their focus on "quality, protecting the brand. Their success generated a lot of revenue that was used to invest in new talent." Christine White, an entertainment attorney, remembered the impact of OutKast, a Grammy Award-winning duo formed in Atlanta in 1992, and the rise of Southern hip-hop as a distinctive sound: "Prior to OutKast, hip-hop was dominated by the New York and Los Angeles urban youth. OutKast brought a high level of attention to the sound of urban young black people in the South, demonstrating that 'Southern' was not the same as 'country.'"[32] "They [OutKast] were the first to wear the baseball caps with the "A" and make references to Atlanta neighborhoods, to our community in the music. It gave us a sense of pride, and people in Atlanta embraced the sound, the quality instrumentation, the melodies," remembered Shanti Das.[33] Atlanta continued to consume music from New York and Los

---

[31] Ibid.

[32] Christine White, telephone interview by the author, 29 November 2015.

[33] Shanti Das, telephone interview by the author, 29 November 2015.

Angeles, but increasingly the city replaced that music with its own sound and began to export the Atlanta sound. Urban writer Jane Jacobs described how the local economies of cities grow through *export replacement*. "Cities that replace imports significantly replace not only finished goods but, concurrently, many, many items of producers' goods and services."[34] Thus, CNN and hip-hop became examples of Atlanta's development as a city capable of producing for a global economy. The city developed its own entertainment and media, challenging New York in news and music. As the capacity to produce entertainment and media expanded, more producers were attracted to Atlanta.

The base of talent attracted Tyler Perry, a producer of movies and popular television programs, including two comedy shows for Turner Broadcasting. Perry moved to Atlanta in 1992 to begin writing and producing plays. His commercial success led to the formation in 2008 of Tyler Perry Studios, the first major film studio in the US owned by an African American. Tyler Perry Studios occupies several buildings near the airport.[35]

Atlanta developed a reputation as the Motown of the South. Music producers such as Dallas Austin and filmmakers such as Rob Hardy and Will Packer combined Atlanta's tradition of African-American entrepreneurship with black cultural consciousness, creating music and film that expressed the culture of an urban South. Lomax's dream was coming true. The talented young people in Atlanta were finding a way to create studios and production companies—creating an economy around arts and culture.

---

[34] Jane Jacobs, *Cities and the Wealth of Nations: Principles of Economic Life* (New York: Random House, 1984) 38.

[35] Jared W. LaCroix, "Tyler Perry," *New Georgia Encyclopedia*, 19 February 2016.

The Cultural Olympiad

Atlanta's cultural legacy was an important part of the city's presentation of the Olympic Games in 1996. The Cultural Olympiad has its roots in the Paris Games of 1906. The original concept involved performers in artistic competitions and evolved into a showcase for the arts and culture of the hosting region. In Atlanta, this was expressed as the city competed for serious recognition as a community rich in the arts. As the city prepared to host the world, this was an opportunity to showcase the creative genius of African Americans and their contributions to American art. The Atlanta University Art Collection was rediscovered as one of the city's precious heirlooms and funds were allocated by the Cultural Olympiad to renovate a gallery for proper display of the collection for the guests who would be arriving from around the world.[36] Cultural historian Richard Long attributes the renovation of the galleries to the persistence and vision of Tina Dunkley, who came to Atlanta to serve as director of the art gallery at Georgia State University, but who was drawn to the collection she found in the basement of the Trevor Arnett Library of Clark Atlanta University (CAU). President Thomas Cole invited her to CAU where she oversaw the restoration of the gallery and developed a series of projects to document and tour the collection.

The High Museum invited J. Carter Brown, the director emeritus of the National Gallery of Art in Washington, DC, to curate a special exhibit for the 1996 Olympics. The exhibit, "Rings: Five Passions in World Art" included significant works of art from nearly every major world culture and great museums from the Hermitage in Russia to the Tokyo National Museum in Japan.[37]

Accompanying the "Rings" exhibit was an equally important exhibit showcasing the African-American culture of the South. "Souls Grown Deep" was conceived by Atlanta art collector William Arnett, who had

---

[36] Brenda Thompson, "A Collectors View," in Dunkley and Cullum, eds., *In the Eye of the Muses*, 8–9.

[37] Roberta Smith, "Esthetic Olympics, In 5 Shades for 5 Rings," *New York Times*, 4 July 1996.

spent a number of years collecting the art of self-taught African-American artists. Jerry Thomas, legal adviser to Arnett, remembered the tension and controversy around the "Souls Grown Deep" exhibition:

> Many in Atlanta wanted to show the world it dealt with world class Western art. There was real resistance to showcasing the work of self-taught, uneducated black people. But this art was the visual representation of the culture that produced the civil rights movement, the culture of John Lewis and Coretta Scott King and Fannie Lou Hamer. This was the culture of the rural churches around Thomasville, Georgia, that taught Andrew Young to be a leader. This was authentic culture of the South.[38]

The art critic of the *Los Angeles Times* wrote,

> The engrossing exhibition is "Souls Grown Deep: African-American Vernacular Art of the South," organized by the Carlos Museum at Emory University but handsomely installed in out-of-the-way galleries in City Hall East. The sprawling show expands upon a groundbreaking display of black American folk art that traveled the United States in the early 1980s. Some 500 works by 30 self-taught Southeastern artists have been selected, chiefly from the collection of Atlanta resident William Arnett. Among them are paintings and sculptures by such celebrated figures as James "Son" Thomas, Bessie Harvey, Mose Tolliver, Thornton Dial and Nellie Mae Rowe, together with those of compelling younger artists new to me, including Lonnie Holley and Mary Tillman Smith.[39]

The "Souls Grown Deep" exhibit did for African-American self-taught artists what the Atlanta University Annuals had done for trained artists. It was a turning point in the recognition of these artists. Arnett later developed a catalogue on the exhibit with a foreword from Andrew Young, who wrote, "'Souls Grown Deep: African-American Vernacular Art of the South' documents and celebrates the achievements of visual

---

[38] Jerry Thomas, interview by the author, 25 November 2015.

[39] Christopher Knight, "Wins, Losses of Olympic Proportions," *Los Angeles Times*, 4 July 1996.

artists who, in the preacher's style, were moved to speak and called out to the world."[40]

The arts were nurtured in Atlanta, for black and white, creating a synergy of tolerance, technology, and talent that is critical to attracting and holding the workers who set the pace in a modern economy. As tolerance, technology, and talent converged in Atlanta, the effect prompted economic and population growth. One important outgrowth of a climate that attracted the creative class was the transformation of the communication industry and the emergence of an entirely new industry for the city—entertainment. CNN, Turner Broadcasting System, Cox Communications, public investments in the arts, the emergence of a distinct music scene for hip-hop and R&B have resulted in a film and entertainment industry that produced an economic impact statewide of more than $6 billion in 2015, 75 percent of that in the city of Atlanta, according to LaRonda Sutton, director of the city of Atlanta's Office of Entertainment.[41] In a series of events that reflects the "Atlanta Way," the first tax incentives that nurtured the film industry in Atlanta were proposed by African-American music producer, Dallas Austin, to Georgia's Republican governor, Sonny Perdue.

Atlanta's creative ideas, policies, and practices around tolerance and human rights were transmitted to international audiences. The ideas that emanated from Atlanta gave it an impact and influence far beyond its economic power and amplified the "soft power" of the United States. Joseph Nye, former dean of the Kennedy School of Government, Harvard University, uses the term "soft power" as "the ability to get what you want through attraction rather than coercion or payments. It arises from the attractiveness of a country's culture, political ideals and policies."[42]

---

[40] Andrew Young, "Life Behind the Wall: A Call to Respond," in Paul Arnett and William S. Arnett, eds., *African American Vernacular Art of the South*, vol. 1 of *Souls Grown Deep* (Atlanta: Tinwood Books, 2000) 4.

[41] *Atlanta Business Chronicle*, "Atlanta's booming film industry will only continue to grow," 13 November 2015.

[42] Joseph Nye, *Soft Power: The Means to Success in World Politics* (New York: Public Affairs, 2004) preface.

Nye refers to Coca-Cola and CNN as examples of soft power derived from the appeal of American culture. Coca-Cola® was the first American consumer product to be available around the world. So dedicated is the company to global market penetration that rather than withdraw from South Africa during the anti-apartheid sanctions campaign, the company turned the bottling operation over to ownership by black South Africans. The strategy was developed by Carl Ware, a former president of the Atlanta City Council who joined the Coca-Cola Company in 1979. [43] Since its founding, CNN has represented the American values of free speech and an open society around the world.

The quiet and relentless work of the Carters as they travel the globe, connecting with people in nations such as China, Egypt, and Panama around elections and democracy; Ghana and South Sudan around Guinea worm eradication; and Colombia, Liberia, and Cyprus to promote peace. The Carters' work has benefited millions of people in more than eighty countries.[44] The global goodwill generated by this work of a former American president and his devotion to the work of the Carter Center in waging peace, fighting disease, and building hope is immeasurable.

The unique contribution of African Americans in arts and entertainment, the Carter Center, and the communication platform that was CNN have all been critical components of Atlanta's ability to be a presence on the global stage. Among Atlanta's most significant exports in recent years have been its culture and values. The city's diversity has been its signature brand as Atlanta moved from rejecting hate to embracing difference, inclusion, and love.

Atlanta has no more influential cultural export than the vision of Dr. Martin Luther King, Jr., and the inspiration of his nonviolent movement to end racism, war, and poverty. Around the globe, when people stand for peace and justice, one can discern the influence of Dr.

---

[43] Carl Ware (former member of Atlanta City Council and senior vice president, Coca-Cola Company), video interview, 22 April 2014.

[44] Trip Reports by Former President Carter, http://www.cartercenter.org/news/trip_reports/index.html.

King. His anthem "We Shall Overcome" was sung when the Berlin Wall came down, it was sung by the solidarity movement in Poland, and during the pro-democracy Tiananmen Square protests in China. In 2011, an Egyptian human rights activist translated into Arabic a comic book on Dr. King and the Montgomery Bus Boycott for circulation among young Egyptians.[45] King's legacy and vision are of the United States living up to its best and highest ideals, "the true meaning of its creed, that all [people] are created equal."[46] In his lifetime, he expanded that vision to include all the people of the world. Accepting the Nobel Peace Prize on Human Rights Day, December 10, 1964, Dr. King said,

> After contemplation, I conclude that this award which I receive on behalf of that movement is a profound recognition that nonviolence is the answer to the crucial political and moral question of our time—the need for man to overcome oppression and violence without resorting to violence and oppression. Civilization and violence are antithetical concepts. Negroes of the United States, following the people of India, have demonstrated that nonviolence is not sterile passivity, but a powerful moral force which makes for social transformation. Sooner or later all the people of the world will have to discover a way to live together in peace, and thereby transform this pending cosmic elegy into a creative psalm of brotherhood. If this is to be achieved, man must evolve for all human conflict a method which rejects revenge, aggression and retaliation. The foundation of such a method is love.[47]

Emma Darnell, the first woman to head a cabinet agency in the city reflected,

> We have folks coming here from all over the world…it's an intangible something here that basically is something spiritual. I believe that as long as we have it we'll always be different and we'll always be stronger and we'll always survive. You know, it's not the skyline, not the Olym-

---

[45] David A. Love, *The Griot*, 2 February 2011,
http://thegrio.com/2011/02/02/eygptians-draw-inspiration-from-civil-rights-movement-comic-book/.
[46] King, *Testament of Hope*, 217.
[47] Ibid., 224.

pics, not the Falcons, not the Aquarium. It's that grave down there on Auburn. And what it represents.[48]

---

[48] Emma I. Darnell (former city commissioner of administrative services and vice chair, Fulton County Board of Commissioners), interview by authors, 31 January 2012, audio, Special Collections and Archives, University Library, Georgia State University.

Coretta Scott King, Bishop Desmond Tutu, Jean and Andrew Young
(Young Family Collection)

Ted Turner, Jane Fonda, and Herman Russell
(Russell Collection)

11

The Olympic City—The World Comes to Atlanta

At 7:47 a.m. on September 18, 1990, the president of the International Olympic Committee, Juan Antonio Samaranch, stepped to the podium in Tokyo and made the dramatic announcement that "The International Olympic Committee has awarded the 1996 Olympic Games to the city of...Atlanta." These were the surprising and unexpected words that opened a new era in the city. Atlanta was a long shot to win the bid for the 1996 Games. The announcement was a surprise because even though Atlanta was an emerging, progressive Southern city, few people thought it could compete with Athens, Greece, the birthplace of the original Olympics and the site of the first modern Olympics in 1896. With other major cities such as Melbourne, Australia, and Toronto, Canada, also in the competition, many observers did not give Atlanta much of a chance. Sam Williams of the Atlanta Chamber of Commerce recalls naysayers: "Are you kidding? Athens had the Games a hundred years ago, they're gonna get it again, this is the centennial, why are you even bothering to think about it?"[1] Civic leader Laura Jones Hardman remarked, "Of course it was a crazy idea. I mean who in the world would have thought the Olympics would have been here?"[2] In spite of its status as an underdog in the bidding competition, Atlanta's leaders were hopeful. *The Atlanta Journal* had two cover stories ready to go—one saying Atlanta lost and the other saying "It's Atlanta." When the word came from Juan Antonio Samaranch, the winning headline became one of the most famous

---

[1] Sam Williams (initial executive director, Research Atlanta, and retired president and CEO, Metro Atlanta Chamber of Commerce), 6 November 2013, video interview.

[2] Laura Jones Hardman (civic leader and trustee of Emory University), interview by authors, 7 May 2012, audio, Special Collections and Archives, University Library, Georgia State University.

in the newspaper's history. Billy Payne recalls feeling on that day not joyful for the victory, but

> total, complete, almost indescribable exhaustion. The process to get to that particular moment and all the stress associated with it for so many years, then, you mix in the emotions of the moment. You had a sense that the whole city and state was relying on you to hopefully bring home good news. It was certainly the most physically and emotionally draining moment of my life.

Atlanta Organizing Committee (AOC) member Charlie Battle said, "I'm excited, I'm elated. I'm shell-shocked. I can't express it. I'm at a loss for words." Next, the organizers, Billy Payne, Andrew Young, Charlie Battle, and others faced the monumental task of staging the Olympic Games.[3]

Major League sports were a winning strategy to help solidify Atlanta's reputation as a city of national importance. The physical sports infrastructure would aid the city's pursuit of the Olympic Games and the ultimate goal of becoming an international city. The long and arduous road to the games began in 1987 with a partnership of civic-minded volunteers, led by attorney Billy Payne. On February 8, 1987, Payne formed the Georgia Amateur Athletic Association with the support of the "Atlanta Nine," Peter Candler, Ginger Watkins, Horace Sibley, Tim Christian, Cindy Fowler, Charles Battle, Jr., Linda Stephenson, and Charles Shaffer for the express purpose of bringing the Olympic Games to Atlanta.[4]

Andrew Young was the next essential supporter of the Olympic vision. "We decided we were going to host the Olympics, not as a city project, but as a private sector venture. There were nine families that said, 'Look, we've been making plenty of money and we're doing well. We

---

[3] Joel Provano and Mike Morris, "Remembering the 20th Anniversary of Atlanta's Olympic Moment," *Atlanta Journal-Constitution*, 17 September 2010, 1.

[4] "The Official Report of the Centennial Olympic Games," ed. Ginger Watkins, Ginger, The Atlanta Committee for the Olympic Games, vol. 1 (Atlanta: 6 Peachtree Publishers, 1997) 6.

want to do something for our city.... And if you will help us, we want to start preparing to bid for the Olympics." Young pledged his support for the Olympics as a public-private partnership, consistent with his vision of public purpose capitalism—public purpose funded with capital from the private sector. He would sanction an Olympic effort based on the model for financing an Olympic Games established by Tom Bradley, the first African-America mayor of Los Angeles during the 1984 games with businessman Peter Ueberroth as the chair of a non-profit corporation having responsibility for raising the funds and managing the games. Ueberroth went on to be Commissioner of Baseball.

To sustain a privately funded venture, Billy Payne needed the support of the Metro Atlanta Chamber of Commerce. He presented his vision to the executive committee of the Chamber. Developer Blaine Kelley was present for the meeting.

> Payne said, "It's time for Atlanta to go after the Olympic Games," and he said, "Here's why I think we can do it, and I think we can do it without government money. But I am coming to you first, the Atlanta Chamber of Commerce, to see what you think." And I was in the room and we were asked, "Those of you who are here, are you willing to put up the seed money to begin to make this happen?" And the Executive Committee, to a person, including me, agreed to each put up $10,000 and that was the seed money that got Billy Payne started.[5]

Having won local support, the "Atlanta Nine" began to move through the process of winning designation from the US Olympic Committee as the United States contender for the Games, before moving to compete for final designation by the International Olympic Committee.

For decades, Atlanta's leaders had carefully built a culture of cooperation and an infrastructure for a modern city. Atlanta's approach to its Olympic bid highlighted the culture of Southern hospitality and the city's civil rights legacy, as well as the facilities. The bid documents in-

---

[5] Blaine Kelley (retired developer and CEO, Landmarks Group), interview by authors, 20 January 2012, audio, Special Collections and Archives, University Library, Georgia State University.

cluded a video with appearances by Andrew Young and Martin Luther King III, son of the civil rights leader. Atlanta's strengths were cited: "a world class airport; existing sports venues;... ample hotel rooms, an extensive rapid rail and bus transportation system; experience handling large masses of people because of the city's large convention industry."[6]

In September 1987, Atlanta's bid documents were delivered in person to the US Olympic Committee headquarters in Colorado Springs with the personal touch that would characterize Atlanta's vision and strategy for winning and hosting the Games.

Atlanta was among fourteen US cities vying to participate in the bidding to the IOC. In January 1988, the executive board of the US Olympic Committee met in Atlanta, and the welcome extended to the delegates helped to narrow the field to Atlanta and the Twin Cities—Minneapolis-St. Paul. In April 1988, Atlanta was selected by the US Olympic Committee as the US candidate city to host the 1996 games. In November, the Atlanta Committee for the Olympic Gamers (ACOG) was formed with Andrew Young as chair and Billy Payne as president. The groups' Olympic games logo was entitled, "Atlanta: A Star on the Rise," with five "A's" as a star formation for Atlanta's attributes: access, accommodations, ability, athletics, and attitude.[7] The next step was the development of an official bid to present to the IOC. Four other cities also wanted to host the Olympic Games, including Athens, Greece, the site of the revival of the modern Olympic movement in 1896.[8]

The team of Billy Payne, Mayor Young, and the other AOC members had the task of convincing the world that their city was a worthy candidate for the Olympics. Young's extensive network of international friends got to work lobbying Olympic Committee members in countries like Japan, Germany, and the Netherlands. Young explained his role:

[6] Watkins, *Official Report of the Centennial Olympic Games*, 7.
[7] Ibid., 9.
[8] Maria Saporta, "The Atlanta Olympics '96: What it means to business," *Atlanta Journal-Constitution*, 18 September 1990, A-6.

I got the African countries and the Caribbean countries. Roberto Goizueta of Coca-Cola got the Hispanic countries. There were six countries for people of Indian descent, and in our case, R. K. Sehgal[9] invited
all of them to his house. Atlanta's Polish community invited the Polish
delegates. We had the Chinese community here invite Chinese from
Taiwan, Singapore, Hong Kong, and Mainland China—all at one
time. And so, the bid just had to be orchestrated.

Atlanta's Official Bid for the 1996 Olympic Games was a two-volume
document outlining details for the city's plans to host the event, including proposals for all aspects of the Games, including venues for sporting
competitions, financial support, and accommodations for guests. The bid
highlighted the fact that Atlanta was an experienced convention city with
more than 50,000 hotel rooms and more under construction. Another
selling point was transportation with a huge, world-class airport and rapid rail system to downtown. The bid also mentioned the city as the
birthplace of Martin Luther King, Jr., and Atlanta's proud, peaceful history of civil rights. Early corporate support for the AOC came from local
corporations such as the Coca-Cola Company and the Citizens and
Southern National Bank (later, Bank of America). Their efforts merged
with other groups such as the Atlanta Track Club, which staged a five-
kilometer race with all of the participants wearing AOC T-shirts to impress a visiting delegation of IOC members in September 1989. The race
showed the strong support of local amateur athletes for Atlanta's bid and
was hailed as the largest race of that distance in the world. If IOC delegates could not come to Atlanta, then members of the local organizing
committee traveled throughout the world to meet individually with IOC
delegates and press for their support for Atlanta's bid. Mayor Young's
reputation as former US ambassador to the United Nations was an asset

---

[9] R. K. Sehgal is an accomplished business executive serving as chief executive officer and chairman of Law Companies, vice chairman and chief executive
officer of H. J. Russell & Company, Commissioner of Georgia, Industry, Trade
and Tourism, and an international advisory board member of First Data Corporation.

in the pursuit of votes.[10] One IOC delegate who supported the city's efforts was Anita DeFrantz, a former member of the US rowing team and Olympic athlete. DeFrantz summarized Atlanta's bid: "This was the message to the world: Come to Atlanta, the American South is a part of the world you have not visited. We have great traditions here of family and faith and community, and we can take care of your athletes when they come here and meet their test with history."[11]

In September 1990, the IOC held its selection meeting in Tokyo, where a large delegation (more than 350 people) from Atlanta was on hand to represent the city. While a specially selected band played and a youth choir sang, representatives of the AOC such as Billy Payne and Andrew Young lobbied intensely on behalf of the city. The members of the IOC deliberated for two days, with many members favoring Athens as a sentimental choice over Toronto, Manchester, and Melbourne. Finally, the delegates made a selection, and IOC president, Juan Antonio Samaranch, made the dramatic announcement that the Olympic Games were awarded to Atlanta. A crowd of several thousand people gathered in Underground Atlanta to watch the news of the announcement, and many others joined them in a day-long celebration. There was a ticker-tape parade down Peachtree Street with more than a half million people welcoming Billy Payne, Mayor Andrew Young, and other delegates as they returned from Tokyo.[12]

Maynard Jackson returned to office as mayor following two four-year terms by Andrew Young. Jackson had a vision for the city and the opportunity provided by the Olympics. Jackson described the challenge of preparing for the Olympics as climbing the "twin peaks of Mount

---

[10] Atlanta Committee for the Olympic Games, *Welcome to a Brave and Beautiful City*, vol. 1, and *Atlanta: A City of Dreams*, vol. 2, Atlanta's Official Bid for the 1996 Olympic Games (Atlanta: Peachtree Publishers, 1990).

[11] Anita DeFrantz (former Olympic athlete and medalist, member of the International Olympic Committee), video interview, 8 March 2014.

[12] Bert Roughton, Jr., and Karen Rosen, "City explodes in thrill of victory as Athens is defeated on 5th vote," *Atlanta Journal-Constitution*, 18 September, 1990, A-1.

Olympus." The first peak symbolized the effort to put on the Games themselves, while the second represented the effort to improve Atlanta in significant ways. For Mayor Jackson, this improvement meant using the Olympics as an opportunity to revitalize some of the city's low-income neighborhoods. The task of putting on the Olympics fell to the AOC, which expanded and became the Atlanta Committee for the Olympic Games (ACOG). In an unprecedented move, Billy Payne moved from his position of leadership on the bid committee to become the head of ACOG charged with the tasks of raising the money, building the venues, and staging the Olympics.

Mayor Jackson's commitment to using the Olympics to improve the city led to the creation of another organization, the Corporation for Olympic Development in Atlanta (CODA). Jackson had a difficult time finding someone to head CODA and an even more difficult time finding money to support the work of the organization. Long-time city employee Clara Axam accepted the position, but when she reported to her office, she was the only staff member. The following day, she had her mother come to the office in order to answer the phone. To overcome the lack of resources, Axam used student and faculty volunteers to survey neighborhood leaders. Mayor Jackson proposed a special tax on tickets for sporting events in the city to fund CODA, but when that failed to gain support, he suggested adding a one-cent sales tax. Neither proposal was given serious consideration by the Georgia legislature. Without public sector support and with limited contributions from businesses and foundations, CODA largely abandoned its neighborhood redevelopment program. It focused the limited funds it was able to raise on improving sidewalks, lighting, and signage, as well as planting street trees on streets near Olympic venues. CODA also placed public art in several plazas and parks that were highly visible during the Olympic Games. Combined with the cultural Olympiad this expanded the environment for art in Atlanta.[13]

---

[13]Clara Axam (former president, Corporation for Olympic Development in Atlanta and consultant), interview by authors, 13 November 2012, audio, Special Collections and Archives, University Library, Georgia State University.

The challenge of raising money was not limited to CODA. The task of building venues and other expenses would run to more than $1.58 billion—of which around $650 million would go to construction costs. Unlike previous Olympics in Montreal, Seoul, and Barcelona, public sector support for the Olympics in Atlanta was limited. In the federal system in the United States, local governments are largely on their own to finance events such as the Olympic Games. In other parts of the world, cities receive support from their national government in order to pay for the development costs associated with Olympic preparation. The Olympics are regarded as an event that will showcase not only the host city, but also a nation such as Korea or Spain that seeks to attract visitors and investment. ACOG had to follow the example of Los Angeles and rely on the sale of broadcasting rights, ticket sales, and corporate sponsorships to finance the bulk of the construction and operating expenses. ACOG formed an array of partnerships and official licensing agreements with 110 companies for products ranging from imported cars (BMW and Nissan), domestic cars (General Motors), watches (Swatch), salad dressing (Vidalia Onion Vinaigrette), clothing of all sorts, and sports equipment. As a result of this corporate support, the Atlanta Olympic Games did not run up the public debt incurred by Montreal in 1976. The state of Georgia contributed some assistance for security and for the construction of the Olympic Village, which would later be converted into dormitories for local public universities. The federal government also made a contribution for security, transportation, trees, and infrastructure improvements.[14] While these efforts to raise money did not provide the sort of windfall profit that the 1982 Los Angeles Olympics generated, ACOG did generate a small surplus of $10 million after all costs were paid. This money was divided between the IOC and the USOC.

Since the start of construction on Atlanta's airport, Mayor Jackson insisted on 20 percent minority contractor or joint ventures in all public works. This percentage had been increased to 35 during Andrew Young's administration. When the Olympic contracts were put out for bid, the

---

[14] Newman, *Southern Hospitality*, 260–61.

minority business development requirement was increased to 40 percent. The Equal Employment Opportunity Program of the Atlanta Games was developed in 1991 and approved by ACOG, becoming one of the first policies adopted after the awarding of the Olympics to the city. When several white business firms complained, Andrew Young, who was no longer mayor but was a key leader in ACOG, reminded them that the Olympic construction program was adding to the growth of Atlanta. The remaining 60 percent of the contracts in a growing city would benefit everyone. Young's diplomatic skills convinced the business leaders to proceed without delay. The 40 percent minority contracting requirement gave opportunities for many new African-American and women-owned businesses to compete successfully for Olympic-related projects. For the first time in Olympic history, all venues in Atlanta were also required to comply with federal Americans with Disabilities Act (ADA) require-ments for accessibility. According to former city attorney and lawyer for ACOG, Marva Brooks, this requirement was a new phase in the civil rights movement. Brooks had served Maynard Jackson in the implemen-tation of policies to include minority businesses in city contracts and was sensitive to Andrew Young's reputation as a civil rights leader. As the first African-American woman to serve as Atlanta's city attorney, she embraced the ADA requirements as another stage in the city's journey to create a genuinely inclusive community. While the ADA requirements added complexity to the design and construction of projects such as the Centennial Olympic Stadium, the result was greater convenience for spectators with mobility challenges.[15]

Brooks helped to guide the Atlanta bid for the Olympics. When the contracts arrived from the International Olympic Committee, there were two copies, one in English and the other in French. Brooks, who had studied French, knew that the French version was more punitive than the English version. She carefully read the French version and helped the city to negotiate more favorable terms from the IOC. Brooks left city

---

[15] Marva Brooks (former city attorney), interview by authors, 7 March 2012, audio, Special Collections and Archives, University Library, Georgia State University.

government in 1990 and moved into private legal practice with the Atlanta law firm of Arnall Golden Gregory, LLP. A year later, Brooks became associate general counsel for ACOG, retaining the position from 1991 until 2000, when ACOG had completed all reports and distributed its assets. Books and Shirley Franklin were the two highest ranking women involved in the Atlanta Olympics. Brooks returned as a partner with Arnall Golden Gregory until her retirement. In 2007, Marva Brooks received the Margaret Brent Award from the American Bar Association for her lifetime of service to the legal profession.[16]

Shirley Franklin began her active participation in the city when she served as a volunteer in Maynard Jackson's 1973 campaign for mayor. Jackson appointed Franklin to serve in his administration as commissioner of cultural affairs. Andrew Young recognized Franklin's experience working in city hall, so he asked her to lead the transition team prior to Young's taking office as mayor. Once in office, Young named Franklin to the position of chief administrative officer, the first woman to serve in this capacity. Her knowledge of how to get things done in the city made Shirley Franklin a valuable member of the leadership team at ACOG. Her official title was vice president of external relations. In this capacity, Franklin worked closely with Marva Brooks and others to implement the Equal Employment Opportunity Program. Brooks and Franklin say that ACOG provided full participation of small, minority, and women-owned businesses in virtually every aspect of the Olympic preparation from design to execution. Much of this participation occurred on the construction of the facilities, achieving record levels of private sector work. Additionally ACOG created successful construction- and sports broadcasting-training programs and incorporated area artists and arts organizations in a variety of special events. In 2001, Shirley Franklin ran

---

[16] "2007 Margaret Brent Awards, Marva Jones Brooks," American Bar Association, http://www.americanbar.org/content/dam/aba/migrated/women/ bios/BrooksBio.authcheckdam.pdf (accessed 9 September 2015); John Manasso, "Former City Attorney shaped city, paved way for women," *Atlanta Business Journal*, 24 September 2007, http://www.bizjournals.com/atlanta/stories/ 2007/09/24/smallb5.html (accessed 9 September 2015).

for mayor and was elected, becoming the first African-American female to serve as mayor of a large Southern city. Franklin credits the mentoring of Maynard Jackson and Andrew Young for her election. In that office, Franklin led an overhaul of the city's dilapidated sewer system, instituted many efficiencies in Atlanta's government, and developed a tough new city ethics policy to promote honesty and transparency for city employees and those who do business with the city.[17]

Local politics also played a role in the planning for the Olympics. After a single four-year term, Maynard Jackson decided in 1993 that he would not seek reelection later that year. In a relatively brief campaign, city council member Bill Campbell was elected mayor. While there was some promise of his administration continuing the close partnership that had existed with the city's business leaders, there was also concern about preparations for the Olympics. One of these concerns was the desire to build a permanent legacy of the Centennial Olympic Games in downtown Atlanta. Following a lunch meeting between ACOG president Billy Payne and the chairman of the Coca-Cola Company, Roberto Goizueta, the two men proposed the redevelopment of an area west of downtown that was filled with warehouses, a few small businesses, and several shelters for the homeless. In a complex public-private partnership, the land for a new park was acquired by the state of Georgia with funds contributed by the business community. The sale of commemorative bricks used in the sidewalks of the park provided additional financial support for the project. The Centennial Olympic Park was located near the state-operated Georgia World Congress Center, so that the construction and maintenance of the new park were the responsibility of the state. This freed the project from any potential delay by the city. With such strong support from business leaders, the new mayor, Bill Campbell, also supported the new park and hailed it as part of an effort to revitalize the area around it after the Olympics. Centennial Olympic Park was a popular gathering place for spectators during the Games. Unlike

---

[17] Shirley Clarke Franklin (former mayor, City of Atlanta), video interview, 1 May 2015.

the competition venues, there was no admission price, so thousands of people packed into the park from its opening in the mornings until late at night. ACOG built an Olympic "Fountain of Rings," whose jets of water were choreographed to lights and music. The fountain was also popular with children and adults as a place to splash and cool off during the warm summer days and nights. Olympic sponsors put up temporary pavilions in the area, and AT&T constructed a stage and amphitheater in the park for concerts.[18]

An entrepreneur and close friend of Mayor Bill Campbell convinced the city leaders that the Olympics could provide an opportunity for revenue from sales in kiosks and vending carts on city streets, parks, and sidewalks. Under the contract with the city, Atlanta's government would receive at least $2.5 million from the sales by vendors operating on public property. IOC officials, visiting journalists, and many of the vendors were unhappy with the program, which lined the sidewalks with temporary wooden stalls offering food and souvenirs. The vendors who were sold rights to locations on streets that failed to attract crowds filed claims against the city for more than $25 million. The stalls operated by the vendors on busy streets obscured many of the streetscape improvements made by CODA and created an image problem that was criticized by many of the visiting journalists.[19]

One key ingredient in staging the Olympics was the recruitment and training of an army of volunteers that eventually numbered more than 42,000 people. The task of the volunteers was to provide warm Southern hospitality to visitors from the corporate sponsors, IOC and national Olympic officials, and sports federation executives from around the world. Many of the visitors stayed in the official "Olympic Family Hotel," the Marriott Marquis, and other downtown luxury hotels. ACOG's staff included "guides" assigned to escort VIPs during their stay in Atlanta, as well as uniformed volunteer drivers assigned to motor pools located near hotels and venues. Other volunteers provided greet-

---

[18] Newman, *Southern Hospitality*, 272–74.

[19] Ronald Smothers, "Atlanta Vending Contract Angers Olympics' Sponsors," *New York Times*, 12 November 1995, 1, 10.

ings and information, medical assistance, ticket taking, security, translating, help in athletic venues, and a variety of other tasks. Each volunteer was given training, credentials, and a uniform. In spite of the heat and humidity of the Georgia summer, the crowds of visitors, and the traffic jams, the legions of blue, green, and white shirted volunteers were given high praise for providing "gobs of Southern hospitality."[20]

One volunteer who joined the effort during the earliest preparations for the Games was civic leader Dianne Wisner. Lacking a defined role, she saw the need to answer the telephones in the office of the Atlanta Organizing Committee and began coming into the offices early in the mornings to answer calls. One morning she answered a call from country singer Garth Brooks, who wanted to know what he could do to help the Olympic cause. Wisner had heard of the ancient Greek tradition of an Olympic peace in which city-states at war with one another would observe a truce during the Games. There were several ways to update this tradition such as the sponsored program in which local families would open their homes to the families of Olympic athletes. Wisner suggested to Brooks that perhaps another way to continue the Olympic peace tradition would be for the singer to give a performance to raise money for a worthy cause. From that early morning phone call, Garth Brooks agreed to give a personal contribution of one million dollars on behalf of the children of the world through the United Nations Children's Emergency Fund (UNICEF). Brooks also sponsored five concerts in the months leading up to the Olympics that raised a total of $13 million. This money provided 12.2 million children with vaccinations and medical care. In this instance, the ideals of the Olympics shared by one volunteer had an impact on millions of lives.[21]

---

[20] Peter Applebome, "So, You Want to Hold an Olympics," *New York Times*, 4 August 1996, 1, 23.

[21] Dianne Wisner (Olympic volunteer and civic leader), interview by authors, 6 December 2011, audio, Special Collections and Archives, University Library, Georgia State University.

After years of preparation, the opening ceremonies finally began on Friday evening, July 19, 1996. The Olympic Stadium was filled with 83,100 spectators and 172 broadcasters, who beamed television images of the event around the world. The themes of the ceremony honored the one hundredth anniversary of the modern Olympic movement, the civil rights heritage of Atlanta as the birthplace of Dr. Martin Luther King, Jr., and the culture of the region. Athletes representing 197 nations marched into the stadium, and the torch bearing the Olympic flame arrived after a journey of more than 15,000 miles lasting eighty-four days. In a dramatic moment, former Olympic gold medalist and heavyweight boxing champion Muhammad Ali lit the cauldron that would burn throughout the Games. The lighting of the flame marked a return by Muhammad Ali to the city that had given him a second chance in the boxing ring.

The Centennial Games in Atlanta broke several Olympic records. The athletes came to Atlanta from a record number of countries and competed before the most spectators in the history of the Olympics. Almost 11,000 athletes representing 197 nations competed in 26 sports before record crowds of spectators. There were more women athletes competing in Atlanta with almost 4,000 participating in the Centennial Games. An estimated 8 million spectators attended the competition, including preliminary events held in other cities. The worldwide television audience was estimated at 3.5 billion. The traffic management plan arranged by ACOG and the city encouraged most spectators and downtown workers to use the rapid transit system, which operated around the clock with trains packed with riders. More than a million visitors flocked to Centennial Olympic Park and the nearby venues such as Underground Atlanta.[22] Contrary to the dour reports filed by journalists, most spectators seemed to be enjoying the Olympics and Atlanta as they filled downtown with activity throughout the days and long into the nights.

---

[22] Atlanta Committee for the Olympic Games, "Atlanta Centennial Olympic Games Fact Book" (Atlanta: Atlanta Committee for the Olympic Games, 1996).

As a group, the journalists sent from all over the world to cover the Atlanta Olympics found much to criticize. Most housing for the journalists was scattered throughout the metropolitan area at a considerable distance from downtown where ACOG established an International Broadcast Center at the Georgia World Congress Center and a Main Press Center in Peachtree Center's Inforum building. Buses and drivers from other cities were to provide transportation for the journalists. During the early days of the Games, busloads of journalists were lost or late arriving at the competition venues due to the breakdown of the buses or the unfamiliarity of the drivers with the city's streets. Another inconvenience was the failure of the computer system to provide instant reporting of the results of athletic competitions. The computer company was a major corporate sponsor of the Games and had promised the timeliest reporting of data from the competitions in the history of the Olympics. The failure of the system added to the frustration of journalists covering the event. Stories filed from Atlanta described the Games as too commercialized and described the city as a cheap carnival with the many vendors selling their wares on public property.[23]

Atlanta did not compare favorably in many ways with the host city for the 1992 Olympics, Barcelona, whose charms and architectural heritage were augmented with a $10 billion makeover financed by their national, state, and local governments. In contrast, Atlanta was a young city of the New South, lacking a long history of design and offering a tourism industry focused on the convention business. Atlanta was not a vacation destination with large numbers of attractions for visitors. Instead, it was a city built on transportation and commerce, and its businesslike approach to the task of hosting the Olympics was not understood or appreciated by many of the press corps.

Just before 1:30 a.m. on July 27, the ninth day of the Games, as crowds listened to a concert in Centennial Olympic Park, a pipe bomb exploded, spraying shrapnel that caused two deaths and more than a hundred injuries. The mood of the Games changed as memories were

---

[23] *Atlanta Journal-Constitution*, 6 August 1996, Special Edition, 1–6.

stirred of the terrorist attack on the 1972 Olympics in Munich. While competition continued the next day, the park remained closed for three days before it reopened with a memorial service led by Andrew Young. Summoning the voice of minister, civil rights leader, elected public official and international diplomat and speaking without notes as he always does, Young gave a speech that many say was among his best as it summarized the ideals and possibilities of the Olympics:

> We are here to proclaim a victory. We are here not to wallow in tragedy, but to celebrate a triumph, a triumph of the human spirit. We are here to remember the lives of Alice Hawthorne and Melih Uzunyol. Two wonderful citizens, one from America and one from Turkey, who sought to come here to celebrate with 197 nations of the world—the possibilities of this planet living together into the twenty-first century, with a new measure of peace and prosperity.
>
> We are here because the 111 victims of a tragic and ruthless incident lay in the hospital. And as Jesse Jackson and I visited with them yesterday, we did not find a single proclamation of despair. We didn't see a single incident of resentment. If there was a triumph of the human spirit it was in the young people from Georgia, from Connecticut, from Kentucky, from England, from all over the world, who were the victims of this incident. People who were only looking forward to getting on with their lives, and many of them hoping to get out of the hospital in time to get back to the Games.
>
> We are here because the athletes said that they had not come except to compete peacefully on the fields of athletic endeavor. And, indeed, we have seen some remarkable triumphs, from the young and old, from one part of the world and the other, seeking to celebrate their triumph over their own minds and bodies and spirits, representing the best that their nations and this planet can put forward.
>
> So, we are here on what will be a memorable occasion. Indeed, it will be an unforgettable occasion. It's unfortunate that our lives are too often defined by the tragedies and suffering that we experience. And, yet, it's because those tragedies and those sufferings have often been the incidents which bring us to our senses and remind us who we really are.
>
> Yes, we enjoyed the frivolity we loved in this park. We still love this park. We will love this park into the future.
>
> This has been in every sense of the word a people's park. You didn't have to have a ticket to come here. You could meet with all of the people from all over the world. And people from all over the world

came to this park. More than a million people enjoyed this park in the days that it was open. And we didn't have a single incident, a single fight, people didn't even get too drunk.

We learned to celebrate the joy of humanity. And we learned that we were brothers and sisters regardless of our race, regardless of our religion, regardless of our national origin.

And, unfortunately, some people felt like they didn't belong. Like they weren't invited, but the whole world was welcome here. And the whole world remains welcome here, and we want everybody to know that there's no need in being alienated from that loving community.

There is nothing that keeps you out except an unwillingness to open your heart, and open your mind to the love and fellowship that this planet offers to all of its citizens.

Unfortunately, had it not been for the tragedy of Saturday morning, we—all of us—might have taken this joy for granted.

We are the privileged of the world. We are the brightest and best of all the nations on the face of the earth. And, we come together in peace because we know an enormous level of prosperity.

And, we might not have taken account and given thanks for all of our blessings we may have taken them for granted had it not been for this, what we felt to be needless, certainly unearned suffering. But, Martin Luther King, Jr., reminded us that unearned suffering is always redemption.

There is no religion on the face of the earth that doesn't give recognition to the power of the suffering servant. Religion speaks to the need for renunciation of the things of this world. That you might be lifted up into a new power of the human spirit of a divine spirit that really is the basis of our unity.

And so we say to those who suffered here, that we assure you that your suffering is not in vain. We assure you that we the children of the world will learn new lessons from this experience. And we are sure that the twenty-first century will remember the joy, the wonderful, the celebration, the vitality of the people of the earth who gathered in this park. And that we will define the future, not with hatred, not bitterness, not alienation, but with joy, happiness.

The celebration that we see here this morning, we have been wonderfully blessed by our presence together. I don't know what the future holds. But I know you represent the future. You are the people of the future.

You are the people who can solve all of the problems of the planet together and who have no need for hatred and violence.

We love you. We thank you. God bless you.[24]

Young was correct in saying that the Games would go on and that the Centennial Olympic Park would become a favorite place for residents and visitors to enjoy. The act of the lone terrorist, Eric Rudolph, could not stop the pleasure people found in the park and the competition sites. While there were no further incidents to mar the Games, violence continues to affect other cities and other athletic competitions. After the park bombing in Atlanta and the Boston Marathon bombing, the issue of security for major athletic events such as the Olympics has become a major concern for cities thinking about bidding for future mega-events.

After seventeen days, the Olympic flame was extinguished in the closing ceremony. Near the end of the event, the president of the IOC, Juan Antonio Samaranch, addressed the crowd and said, "Well done, Atlanta!" and adding that the Games were "most exceptional." In closing the four previous Olympic Games, Samaranch had proclaimed each of them to be the "best ever." Whether Samaranch was responding to the act of terrorism in the park or the organizational problems ACOG experienced, many residents of Atlanta felt that the city was damned by his faint praise. The IOC's criticism and the reaction of local residents became part of the Olympic legacy in the city.

In spite of some negative publicity, more than 2 million people visited Atlanta during the Games. With worldwide attention focused on the city more than 19 million visitors came to Atlanta during 1996. This boost in tourism continued in the years following the Olympics with a significant increase in the number of international visitors. Economic investment in tourism-related businesses also benefitted from the Olympics. For example, at the time of its successful bid, the area had 50,000

---

[24] Maria Saporta, "Remembering Atlanta's Olympic moment 16 years ago when Andrew Young appealed to city's heart," *Saporta Report*, 30 July 2012, http://saportareport.com/remembering-atlantas-olympic-moment-16-years-ago-when-andrew-young-appealed-to-citys-heart/ accessed 31 July 2012.

hotel rooms, a number which increased to more than 60,000 by 1996. Instead of a slowdown in the pace of investment in new hotels, the four years after the Games saw an increase to more than 87,000 hotel rooms.[25] As Mayor Young observed, each of these rooms meant a new job opening in metropolitan Atlanta, contributing to the employment and population growth of the area.

The biracial public-private partnership that had functioned for several decades in Atlanta's leaders accomplished the complex task of hosting an event the size of the summer Olympics. Following the Games, the chamber of commerce established the Atlanta Sports Council to cultivate the business of sports in the city. This led to other opportunities to host athletic events such as the 2000 Super Bowl of the National Football League, the National Collegiate Athletic Association championship games for men's basketball in 2002, and a variety of other accomplishments. One of these was the decision to relocate the College Football Hall of Fame to the city. The Atlanta Sports Council also works with the Atlanta Convention and Visitors Bureau to attract sports-related conventions to Atlanta. Examples of these include the meetings of sports federations and the organizations of sports equipment manufacturers.[26]

There were physical legacies of the Games in Atlanta, such as the construction of new apartments and the conversion of older buildings into lofts in the downtown area. The mayor's office and business leaders had long sought this goal, but the jumpstart of Olympic visitors encouraged developers to invest in downtown housing. This housing boom also

---

[25] Atlanta Convention and Visitors Bureau, "Annual Report: Atlanta Convention and Visitors Bureau" (Atlanta: ACVB, 1996 and 2000).

[26] Stan Kaston, Robert Dale Morgan, and Janet Marie Smith, "The Olympic Games: Seventeen Days of Sports or More?" in *The Olympic Legacy: Building on What Was Achieved*, ed. Research Atlanta, Inc. (Atlanta: Policy Research Center, Georgia State University, 1996); Len Pasquarelli, "Atlanta lands 2000 Super Bowl," *Atlanta Journal-Constitution*, 1 November 1996, F-1; and Tim Tucker, "Securing the city's spot as super-host for events The Atlanta Sports Council, a key player in landing the 2000 Super Bowl, has plans for a lot more," *Atlanta Journal-Constitution*, 19 January 1997, F-2; *Atlanta Journal-Constitution*, 1 November 1996, F-1; 19 January 1997, F-2.

extended northward along Peachtree Street through the areas of Midtown and Buckhead. The Olympic Stadium was reconfigured and renamed to become Turner Field, the home of the Atlanta Braves until the team relocated to suburban Cobb County after the 2016 baseball season. Local colleges and universities, both public and private, received new or improved athletic facilities and student housing as a result of the Games. For example, the Olympic Village that housed athletes during the Games became dormitories for Georgia State University and Georgia Tech. More recently, Georgia State transferred the dorms to Georgia Tech and constructed new housing facilities downtown, increasing the number of residents in the area.

With its location near the Georgia Dome and the Georgia World Congress Center, Olympic Centennial Park was another important legacy of the Games. The city's leaders hoped the park would serve as a magnet for investment in a previously run-down area. Their hopes were slowly realized after the Olympics as restaurants, hotels, condominiums, and tourist attractions such as the World of Coca-Cola, the Georgia Aquarium, the Center for Civil and Human Rights, and other developments were built in the area. Public art and more attractive streetscapes resulted from the investments made by CODA in preparation for the Games.

An intangible—but significant nonetheless—result of the 1996 Olympics was the increased perception of Atlanta as an international city. After the 1996 Olympic Games, few people in the world did not know about Atlanta, and many held a favorable image in spite of criticism by the IOC and international journalists.

The city hosted more than 19 million visitors during 1996, a record number for a single year. Atlanta's leaders capitalized on this momentum, and the city's convention business continued to thrive in the post-Olympic years. According to the Atlanta Convention and Visitors Bureau, in 1998 the city hosted 3,057 meetings attended by more than 3,423,000 people. The growth in the number of conventions prompted leaders to undertake the fourth enlargement of the Georgia World Congress Center since its opening in 1971. When completed in 2002, the expanded convention facility had 1.4 million square feet, making the

World Congress Center competitive in size with newly enlarged convention centers in Orlando and New Orleans. The facility increased hotel occupancy in downtown by enabling Atlanta to host two conventions of fifty thousand visitors at the same time while a third meeting of the same size is setting up. The increased numbers of visitors to the city also boosted related tourism businesses such as restaurants. In 1999, Atlanta could boast of having more than eight thousand restaurants to feed the appetites of tourists and local residents.[27]

The Olympics helped introduce Atlanta to increased numbers of visitors from the US and abroad. These tourists came to the city for the same combination of reasons that served Atlanta throughout its history. As the head of the Georgia Hospitality and Travel Association, Lloyd Webre said, "Organizations prefer Atlanta to host their events for its accessibility, hospitality, and the diversions it has to offer to visitors." Tourism leaders are also proud of the fact that the city is well-known for hosting major events such as the Olympics and the Super Bowl. In 1999, Atlanta hosted 538,000 international visitors, giving the city a ranking of twelfth among US destinations, behind the top locations such as New York, Los Angeles, Miami, Orlando, and San Francisco. Atlanta was increasingly popular with travelers from Canada, France, the United Kingdom, and Latin America.[28]

After the Olympics, Atlanta was also regarded as an international city for business. There are consulates or trade representatives for more than seventy foreign countries in the city. Atlanta is also home to the headquarters of several major international companies, including Coca-Cola, CNN, and Delta Airlines. During Andrew Young's eight years as mayor, 1,100 international companies moved to Atlanta. The growth in international business continued with additional investment by foreign companies in the Atlanta area and local companies that export products

---

[27] Saeed Ahmed, "Conventions draw record numbers to Atlanta this month has been the city's busiest ever, and there's no letup in sight," *Atlanta Journal-Constitution*, 20 July 2000, XJD-1.

[28] Saeed Ahmed and Shelia M. Poole, "International tourism: Atlanta becoming a top destination," *Atlanta Constitution*, 13 September 2000, F-1.

and services around the world. The metro Atlanta area is the driving force behind making Georgia the eleventh-largest exporter among the states in the union and the eighth-largest importer. Almost 15,000 companies in Georgia export goods and services to 230 countries overseas. As the former senior vice president of the Coca-Cola Company Carl Ware said, "If you are sitting in London or Brussels or Johannesburg, and you are looking for a place to invest in the US, Atlanta and Georgia are right at the top of the list for places because of its very friendly environment."[29]

The challenges of multi-culturalism are very much a part of life in Atlanta, but the tradition of black and white partnership and cooperation provides a model for inclusion that fits in a post-Olympic city. Atlanta can also offer lessons to other places on how it has grown from a small country town to a place of international importance. The Olympics were good for the city in a variety of ways. The Games were good for business, for downtown, for the city's colleges and universities, and for the people of Atlanta. The Olympics were a major event that showed once again that the "Atlanta Way" is a special part of the city. Civic leader Laura Hardman said, "That's what's great about the 'Atlanta Way.' You just think it can happen and it does, but not without a lot of work and a lot of effort, but most of all, teamwork. It can't be done by one person. And that's the realization that it takes everyone working together and people will pull together."[30] A significant element in this process was the ability to move beyond a history of segregation as elected officials worked with business leaders of all races. Carl Ware summed it up this way: "The lasting importance of the Olympics was the way our city and business leaders worked together and formed a model on how you get something like that accomplished. That was a monumental task and that too became the 'Atlanta Way' of getting things done."[31]

Another Atlanta leader, Lisa Borders, described Atlanta after the Olympics in this way: "The view of Atlanta is we're the New South,

---

[29] Carl Ware (former member of Atlanta City Council and senior vice president, Coca-Cola Company), video interview, 22 April 2014.

[30] Hardman, interview, 7 May 2012.

[31] Ware, interview, 22 April 2014.

we're the international city. We dubbed ourself so, but there was a lot of hard work to make it so that people would see us on an international stage, not just on a national stage." Lisa Borders is the granddaughter of one of the great black preachers and civil rights leaders in Atlanta, William Holmes Borders. Her father had a long and distinguished career as a physician, and her mother was a civic volunteer. Lisa has leadership experience as head of the Cousins Foundation, the Grady Healthcare System Foundation, the president of the Atlanta City Council, a vice president of the Coca-Cola Company, and commissioner of the WNBA. She represents the kind of intergenerational leadership that has helped shape Atlanta. She says that the city has been strategic in the past to recognize its importance as a transportation crossroads. As she phrased it, "We are the gateway to what we call the New South."[32]

The struggles over civil rights, risks and gambles over the development of the city's infrastructure, and negotiations over participation in the city's political and economic life bore fruit in the gathering of the world in Atlanta in 1996. Prior to the civil rights movement and the integration that resulted, Atlanta could not have elected Maynard Jackson and Andrew Young to the leadership of the city. Young's international relationships were crucial to the city's winning bid, as was its identity as the home of Martin Luther King, Jr. The city's traditions of hospitality, inclusion, civic pride, volunteerism, and public-private partnership proved to be invaluable assets in the pursuit of the Olympic dream. Atlanta had grown from the capital of a New South into a gateway city, welcoming the world.

Atlanta's report on the Olympic Games opens with these words from Billy Payne: "For seventeen days in the summer of 1996 the world came together in peace and harmony in Atlanta for what became the

---

[32] Lisa M. Borders (chair of the Coca-Cola Foundation and vice president of Global Community Connections for the Coca-Cola Company), interview by authors, 10 February 2012, audio, Special Collections and Archives, University Library, Georgia State University.

largest gathering of athletes and nations in Olympic history.... We celebrated the magnificence of our common humanity."[33]

---

[33] Watkins, *Official Report of the Centennial Olympic Games*, Forward, v.

Anita DeFrantz (far left) at International Olympic Committee meeting
(Courtesy IOC)

Atlanta Organizing Committee Members: (from the second on the left) Billy Payne, Andrew Young, and Maynard Jackson *(Young Family Collection)*

Atlanta Olympic Committee press conference: Andrew Young, Billy Payne,
Maynard Jackson; back row, Councilmembers Mary Davis, Jim Maddox, President
Marvin Arrington, and Bill Campbell *(AARL, Andrew Young Papers)*

Andrew Young and Maynard Jackson during AOC bid
(AARL, Andrew Young Papers)

12

Lessons from the Making of Modern Atlanta

The making of modern Atlanta is an extraordinary story. This Southern city that was once bound by the shackles of segregation, trans-
formed itself into a global city impacting world affairs. It is the story of
a handful of visionary leaders, black and white, who formed the city's
first biracial coalition in the 1940s. Change is never easy, but it was a
battle they were willing to take on, that they had to take on to put Atlanta on a path to a brighter future.

The world can learn a lot from Atlanta making every one a part of
the deal. And if the deal is going to succeed, it has to include everyone
from the rich to the least of these God's children in some way. In order
for everyone to have a stake in the progress and prosperity of the city,
you leave anyone out, they are liable to try and mess it up for everyone.

It is also significant that we were able to do this by creating public-private partnerships that I came to call public-purpose capitalism.
This is where the public identified the problem and the private sector
produced the money, the management, and the partnership created opportunities for all our citizens. This enabled us to keep our taxes low,
and not raising government funding. Some call this the "Atlanta Way,"
but I am convinced this governing philosophy and policy framework
can work anywhere on the planet in any city and in any state or nation.
                                                              —Andrew Young

What is the message from Atlanta's past, making a modern international
city out of a sleepy provincial town that can be helpful to a new generation of leaders in the city and in other places? A number of important
lessons emerge from the experiences and reflections of scores of civic,
business, philanthropic, educational, civil rights, and community leaders
who were interviewed for this book.

—First, recognize the city's core competencies and build from
strength: in the case of Atlanta, transportation and tolerance.

—Second, craft a governing coalition that includes business, philanthropy, and diverse racial, cultural, and other historically marginalized groups.

—Third, the quality of elites matter. Civic, business, and philanthropic leaders must cultivate an ethic of community service.

—Fourth, pair economic growth with expanded opportunities for disadvantaged communities.

—Fifth, sustain the coalition and the vision by mentoring new leaders.

Core Competencies—Transportation and Tolerance

Atlanta's core competency rests on the twin pillars of transportation and tolerance. Core competencies in management terms are the assets that allow Atlanta to bring value to the marketplace, in economic terms; these are the source of Atlanta's comparative advantage. It is critical that leaders understand the source of their city's economic value. Transportation is moving people, goods, and services from one place to another and has been the life-blood of Atlanta. Tolerance is an atmosphere that accepts difference. Transportation and tolerance have grown and evolved as Atlanta has grown. Atlanta began with a stake in the ground, marking the southernmost point of the Western and Atlantic railroad. Transportation is its reason for being. As a consequence of the railroad network, the Confederate Army kept a munitions depot in Atlanta. The munitions depot and supply lines meant that Atlanta would be occupied by the Union forces at the end of the Civil War. Across the South, abolitionist school teachers and missionaries followed the Union Army to serve the needs of African Americans newly released from generations of slavery. Atlanta became host to such missionaries, educators from the American Missionary Association who rejected not only slavery but also the philosophy of white supremacy that was used to justify it.

In Atlanta, transportation infrastructure that invited the Union presence created an environment whereby racial moderation could be practiced. The Union occupation protected institutions dedicated to the uplift of African Americans from white supremacist backlash and allowed these institutions to put down deep roots. By the late nineteenth century, African-American progress could be showcased with a pavilion at the Atlanta Exposition, and Henry Grady, the prophet of the New South, was able to use moderation on race as a comparative advantage for Atlanta in soliciting investors. The narrative of the New South, where former slaves and former slave owners "cast down their buckets" to live together in a mutually beneficial, if not harmonious, manner took hold in Atlanta. Henry Grady, the white editor of the *Atlanta Constitution* and Booker T. Washington, the African-American president and founder of Tuskegee Institute, were both advocates for this narrative.

William B. Hartsfield emerges as a pivotal Atlanta leader who grasped the significance of tolerance and transportation at a critical time for Atlanta's future prosperity. In preparing the city the take the lead on air transport within the region, he demonstrated an understanding that Atlanta was a transportation center, not simply a railroad hub. Hartsfield is also credited with coining the phrase "a city too busy to hate" at a time when other Southern cities were using violence to hold back the tide of history that was the civil rights movement. Former Atlanta mayor Shirley Franklin learned from her experience working with Maynard Jackson and Andrew Young, that governing decisions have to be rooted in the culture of a community if they are to be sustained.[1]

In Atlanta, the culture of tolerance is rooted in the city's early history as a town of carpetbaggers, Union troops, African-American educators and business leaders, and enterprising white business leaders with New South aspirations. Hartsfield and John Wesley Dobbs, leaders of the Atlanta Negro Voters League, initiated a political coalition that became the core of a pro-growth governing regime in the city.

From Hartsfield to the Olympic era, each successive mayor has built upon the pillars of transportation and tolerance, expanding upon these core competencies, building from strength. Mayor Ivan Allen governed during the student sit-in and civil rights era. As evidence of its culture of tolerance, Atlanta was desegregated without the violence that was seen later in Birmingham. Allen further enhanced the city's reputation for

---

[1] Franklin, video interview, 1 May 2015.

racial tolerance by testifying in Congress in support of legislation to end racial segregation in public facilities, employment, and education. The impact of Allen's leadership was critical to Atlanta's emergence as an economic force as business leaders supported the mayor's growing commitment to racial tolerance. Marc Morial, former mayor of New Orleans, observed, "Look, Atlanta, but for civil rights, but for economic inclusion, CNN, Coca-Cola, UPS, Georgia Pacific—you name any of these big companies that have either relocated to Atlanta or have grown in Atlanta—that could not have happened if the social and political order of 1960 remained. It changed and when it changed, it changed the economic fortunes of Atlanta."[2] Allen also expanded the public infrastructure of the city, including a modern airport terminal, major league stadium and team, a convention center, and expanded interstate road network.

Mayor Sam Massell, the city's first Jewish mayor, initiated affirmative action for minority contracting in the city and hired the first African Americans for senior posts in city government. He was an advocate for rapid transit and led a successful ballot referendum that enabled the city to build a rapid rail system, connecting the airport and some suburban areas to the downtown business district.

Mayor Maynard Jackson, the grandson of John Wesley Dobbs, expanded the concept of racial tolerance to include economic and cultural equality. Jackson pioneered the concept of minority-majority joint ventures to promote inclusion for minorities and women in city contracts, and he established a role for city government in supporting the arts in diverse communities. He developed the first bureau of cultural affairs, transforming the city's relationship to the arts. Moving from racial tolerance to inclusion in the city's economic and cultural life, Jackson contributed the important twin pillars of the "Atlanta Way"—tolerance and transportation—in his approach to the Atlanta Airport, and a new, state-of-the art terminal was built with minority business participation in joint ventures in every aspect of the airport from bond-selling to design to

---

[2] Marc Morial (former New Orleans mayor and current president, National Urban League), video interview, 2 July 2013.

concessions. When faced with opposition, Jackson demonstrated his resolve by stopping airport construction until the white business community acceded to the joint venture program. His success embedded racial inclusion, not just in the "Atlanta Way" of politics, but the "Atlanta Way" of business, linking the practice of tolerance to the city's economic engine—the Atlanta Airport.

Mayor Andrew Young, former US ambassador to the United Nations and close associate of Martin Luther King, Jr., took the concept of tolerance to serve as Atlanta's comparative advantage at a global level. As mayor, Young represented the movement for racial tolerance and inclusion led by Dr. King. When he invited the world to Atlanta, he burnished the city's reputation for inclusion even further, melding it with the legacy of Dr. King and his own reputation as President Carter's ambassador to the United Nations. Young worked with the city's hospitality industry to insure that everyone from international business travelers to teenagers attending a family reunion were treated with respect and Southern hospitality. He worked to bring international air carriers into the Atlanta airport and to encourage Delta Airlines to expand its international flights. In the years following the Olympic Games, the Atlanta airport grew to be the world's busiest.

Atlanta's mayors, beginning with William Hartsfield, have built on the city's twin pillars of transportation and tolerance. In addition, practices with respect to tolerance have expanded —to include race, ethnicity, religion, gender, and sexual orientation. This framework, forged by political and government leadership, allowed the city's business, cultural, and non-profit leaders to build a diverse array of enterprises. Transportation and tolerance created an environment that attracted gifted people to Atlanta. For whites, there was the attraction of a dynamic and comparatively open city. For African Americans, the city's racial tolerance offered safety, relative to the repression and violence of rural areas and smaller cities, as well as opportunity. International business investors also found a city open to people of diverse nationalities that combined with one of the world's largest airports was a tremendous advantage in an increasingly global economy. Atlanta was becoming not simply a Southern dish of black-eyed peas and rice, but a rich gumbo of races, creeds, and cultures.

Creativity thrives in an atmosphere of tolerance and Atlanta's rich soup of diversity and led to an environment that generated new ideas, new ways of doing things, and new ways of being.

Craft an Inclusive Governing Coalition

Atlanta's leaders crafted a governing coalition that included historically marginalized groups, especially African Americans. This coalition was born as the city's white leaders were pushed to back up the reputation for tolerance with actions. African-American leaders tested the city's reputation for tolerance and demanded schools, equal pay for teachers, black police officers, parks and recreation spaces, and an end to segregation, and they used their voting strength to win concessions for their community. They demonstrated an ability to block measures when benefits to the black community were insufficient. The white business community wanted profitable enterprises, and the African-American community wanted jobs and economic opportunity. Together, they crafted a pro-growth governing coalition that supported the bonds, taxes, and other government-backed strategies to give Atlanta an infrastructure to promote the city's growth.

Tolerance and its more robust sibling, inclusion, is key to the "Atlanta Way." City leaders were creative in their approach to the challenge of expanding understanding across communities and working through tension and conflicting interests. Atlanta's business leaders—black and white—developed formal structures for managing the competing interests of different groups. At its inception, the Action Forum was a remarkable expression of the willingness of Atlanta leaders to reach across racial barriers. An equal number of black and white business leaders met monthly to discuss key issues and find innovative solutions to sensitive matters such as school desegregation. The Metro Atlanta Chamber of Commerce reached out to black business leaders Jesse Hill and Herman Russell and worked closely with Mayor Young as it did with its former president, Ivan Allen. Later, the downtown business group Central Atlanta Progress was formed and, more recently, the Atlanta Committee for Progress, which carries on the tradition of working behind the scenes to keep a diverse group of business leaders working cohesively on key issues.

The 1996 Olympic Games were the ultimate economic growth opportunity—possible only because of the biracial coalition in Atlanta, Mayor Andrew Young, and the legacy of Martin Luther King, Jr., Billy Payne, and the Metro Atlanta Chamber of Commerce were essential players in winning the Olympics, but Atlanta's civil rights legacy and the leadership of Andrew Young and Maynard Jackson are what made the difference in Atlanta's successful bid for the Centennial Olympic Games—once again, tolerance and inclusiveness and Atlanta's other pillar—transportation—were Atlanta's comparative advantage.

Community Service

The civic-mindedness of the elites in a community makes a tremendous difference in what can be accomplished. Civic, business, and philanthropic leaders must cultivate an ethic of community service if a city is to thrive and meet significant challenges. People with social networks, influence, moral stature, and the ability to mobilize resources must be willing to use those resources to improve the well-being of the city. Atlanta leaders have had a wonderful example in Robert Woodruff and the Woodruff Foundation. Woodruff demonstrated a willingness to act in the city's interest at critical times, from helping to pay city workers during the Depression to providing financial resources to the city during the international funeral for Dr. Martin Luther King, Jr.

Business, civic, and philanthropic engagement in civic projects have resulted in the Woodruff Arts Center, the Carter Center, the King Center, the revitalization of the Atlanta Zoo, the renovation of Underground Atlanta, and the transformation of public housing projects such as East Lake Meadows into vital mixed income communities. Atlanta leaders volunteer their time, talent, and resources to create better solutions for the city, often with no benefit to themselves. White real estate developer Blaine Kelley recognized that the 1968 assassination of Dr. King was a turning point for the city of Atlanta. People recognized that Atlanta was the home of the civil rights movement and that pricked our consciences, to think about what's decent, what's humane, what's fair, and that happened first and foremost in this city compared to any other city in the world.... Atlanta's uniqueness is it is not only a successful business city and a successful education city and all that, but we're unique like no other in the world and that we're the headquarters for Centers for Disease Control, the King Center, the King Chapel, the Woodruff Foundation, the CARE, and there's no other city which has this combination of serving others in the constructive way that Atlanta does. And it's volunteer.... And so, I'd say we've grown to have quite a heart here. So I say maybe we're the city with a heart.[3]

Kelley and his wife, Sylvia Sanders Kelley, are examples of the volunteer leadership in Atlanta. She has provided leadership in education, religion, and human rights while he served as head of the chamber of commerce, Central Atlanta Progress, and the Advisory Board at the MLK Center for Nonviolent Social Change. Dr. Benjamin Mays, Jesse Hill, Jean Childs Young, John Portman, and Ivan Allen III are a few of the leaders included in this book who represent the ethic of community service that characterizes the "Atlanta Way."

Economic Growth and Opportunity

Atlanta's governing coalition is based on economic growth. To sustain the coalition, economic growth must be accompanied by expanded opportunities for disadvantaged communities, especially the African-American community or those voters will abandon the coalition. Since the 1920s the black community in Atlanta has been consistent in rejecting ballot measures that have no clear benefit to the black community. The coalition will lose the support of African-American voters if the benefits of economic growth are not perceived to extend to the black community.

---

[3] Blaine Kelley (former developer and CEO, Landmarks Group), interview by authors, 20 January 2012, audio, Special Collections and Archives, University Library, Georgia State University.

Mayor Massell understood the basis of the coalition and persuaded black voters to support MARTA by creating a proposal that permitted him to demonstrate the clear benefits—lower fares, minority contracts, and hiring. Andrew Young, then the chair of the community relations commission, called it a "Fairness Formula."

Mayor Jackson was driven by both principle and politics to require minority contracting in the construction of the new Atlanta airport terminal, merging the twin pillars of tolerance and transportation. In the Jackson era, African Americans in Atlanta had high-quality education because of the Atlanta University Center, but because of the legacy of segregation, they had little access to middle-class jobs in private companies. Jackson used the power of his position to open opportunities for African Americans in companies doing business with the city, especially financial institutions. In doing so, he protected the pro-growth coalition, much as President Franklin Roosevelt protected capitalism with the New Deal. Neither received appreciation from the greatest beneficiaries of their policies—big business.

Mayor Young coined the term "public-purpose capitalism" to describe his approach to using private sector resources to attain public sector goals. The public-purpose vision, enhancing economic opportunity for disadvantaged citizens, was a core value behind Mayor Young's economic development projects. Examples include the Lakewood Amphitheatre project as an ideal—where the local residents were able to benefit from a development project by becoming small-business owners rather than simply low-wage employees.

The pro-growth initiatives such as the MARTA system and Grady Hospital that created and helped sustain the economy of the Atlanta region are successful due to the support of the voters of the city of Atlanta and the counties of Fulton and DeKalb. The support of black voters in each of the three jurisdictions determined the outcome of pro-growth measures. The pro-growth coalition must insure that these voters perceive a genuine benefit for the additional fiscal responsibility they accept if the pro-growth agenda is to continue.

Pro-growth may need to yield to smart growth as the reality of global climate change and the scarcity of water resources affect Atlanta.

This shift from a prodigious use of land and water to conservation will make it more difficult to share resources with those who have yet experience material benefits from Atlanta's pro-growth posture. In addition, the poor and disadvantaged may not be essential for a governing coalition in Atlanta's future, but a governing coalition that is insensitive to the unmet needs in its community will lack moral authority. The absence of moral authority will eventually erode the ability to mobilize a community for the common good. Historically, Atlanta has been unable to enact policies to spur economic growth in the absence of support from African-American voters.

Mentor New Leaders

Atlanta leaders have sustained a practice of mentoring future leaders for the city. This mentoring practice has been instrumental in sustaining the "Atlanta Way," transmitting the culture of tolerance, inclusion, and creative problem-solving to subsequent cadres of leaders. Dr. Martin Luther King, Jr., was mentored by Dr. Benjamin Mays. He, in turn, was a mentor to Andrew Young, whose legacy included mentoring the two most recent mayors, Shirley Franklin and Kasim Reed.

Mentoring within the Atlanta Police Department provides a unique example of sustaining and expanding Atlanta's culture of tolerance and inclusion through mentoring. Chief Herbert Jenkins, the city's long-time white police chief under mayors Hartsfield and Allen, mentored one of his successors, Morris Redding. Chief Redding, a white officer with ties to the civil rights community, led the police department under Mayor Young. Redding, in turn, provided opportunities and mentoring for two younger African-American officers, Beverly Harvard, who was promoted by Redding to become the first female deputy chief and later became police chief under Mayor Bill Campbell. She was the first African-American female to head a major city police department. The other officer mentored by Redding, George Turner, serves as chief under

Mayor Kasim Reed.[4] Redding saw his promise and assigned the young officer, George Turner, to Mayor Andrew Young's security detail. The opportunity to spend time watching Young in meetings is how Chief Turner says he learned to be the leader required to become head of the department.[5]

The informal mentoring process has been important to the city. Virtually every person interviewed offered examples of people who had tutored them in the "Atlanta Way." Jesse Hill, Benjamin Mays, John Portman, and Robert Woodruff were among private and non-profit leaders who emerged from the interviews as influential mentors.

Ivan Allen III, the son of the mayor and a third-generation civic leader, was steeped in the "Atlanta Way" but recognized the problem of sustaining the vision and practices that made Atlanta special. He created a program called Leadership Atlanta in 1969 while he was serving as New Programs Chair of the Metro Atlanta Chamber of Commerce. Leadership Atlanta separated from the Chamber of Commerce in 1977 to become a separate program called the Atlanta Leadership Development Foundation. For many years the co-director of the program was Elaine Alexander, who recalled that Leadership Atlanta is one of the success stories in the city that helps to create a new generation of leaders. Alexander and her African-American co-director, Myrtle Davis, devised a program to promote a diverse leadership network for the city. Elaine Alexander observed, "Government, education, social service, law, banking. And when I think of how we used to do it.... I mean we kept graphs.... We had the different categories on top and we had squares under each—white male, black male, white female, black female—and we put the names of the applicants, so the first thing you saw was their

---

[4] Morris Redding (retired chief of police, City of Atlanta), interview by authors, 8 March 2013, audio, Special Collections and Archives, University Library, Georgia State University.

[5] George Turner (police chief, City of Atlanta, 2011–), interview by authors, 17 February 2012, audio, Special Collections and Archives, University Library, Georgia State University.

professions. And then the goal was to have a balanced class."⁶ While
there are now more than one thousand similar local leadership programs
across the US, Leadership Atlanta is the oldest sustained program in the
nation and has served as a model for many other communities. In 2004,
the foundation created a program for promising young professionals aged
25 to 32 called LEAD Atlanta. LEAD Atlanta combines leadership development and community education into an eight-month program. According to its website, "Leadership Atlanta leveraged one of Atlanta's
greatest assets—the tradition of cooperation among its businesses, community organizations, and public officials."⁷ The structure of Leadership
Atlanta echoes the Action Forum—black and white co-chairs, equal
numbers of blacks and whites in the group. Leadership Atlanta affirms
and rewards civic engagement—only applicants with a track record of
community service have any chance of being accepted to the prestigious
program.

Atlanta has a cadre of younger leaders, who through formal and informal mentoring and leadership development espouse the core values of
the "Atlanta Way." Several of these younger leaders were asked to give
their perspective on the "Atlanta Way." Current mayor, Kasim Reed, an
African-American man, was an undergraduate student at Howard University when he met Andrew Young, also a graduate of Howard. Young
recognized the leadership potential of this youthful student from Atlanta
and served as a mentor to him, helping Reed become a member of the
Georgia State Senate and mayor of Atlanta. When asked about the "Atlanta Way," Reed replied, "We have chosen cooperation over conflict.
And that is why I think we are one of the most successful cities and one
of the leading cities in the world."⁸

---

⁶ Elaine Alexander (former director, Atlanta Leadership Development
Foundation), interview by authors, 24 February 2012, audio, Special Collections
and Archives, University Library, Georgia State University.
⁷ "Our History, 1969–2016," www.leadershipAtlanta.org/About/History
(accessed 25 November 2015).
⁸ Kasim Reed (mayor, City of Atlanta), video interview, 21 November
2013.

Alex Si-chi Wan, the first Asian-American member of the Atlanta City Council and representing a district that includes the Midtown area, replied, "When I think of the term the 'Atlanta Way,' there are several things that come to mind. The first one is dreaming big and thinking big and bold and not being afraid to hope for things."[9] Another view came from Duriya Farooqui, a Muslim woman who came to work in city government soon after graduating from the Kennedy School of Government, Harvard University. After serving as a policy planner during the administration of Mayor Shirley Franklin, Farooqui became the chief operating officer of the city under Mayor Kasim Reed. When asked about the "Atlanta Way," she replied, "We already have the third-highest concentration of Fortune 500 companies. Atlanta is a great place to start a business and raise a family, and that is going to continue to be a great asset for people who want a high quality of life and growth opportunities and a great future."[10] Her comments capture the facet of Atlanta as a growing city that is open for business.

When asked about the future of the city, Michelle Nunn, a white woman and fifth-generation Georgian, who serves as the president and CEO of CARE, USA, said, "I see a bright future based upon the arc of our own history, based upon the traditions, the lessons that we have learned around social change, social movements and also economic development entrepreneurship, future oriented leadership, things like the Atlanta Beltline that are helping to reimagine our city."[11] Nunn speaks as a leader in the important nonprofit and philanthropic sector of Atlanta. Before becoming head of an international nonprofit, she was executive director of Hands-On Atlanta, a local volunteer-based organization that merged with the national Points of Light Foundation. Her vision recalls

---

[9] Alex Si-chi Wan (first Asian-American member of the Atlanta City Council, District 6), video interview, 21 November 2013.

[10] Duriya Farooqui (principal, Bain & Company, and former chief operating officer, City of Atlanta), video interview, 21 November 2013.

[11] Michelle Nunn (president and CEO, CARE, USA), video interview, 1 May 2015.

the lessons learned from the civil rights movement that serve as guidance for the future.

Sam Zamarripa, the first Hispanic member of the Georgia State Senate, reminds us, "The questions around ethnicity and race are going to be a lot more complicated, but the fundamental issue is still the same: can people work together; can people get along; can people collaborate, do people have a shared and common vision?"[12]

Stacey Abrams, an African-American woman and the minority leader in the Georgia House of Representatives, calls us to the work left to be done: "We have to lift up every member of our society and we have to do it together and harness our energies. We also have to recognize that we have a creativity and a vision that can transform the South and, then, transform the nation."[13] Abrams's vision echoes the dream of inclusiveness, moving beyond tolerance to the Beloved Community envisioned by Martin Luther King, Jr., and the importance of creativity to the city's future.

The diversity of these highly placed leaders is evidence of the critical role that tolerance and inclusion have played in the growth and development of Atlanta. This cultivation of diversity that has evolved as a result of our history and politics has been Atlanta's true secret formula.

The "Atlanta Way"

Atlanta was able to grow and thrive, emerging in the twenty-first century as one of the top ten metropolitan areas in the United States, in terms of population, and with the world's busiest airport, by building upon the twin pillars of transportation and tolerance. Atlanta's culture of tolerance had its roots in the Reconstruction era and was the basis for crafting a governing coalition of white and black leaders. The economic growth that resulted from the efforts of the governing coalition was

---

[12] Sam Zamarripa (first Hispanic member, Georgia State Senate, business and civic leader), video interview, 15 November 2015.

[13] Stacey Abrams (minority leader, Georgia House of Representatives), video interview, 21 November 2013.

shared in an intentional manner with members of disadvantaged communities, through community benefit arrangements, and programs for minority and female-owned businesses. Intentional inclusion in an array of initiatives ranging from the Action Forum to joint ventures to Leadership Atlanta became part of the Atlanta way of doing things. Formal and informal mentoring and leadership development structures were instituted to sustain the policies and practices of the coalition into the future. These practices can be adapted by a new generation of leaders in Atlanta and in other communities.

Atlanta began as a railroad hub, evolving into an airplane and general transportation hub. Conceptually, transportation has expanded from railroads to the airport and the physical movement of people, goods, and services to evolve to a transmission of ideas, concepts, and values, as evidenced by CNN, the Carter Center, and the King Center. The city is poised to invest in the physical infrastructure, arts, culture, and human capital to expand further a media, entertainment, and information technology hub.

Ultimately, Atlanta's way of doing things comes back to the city's culture of tolerance. This has been Atlanta's comparative advantage. Without the culture of tolerance, Atlanta could not have made the investments in modern infrastructure that allowed it to build on the foundation laid by the railroads. The city has not always lived up to its reputation as a "City too Busy to Hate," but it was always able to adjust course and continue to make progress. As the city has moved from railroads to airplanes to digital airwaves in its business infrastructure, an equivalent evolution must take place in its moral progress. Atlanta has moved beyond tolerance to inclusion. The challenge today is to reach toward a culture that truly celebrates diversity in all its forms embracing the vision of Dr. King's "Beloved Community."

Andrew Young, Shirley Franklin, and Sam Massell
(Young Family Collection)

Anne Cox Chambers and Andrew Young at Atlanta Press Club
(Courtesy Atlanta Press Club)

Charlie Loudermilk and Andrew Young
(Young Family Collection, photo by John Glen)

Jesse Hill, Charlie Loudermilk, John Portman, Shirley Franklin, Andrew Young,
AJ Robinson, and John Lewis at dedication of Young statute, 2008
(Young Family Collection)

Kasim Reed, Duryia Farooqui, Billye Aaron, Sharon Campbell,
Carolyn and Andrew Young raise funds for UNCF *(Courtesy UNCF)*

Mayors Allen, Massell, Campbell, Jackson, and Young
(Young Family Collection)

Stacey Abrams, Shirley Franklin, Andrew Young, Harvey Newman, Ravi Perry, and
Andrea Young at the Congressional Black Caucus Annual Legislative Conference
(Willie Tucker)

Andrew Young (holding proclamation), accompanied by Carolyn Young
and family members, honored by Atlanta City Council, 2012
(Willie Tucker)

Bibliography

Allen, Frederick. *Atlanta Rising: The Invention of an International City, 1946–1996*. Atlanta: Longstreet Press, 1996.

————. *The Secret Formula: How Brilliant Marketing and Relentless Salesmanship Made Coca-Cola the Best-Known Product in the World*. New York: Harper-Business, 1994.

Allen, Ivan, Jr., and Paul Hemphill. *Mayor: Notes on the Sixties*. New York: Simon and Shuster, 1971.

Amaki, Amalia and Andrea Barnwell Brownlee. *Hale Woodruff, Nancy Elizabeth Prophet and the Academy*. Seattle and London: Spelman College Museum of Fine Art in association with University of Washington Press, 2007.

Atlanta Committee for the Olympic Games. *Atlanta Centennial Olympic Games Fact Book*. Atlanta: Atlanta Committee for the Olympic Games, 1996.

Atlanta Committee for the Olympic Games. *Welcome to a Brave and Beautiful City* (vol. 1) and *Atlanta: A City of Dreams* (vol. 2). Atlanta's Official Bid for the 1996 Olympic Games. Atlanta: Peachtree Publishers, 1990.

Atlanta Convention and Visitors Bureau. "Annual Report: Atlanta Convention and Visitors Bureau." Atlanta: ACVB, 1970, 1975, 1980, 1996, and 2000.

Atlanta Convention and Visitors Bureau. "Atlanta Convention and Visitors Bureau: Fact Sheet." Atlanta: ACVB, 1987.

Ayers, Edward L. *The Promise of the New South: Life after Reconstruction*. New York: Oxford University Press, 1992.

Bacote, Clarence Albert. *The Story of Atlanta University: A Century of Service, 1865–1965*. Atlanta: Atlanta University, 1969.

————. "The Negro in Atlanta Politics." *Phylon: The Atlanta University Review* 16/4 (Fourth Quarter 1955): 329–32.

Banks, Manley Elliott. "A Changing Electorate in a Majority Black City: The Emergence of a Neo-Conservative Black Urban Regime in Contemporary Atlanta." *Journal of Urban Affairs* 22 (Fall 2000): 265–78.

Barton, Bruce. "The Church that Saved a City: How Atlanta Found Itself after the Race Riots." *The Congregationalist and the Christian World* 99/45 (5 November 1914): 587–88.

Bayor, Ronald H. *Race and the Shaping of Twentieth-century Atlanta*. Chapel Hill: University of North Carolina Press, 1996.

Blicksilver, Jack. "The International Cotton Exposition of 1881 and Its Impact Upon the Economic Development of Georgia." *Cotton History Review* 1 (1960): 175–94.

Boone, William Henry, Jr. "The Atlanta Community Relations Commission." MA thesis, Atlanta University, 1969.

Braden, Betsey and Paul Hagan. *A Dream Takes Flight: Hartsfield International Airport and Aviation in Atlanta*. Atlanta and Athens: Atlanta Historical Society and University of Georgia Press, 1989.

Brimmer, Andrew F. and F. Ray Marshall. *Public Policy and Promotion of Minority Economic Development: City of Atlanta and Fulton County, GA*. Washington, D.C.: Brimmer and Marshall, 1990.

Burton, Orville Vernon. "Born to Rebel." In *Walking Integrity: Benjamin Elijah Mays, Mentor to Martin Luther King, Jr.* Edited by Lawrence Edward Carter, Sr., Macon, GA: Mercer University Press, 1998. 33–80.

Carter, Edward R. *The Black Side: a partial history of the business, religious, and educational side of the Negro in Atlanta, Ga.* 1894. Reprint. Freeport, NY: Books for Libraries Press, 1971.

Clarke, Edward Young. *Illustrated History of Atlanta*. 1877. Reprint. Atlanta: Cherokee Publishing Company, 1971.

Cooper, Walter G. *The Cotton States and International Exposition and South, Illustrated*. Atlanta: Illustrator Company, 1896.

Crimmins, Timothy J. "The Crystal Stair: A Study of the Effects of Caste and Class on Secondary Education in Late Nineteenth-century Atlanta, Georgia." *Urban Education* 8 (January 1974): 4014–21.

Darnell, Tim. *The Crackers: Early Days of Atlanta Baseball*. Athens: Hill Street Press, 2003.

Davis, Deborah. *Guest of Honor: Booker T. Washington, Theodore Roosevelt, and the White House Dinner That Shocked a Nation*. New York: Atria Books, 2012.

Davis, Harold E. *Henry Grady's New South: Atlanta, A Brave and Beautiful City*. Tuscaloosa: University of Alabama Press, 1990.

Dorsey, Allison. *To Build Our Lives Together: Community Formation in Black Atlanta, 1875–1906*. Athens: University of Georgia Press, 2004.

Doyle, Don H. *New Men, New Cities, New South: Atlanta, Nashville, Charleston, Mobile, 1860–1910*. Chapel Hill: University of North Carolina Press, 1990.

DuBois, W. E. B. "The Negro in Business." In *Fourth Annual Conference on the Condition of the Negro*. Atlanta: Atlanta University, 1899.

———. *The Souls of Black Folk*. New York: Vintage Books, 1990.

Dunkley, Tina Maria and Jerry Cullum. *In the Eye of the Muses: Selections from the Clark Atlanta University Art Collection*. Atlanta: Clark Atlanta University, 2012.

Dyer, Thomas G. *Secret Yankees: The Union Circle in Confederate Atlanta*. Baltimore: Johns Hopkins University Press, 1999.

———. *University of Georgia: A Bicentennial History, 1785–1985*. Athens: University of Georgia Press, 1985.

English, Thomas H. *Emory University, 1915–1965: A Semicentennial History.* Atlanta: Higgins-McArthur Company, 1966.

Eric Hill Associates. *City of Atlanta, Georgia, Report on Relocation of Individuals, Families and Businesses.* Atlanta: Community Improvement Program, 1966.

Fleischmann, Arnold. "Atlanta: Urban Coalitions in a Suburban Sea." In *Big City Politics in Transition.* Edited by H. V. Savitch and John Clayton Thomas. Newbury Park, CA: Sage, 1991. 97–114.

Florida, Richard L. *The Rise of the Creative Class: And How It's Transforming Work, Leisure, Community, and Everyday Life.* New York: Basic Books, 2002.

Friends of Maynard Jackson. *The Jackson Years: On Managing Change, 1974–1982.* Atlanta: n.p., 1982.

Garrett, Franklin M. *Atlanta and Environs: A Chronicle of Its People and Events.* 2 vols. Athens: University of Georgia Press, 1969.

Guy-Sheftall, Beverly and Jo Moore Stewart. *Spelman: A Centennial Celebration, 1881–1981.* Charlotte, NC: Delmar Company, 1981.

Hanson, Elizabeth I. *Margaret Mitchell.* Boston: Twayne Publishers, 1991.

Harlan, Louis R., editor. *The Booker T. Washington Papers.* Vol. 3. Urbana: University of Illinois Press, 1974.

Hartsfield, William B. "Airport Materials." Archive collection. Atlanta History Center.

Hirsch, Paul M. "Atlanta: The City, Metropolitan Region, and the Atlanta M. S. A." Atlanta: Department of Urban Studies, c. 1983.

Holmes, Robert A. *Maynard Jackson, A Biography.* Miami: Barnhardt & Ashe Publishing, Inc., 2011.

Hornsby, Alton, Jr. *Black Power in Dixie: A Political History of African Americans in Atlanta.* Gainesville: University Press of Florida, 2009.

Horton, Nehl. *The Young Years: A Report on the Administration of The Honorable Andrew Young, Mayor of the City of Atlanta, 1982–1989.* Atlanta: n.p., 1989.

Jacobs, Jane. *Cities and the Wealth of Nations: Principles of Economic Life.* New York: Random House, 1984.

———. *The Economy of Cities.* New York: Vintage Books, 1969.

Kaston, Stan, Robert Dale Morgan, and Janet Marie Smith. "The Olympic Games: Seventeen Days of Sports or More?" in *The Olympic Legacy: Building on What Was Achieved.* Commissioned by Research Atlanta, Inc. Atlanta: Policy Research Center, Georgia State University, 1996. 41–48.

Kent, William E. "Underground Atlanta: The Untimely Passing of a Major Tourist Attraction." *Journal of Travel Research* 22 (Spring 1984): 2–7.

Kent, William E., and J. Thomas Chesnutt. "Underground Atlanta: Resurrected and Revisited." *Journal of Travel Research* 29 (Spring 1991): 36–39.

King, Martin Luther, Jr., and James M. Washington, editor. *A Testament of Hope: The Essential Writings of Martin Luther King, Jr.* San Francisco: Harper and Row, 1986.

Kruse, Kevin M. *White Flight: Atlanta and the Making of Modern Conservatism.* Princeton, NJ: Princeton University Press, 2005.

Lefever, Harry G. *Undaunted by the Fight: Spelman College and the Civil Rights Movement 1957–1967.* Macon: Mercer University Press, 2005.

Lewis, David Levering. *King: A Biography.* 2nd edition. Urbana: University of Illinois Press, 1978.

Link, William A. *Atlanta, Cradle of the New South: Race and Remembering in the Civil War's Aftermath.* Chapel Hill: University of North Carolina Press, 2013.

Martin, Charles H. *Benching Jim Crow: The Rise and Fall of the Color Line in Southern College Sports, 1890–1980.* Urbana: University of Illinois Press, 2010.

Martin, Harold H. *William Berry Hartsfield: Mayor of Atlanta.* Athens: University of Georgia Press, 2010.

Mason, Herman Skip, Jr., editor. *Going Against the Wind: A Pictorial History of African-Americans in Atlanta.* Atlanta: Longstreet Press 1992.

Mays, Benjamin. *Born to Rebel: An Autobiography.* Athens: University of Georgia Press, 1987.

McGill, Ralph. *Best of McGill: Selected Columns.* Atlanta: Cherokee Publishing Company, 1980.

———. *The South and the Southerner.* Athens: University of Georgia Press, 1992.

McMath, Robert C. Jr., Ronald H. Bayor, James E. Brittain, Lawrence Foster, Augustus W. Giebelhaus, and Germaine M. Reed. *Engineering the New South: Georgia Tech, 1885–1985.* Athens: University of Georgia Press, 1985.

Mitchell, Margaret. *Gone with the Wind.* New York: MacMillan, 1936.

Moore, Moses N., Jr. "From Atlanta to Brooklyn: The Social Gospel Ministry and Legacy of Henry H. Proctor." American Theological Library Association. *Union Seminary Quarterly Review* 62/3–4 (2010): 52–69.

Negri, Ed, and Michael J. Cain. *Herren's: An Atlanta Landmark: Past, Present & Future.* Roswell, GA: Roswell Publishing Company, 2005.

Newman, Harvey K. "Black Clergy and Urban Regimes: The Role of Atlanta's Concerned Black Clergy." *Journal of Urban Affairs* 16 (March 1994): 23–33.

———. "Hospitality and Violence: Contradictions in a Southern City." *Urban Affairs Review* 35/4 (March 2000): 541–58.

————. *Southern Hospitality: Tourism and the Growth of Atlanta*. Tuscaloosa: University of Alabama Press, 1999.

Nye, Joseph. *Soft Power: The Means to Success in World Politics*. New York: Public Affairs, 2004.

Pomerantz, Gary M. *Where Peachtree Meets Sweet Auburn*. New York: Penguin Books, 1996.

Pooley, Karen Beck. "Segregation's New Geography: The Atlanta Metro Region, Race, and the Declining Prospects for Upward Mobility." *Southern Spaces*. 15 April 2015. <http://southernspaces.org/2015/segregations-new-geography-atlanta-metro-region-race-and-declining-prospects-upward-mobility> Accessed on 14 January 2016.

Preston, Howard L. *Automobile Age Atlanta: The Making of a Southern Metropolis, 1900–1935*. Athens: University of Georgia Press, 1979.

Reed, Adolph, Jr. "A Critique of Neo-Progressivism in Theorizing about Local Development Policy: A Case from Atlanta." In *The Politics of Urban Development*. Edited by Clarence N. Stone and Heywood T. Sanders. Lawrence: University Press of Kansas, 1987. 202–211.

————. "The Black Urban Regime: Structural Origins and Constraints." In *Power, Community and the City*. Edited by Michael P. Smith. New Brunswick, NJ: Transaction Books, 1988. 199–215.

Riani, Paolo. *John Portman*. Washington, DC: American Institute of Architects Press, 1990.

Rovaris, Dereck J., Sr. *Mays and Morehouse: How Benjamin E. Mays Developed Morehouse College, 1940–1967*. Silver Spring, MD: Beckham Publications Group, Inc., 2005.

Sanders, Heywood T. *Convention Center Follies: Politics, Power and Public Investment in American Cities*. Philadelphia: University of Pennsylvania Press, 2014.

Stone, Clarence N. *Regime Politics: Governing Atlanta, 1946–1988*. Lawrence: University Press of Kansas, 1989.

————. "Urban Regimes and the Capacity to Govern: A Political Economy Approach." Journal of Urban Affairs 15/1 (1993): 1–28.

Townsend, James L., and Paul Hagan, editors. *Atlanta International Airport: A Commemorative Book*. Atlanta: National Graphics, 1980.

Trotter, Michael H. *The History of the Atlanta Action Forum*. Atlanta: n.p., 1992.

————. *Research Atlanta: The Early Years*. Atlanta: n.p., 1987.

Underground Festival Development Corporation. "Briefing Paper on the Underground Atlanta Project." 22 December 1986.

U.S. Bureau of the Census. "Population Distribution and Change: 2000–2010." March 2011, Table 3, 6.

U.S. Bureau of the Census. *Seventh Census of the United States, 1850*, vol. 1. Washington DC: Beverly Tucker, 1854.

U.S. Bureau of the Census. *Nineteenth Census of the United States, 1970*. vol. 1. Washington, DC: Government Printing Office, 1972.

Walker, Jack L. "Protest and Negotiation: A Case Study of Negro Leadership in Atlanta." In *Atlanta, Georgia, 1960–1961: Sit-Ins and Student Activism*. Edited by David J. Garrow. Brooklyn, NY: Carlson Publishers, 1989. 69–90.

Wilkerson, Isabel. *The Warmth of Other Suns: The Epic Story of America's Great Migration*. New York: Vintage Books, 2011.

Young, Andrea. *Life Lessons My Mother Taught Me*. New York: Tarcher/Putnam, 2000.

Young, Andrew. *An Easy Burden: Civil Rights and the Transformation of America*. New York: Harper Collins, 1996.

———. "Life Behind the Wall: A Call to Respond." In *African American Vernacular Art of the South*. Volume 1 of *Souls Grown Deep*. Edited by Paul Arnett and William S. Arnett. Atlanta: Tinwood Books, 2000.

Index